Crime, Justice and Human Rights

Leanne Weber
Elaine Fishwick
and
Marinella Marmo

palgrave
macmillan

First published 2014 by
PALGRAVE MACMILLAN

Palgrave Macmillan in the UK is an imprint of Macmillan Publishers Limited, registered in England, company number 785998, of Houndmills, Basingstoke, Hampshire RG21 6XS.

Palgrave Macmillan in the US is a division of St Martin's Press LLC, 175 Fifth Avenue, New York, NY 10010.

Palgrave Macmillan is the global academic imprint of the above companies and has companies and representatives throughout the world.

Palgrave® and Macmillan® are registered trademarks in the United States, the United Kingdom, Europe and other countries

ISBN 978-1-137-29920-8 hardback

ISBN 978-1-137-29919-2   ISBN 978-1-137-29921-5 (eBook)
DOI 10.1007/978-1-137-29921-5

This book is printed on paper suitable for recycling and made from fully managed and sustained forest sources. Logging, pulping and manufacturing processes are expected to conform to the environmental regulations of the country of origin.

A catalogue record for this book is available from the British Library.

A catalog record for this book is available from the Library of Congress.

Typeset by Cambrian Typesetters, Camberley, Surrey

Crime, Justice and Human Rights

Dedicated to the memory of Stanley Cohen,
1942–2013

Contents

SECTION 2 Applying Human Rights in Criminology

SECTION 3 A Criminology for Human Rights

List of Boxes

List of Acronyms and Abbreviations

ACC	African Charter on the Rights and Welfare of the Child
ACT	Australian Capital Territory
AHRC	Australian Human Rights Commission
APF	Asia Pacific Forum
ASBO	anti-social behaviour order
ASEAN	Association of Southeast Asian Nations
ATS	Alien Tort Statute
CAT	International Convention against Torture and other Cruel, Inhuman or Degrading Treatment or Punishment
CCTV	closed-circuit television
CEDAW	Convention on the Elimination of All Forms of Discrimination against Women
CERD	Convention on the Elimination of All Forms of Racial Discrimination
CIA	Central Intelligence Agency
CJEU	Court of Justice of the European Union (previously ECJ)
CPT	European Committee for the Prevention of Torture and Inhuman or Degrading Treatment or Punishment
CRC	United Nations Committee on the Rights of the Child
CROC	Convention on the Rights of the Child
CSW	Commission on the Status of Women
CTC	Count the Costs
ECHR	European Convention on Human Rights
ECOSOC	Economic and Social Council
ECtHR	European Court of Human Rights
EHRC	Equality and Human Rights Commission
EU	European Union
GC	general comment

HRA	Human Rights Act
HRC	Human Rights Committee
HRLC	Human Rights Law Centre
HRMF	Human Rights Measurement Framework
ICC	International Criminal Court
ICCPED	International Convention for the Protection of All Persons from Enforced Disappearance
ICCPR	International Covenant on Civil and Political Rights
ICESCR	International Covenant on Economic, Social and Cultural Rights
ICHRP	International Council on Human Rights Policy
ICPS	International Centre for Prison Studies
ICRC	International Committee of the Red Cross
ICTY	International Criminal Tribunal for the former Yugoslavia
LA	Los Angeles
LAS	League of Arab States
LWP	life without parole
NGO	non-governmental organization
NSW	New South Wales
NTER	Northern Territory Emergency Response
NYPD	New York Police Department
OAU	Organization of African Unity
OHCHR	Office of the United Nations High Commissioner for Human Rights
OVS	Office of Victim Services
SAHRC	South African Human Rights Commission
SIAC	Special Immigration Appeals Commission
TIP	Trafficking in Persons
TJ	Therapeutic jurisprudence
TVPA	Trafficking Victims Protection Act
UDHR	Universal Declaration of Human Rights
UK	United Kingdom
UKBA	UK Border Agency
UN	United Nations
UNHRC	United Nations Human Rights Council
UNICEF	UN International Children's Emergency Fund
UNODC	UN Office on Drugs and Crime
UN TIP Protocol	Protocol to Prevent, Suppress and Punish Trafficking in Persons, especially Women and Children
UNTOC	Convention against Transnational Organized Crime

UPR	Universal Periodic Review
US	United States (adjective)
USA	United States of America
VDPA	Vienna Declaration and Programme of Action
WHO	World Health Organization

Acknowledgements

We would like to express our sincere gratitude to Julia Farrell, who turned our disparate chapters into what we hope is a cohesive book. Kimberly Klein identified US case study material with remarkable efficiency and insight, and Rebecca Powell performed additional research with equal proficiency. Elaine would like to thank her family – Rob, Jim and Tom – for the tea, biscuits and emotional sustenance. Marinella would like to thank her parents, Lucia and Carmelo, for their support over the years. Leanne would like to thank her partner, Tony Kiek, for his gentle reminders about the things that are most important in life.

The authors and publishers would like to thank Thomson Reuters (Professional) Australia Limited www.thomsonreuters.com.au for permission to reproduce material from the chapter 'Criminal Justice and Human Rights', published in M. Marmo, W. de Lint and D. Palmer (eds) *Crime and Justice: A Guide to Criminology*, 4th edn, 2011, Australia; the Institute for Public Policy Research for permission to reproduce an adapted version of a table from T. Lanning, I. Loader and R. Muir, *Redesigning Justice: Reducing Crime through Justice Reinvestment*, 2011; the House of Representatives Hansard for permission to reproduce an extract from a speech given on 10 April 2000; and the Sentencing Project for permission to reproduce a table from C. Mason, *International Growth in Prison Privatization*, 2013.

About this Book

Human rights have been described at various points in history as 'nonsense' by their detractors and as 'secular religion' by their supporters. They are inescapably controversial, but at this point in time many people believe they are indispensable. Human rights provide a set of normative standards against which the performance of governments can be assessed, and are referred to increasingly in the quest for social, cultural and economic justice as well as for the protection of civil liberties. In this risk-conscious age, where security looms large as a political goal, human rights can provide the language and concepts to ask critical questions about the harms, benefits and limits of state action and inaction. Is the security of some people being pursued at the expense of the rights of others? Or are some fundamental rights and freedoms being sacrificed completely in the name of community safety, in a way that will benefit no one in the longer term? We believe that the positioning of criminology in an arena in which individuals and groups encounter the power and the promise of the state makes the critical study of human rights an essential element of contemporary criminological inquiry.

The purpose of this text is to build bridges between the knowledge domains of criminology and human rights. It is aimed at established criminologists and advanced students of criminology with little or no prior knowledge of human rights. While the book is suitable as a text for specialized undergraduate or postgraduate courses in human rights, crime and criminal justice, it has also been drafted with the independent reader in mind. In the first section, we provide a broad, multidisciplinary introduction to human rights concepts, and the law and practice of human rights. In the second section, human rights thinking is applied systematically to a range of well-established topics within criminology and criminal justice. In the final section, we identify some broad research themes within criminology that we believe illustrate the growing relevance of human rights in a globalizing world.

The book does not include important developments relating to the creation of the International Criminal Court and its dealings with large-scale international crimes such as genocide, war crimes and crimes against humanity. Nor does it review the ground-breaking work that is being done by criminologists on transitional justice and peacemaking in international arenas. This is not because we consider these topics to be irrelevant to criminology or insignificant in the wider scheme of things. Rather, it is because important and highly specialized books are already being written on these subjects (see Parmentier and Weitekamp 2007; Stanley 2009; Braithwaite et al. 2010; Savelsberg 2010).

Moreover, these emerging areas of study extend the scope of criminology beyond the usual concern with the maintenance of social order within generally peaceful and stable societies, towards an engagement with fundamental questions of war and peace. While we wish to endorse these developments towards a more globally aware discipline, our focus is deliberately on the more familiar concerns of what we call 'everyday criminology', as it is usually practised within advanced democracies. Instead of seeking to extend the boundaries of criminology to become more globally focused, we are attempting to locate human rights within more well-trodden criminological territory. Rather than seeing human rights as applicable only to distant places with unstable and undemocratic governments, we hope to illuminate some of the connections between domestic criminology and the international human rights arena. This leads us to consider how human rights can be relevant to the operation of criminal law (Chapter 6), crime prevention at the local and national levels (Chapter 7), accountable policing (Chapter 8), and the pursuit of criminal justice (Chapters 9 to 12).

Our approach to the promise and pitfalls of human rights is both circumspect and hopeful. We are mindful of the arrogance of simply assuming the universal acceptance of human rights, the naivety of the unreflective conflation of human rights with the content of human rights law, the danger and hypocrisy of using human rights as a shield while pursuing individual or elite interests, and the limitations of law of any kind in the face of entrenched injustice. Still, we see in human rights an important framing that is becoming essential for criminologists to understand, if not embrace, under conditions of globalization that are transforming both the world and the discipline.

References

Braithwaite, J., Braithwaite, V., Cookson, M. and Dunn, L. (2010) *Anomie and Violence: Non-truth and Reconciliation in Indonesian Peacebuilding*, Canberra: ANU E Press.

Parmentier, S. and Weitekamp, E. (eds) (2007) *Crime and Human Rights*, Amsterdam: Elsevier.

Savelsberg, J. (2010) *Crime and Human Rights*, London: Sage.

Stanley, E. (2009) *Torture, Truth and Justice*, London: Routledge.

Understanding Human Rights

The term 'human rights' can be used in a superficial way that amounts to little more than sloganeering. But if human rights are to count for more than empty rhetoric, it is important to have a sound understanding of the origins and meaning of the term.

In this section we explain the multifaceted nature of human rights — as political philosophy, international law and socio-political practice. We concentrate on the concept and meaning of human rights, initially with minimal reference to criminology, and assume little or no prior knowledge of either human rights law or theory on the part of the reader.

In Chapters 1 to 3 we discuss the nature of human rights as moral standards, as legal constructs and as a basis for political claims, and outline some of the major objections to applying human rights in these contexts.

In Chapter 4 we introduce the idea of collective rights and explain the tensions between individual and group rights. We then relate this discussion to one of the most fundamental principles of human rights — non-discrimination, which is also a core concern within criminology.

Finally, in preparation for Section 2, where we apply human rights thinking systematically to specific areas of criminology, we summarize in Chapter 5 some of the ways in which human rights perspectives are already being applied within criminology.

CHAPTER 1

The Origins and Idea of Human Rights

> **Key concepts**
> Natural rights — Social contract — Universality — Inalienability —
> Indivisibility

1.1 Introduction

Reference to human rights is commonplace in contemporary societies. But what does the term actually mean, and where does it come from? In this chapter we consider human rights as *normative* or moral claims that operate primarily in the space between individuals and the state. Human rights set out rules and standards about how governments and populations should behave. It is their prescriptive character, stating what *should* be, rather than what *is*, that identifies human rights as a system of normative claims.

1.2 What are human rights?

Whatever we think about what human rights are, where they came from and what are their limits, it can be said that 'commitment to human rights is a commitment to a moral vision of how the world should be regulated' (Fagan 2012: 19).

The concept of rights has existed in various forms since ancient times (see, for example, Haas 2008). In modern times, rights came to be associated with individuals rather than collectives, and conceptualized as *human* rights. This way of articulating the relationship between individuals and the state is often traced to social contract theory, as developed by liberal Enlightenment philosophers, most notably British philosopher John Locke. According to Lockean social contract theory, citizens make a notional pact with their rulers to give up some of their individual autonomy (or sovereignty) in return for the provision of collective security. This is a rather risky venture, since governments can misuse the power that has been vested in them by the people. Human rights are intended to be a tool for mitigating this risk of misuse. They express the parameters of that political bargain, and propose limits on the ways that governments can exert their power over citizens. The language of rights is therefore tightly interwoven with the philosophical underpinnings of the liberal democratic state, and can be seen as a kind of citizen's insurance against tyrannical government.

This way of understanding human rights, as a 'bulwark against the state', is quite a negative conception, aimed at ensuring freedom from unwarranted interference by the state with an individual's property, privacy, conscience or liberty. However, in more recent times, particularly since the emergence of the welfare state, residents of liberal democracies have come to expect that governments will intervene more actively on their behalf to promote their security and wellbeing. This has led to a more positive conception of human rights as an agenda of individual entitlements to receive support from the state in relation to health, education and employment, as well as the protection of the classic civil liberties mentioned above. However, since considerable state intervention is needed, including the establishment of a criminal justice system, to ensure that individuals are protected from breaches of their civil liberties, the distinction between positive and negative rights may not be particularly meaningful.

Adherence to particular political ideologies may influence which of these aspects of human rights is emphasized or supported in practice. Forms of liberalism that advocate minimal intervention by government in social and/or economic affairs tend to favour (negative) civil liberties over (positive) welfare rights. The right to work, for example, has little meaning within capitalist systems, where full employment is not considered an objective of government. Welfare liberalism or socialist philosophies advocate state responsibility for meeting human needs, and therefore focus on positive rights such as the provision of housing, jobs and education. In practice, this has sometimes occurred at the expense of civil liberties. It is possible to steer a middle course through these positive and negative conceptions of the role of government with respect to human rights. Former US president, Franklin D. Roosevelt, who was – unusually within the American political context – a strong supporter of social and economic rights, expressed this position as follows: 'The only sure bulwark of continuing liberty is a government strong enough to protect the interests of the people, and a people strong enough and well enough informed to maintain its sovereign control over its government.'

1.3 The philosophical foundations of human rights

Despite the endurance and widespread acceptance of the idea of human rights, it is not an easy matter to establish beyond doubt that we have them. Locke relied on the idea of *natural rights* given to individuals by God, to support his assertion that all human beings possess human rights. This was part of a radical agenda aimed at refuting the doctrine of the Divine Right of Kings in favour of a more democratic form of government that recognized the sovereignty of individuals. The utilitarian philosopher, Jeremy Bentham, famously referred to the idea of human rights as 'rhetorical nonsense – nonsense upon stilts'. Bentham argued instead that laws should be devised by governments to maximize *utility*, an elusive concept that roughly equates to the common good. Critics of Bentham's utilitarianism argue that governance directed single-mindedly at achieving the common good may sacrifice the wellbeing of some individuals for the benefit of others. For example, governments might subject individuals to harsh punishment in order to deter others from committing crimes, regardless of the guilt or innocence of those punished.

German philosopher, Immanuel Kant, argued that individuals must be treated as autonomous moral agents, and therefore as ends in themselves, not as a means to achieve utilitarian objectives. He also claimed that identifying universal moral rules (which he called 'categorical imperatives') that can be derived from pure reason is the best way to provide this protection. This style of moral reasoning is described as *deontological*, meaning that it is based on moral obligations and duties, rather than on a consideration of consequences. While he did not refer to human rights explicitly, our understanding of contemporary human rights owes a large debt to the philosophy of Kant (see Caranti 2012). Liberal theorist, Ronald Dworkin, famously described rights as moral duties that normally 'trump' other considerations, unless a very strong argument can be made that breaching an individual right is necessary to achieve some greater social good (Dworkin 1984). As we shall see in Chapter 2, the drafting of international human rights law often leaves a generous space for consideration of the common good, in recognition of the continued relevance of consequentialist forms of moral reasoning in contemporary governance.

Even after making a convincing case in favour of human rights, it is not a straightforward matter to find a philosophical foundation for them. There is ongoing debate over how the idea of universal human rights might be derived through philosophical reasoning from other concepts such as 'duties', 'needs', 'human nature', 'essential interests', 'shared capacity for suffering', 'human agency' or the goal of securing 'equal individual liberty' (see Fagan 2012). In the face of these conceptual difficulties, postmodern philosophers such as

Richard Rorty have concluded that human rights need not be rationally 'grounded' at all, but can instead be embraced in the spirit of human solidarity (Rorty 1993). Other political philosophers have objected to this 'anti-foundationalism', arguing that a 'quasi-foundational' justification for rights can be established by adopting a 'pragmatic' perspective, accepting that human rights are social constructions, but are none the less real rather than imaginary (Bufacchi 2008). The array of philosophical justifications for the existence and content of human rights is somewhat bewildering to the non-philosopher. Some of these positions delve deeply into what it means to be human, while others reject these considerations as essentialist. Some explanations attempt to sidestep these issues by defining human rights in terms of the functions they perform. Despite the inconclusive nature of these debates, human rights continue to have widespread appeal as practical vehicles for making moral claims. As Conor Gearty notes, 'we have a paradox: the idea of human rights has been reaching dizzying heights in the world of politics and law whilst its philosophical base has been increasingly called into question' (Gearty 2006: 11).

While we do not attempt to get to the bottom of these complex arguments in this book, the way we think about and justify human rights does matter in everyday life. For example, the idea of God-given natural rights sometimes makes an appearance in political debate. In the USA, the Bill of Rights enacted in 1789 after the violent overthrow of British rule is seen by many US citizens as the ultimate or only source of their individual rights. While there is no explicit reference to God in the US Constitution or Bill of Rights, some conservative groups still insist that these documents represent the will of God and therefore cannot be changed. In the political debate about arms control that followed the 2012 Newtown school massacre in the USA, the National Rifle Association has lobbied fervently against restrictions on gun ownership, largely on the basis of Americans' 'God-given rights' under the Second Amendment (see Box 1.1). This example alone illustrates that what we believe our rights to be, and how we justify them, has serious implications for governance and the types of societies we create.

Despite increasing scepticism about the idea of natural rights (but see Feser 2012), Locke's starting point – that universal human rights arise from recognition of the equal dignity and moral worth of all human beings – continues to underpin contemporary understanding of human rights. In practice, while it might fall short of providing a philosophical 'proof', for many human rights supporters it is sufficient to assert that human rights are the rights we have simply by virtue of being human. Whether founded on a belief in God or derived from reason, intuition or solidarity, it is the shared vulnerability to suffering and insecurity that marks the human condition, and renders human

---

Box 1.1   A God-given right to bear arms?

The Second Amendment of the US Constitution reads:

> 'A well regulated Militia, being necessary to the security of a free State,
> the right of the people to keep and bear Arms, shall not be infringed.'

Source: http://www.archives.gov/exhibits/charters/bill_of_rights_transcript.
html.

Disparate interpretations from voices in the US gun control debate:

> 'No government gave [these rights] to us and no government can take
> them away.'
> (Wayne La Pierre, President of the National Rifle Association)

> 'There are absolutes in our Bill of Rights. And they were put there on
> purpose by men who knew what words meant and meant their prohibi-
> tions to be absolute.'
> (Supreme Court Justice Hugo Black, as cited by Wayne La Pierre)

> 'Progress does not compel us to settle centuries-long debates about the
> role of government for all time — but it does require us to act in our time.'
> (President Barak Obama in his inaugural swearing-in address)

Sources: http://www.theblaze.com/stories/2013/01/22/nra-issues-major-
response-to-obamas-inaugural-address-no-govt-can-ever-take-away-our-
god-given-freedoms/; and http://www.breitbart.com/Big-Government/
2013/01/22/Wayne-LaPierre-To-Obama-The-2nd-Amendment-Protects-
God-Given-Rights.

---

rights an important tool for addressing human need. On the other hand, human rights have come increasingly to be understood as being socially and legally constructed, with their particular content open to political debate and amendment as circumstances change.

Dembour (2012) has suggested that contemporary views on the nature of human rights can be divided into four ideal types: the *natural school*, which considers human rights to be 'given', derivable metaphysically either from God or reason; the *deliberative school*, which conceives of human rights as 'agreed' and as an important vehicle for expressing fundamental entitlements; the *protest school*, which sees human rights as 'fought for', stresses practical action to redress injustice, and is less concerned with their philosophical underpinnings; and the *discourse school*, which views human rights as merely 'talked about', accepting that they represent a powerful language to express political claims, while lacking a deep belief in their authenticity. While many human rights thinkers will align themselves with several of these camps, Dembour identifies representative scholars from each school, including Jack Donnelly (natural), Jürgen Habermas (deliberative), Costas Douzinas (protest) and James Nickel (discourse). Key readings from each of these significant thinkers are listed at the end of this chapter.

1.4 Some criticisms of human rights

Several decades ago, feminist legal theorist Carol Smart (1989) observed that '[i]t's almost as hard to be against rights as it is to be against virtue'. While 'rights talk' has become pervasive in many contemporary societies, this statement may not be as applicable now as it was at that time. Serious reactions against human rights approaches are now emerging in liberal democracies that once supported the idea of human rights, and many recent books on the subject conclude with speculations about whether human rights will, or should, survive (for example, Gearty 2006). In addition to these broad political and legal debates, there has always been a range of philosophical objections to the idea of human rights as a way of regulating the relationship between individuals, the state and other collectivities.

For communitarians, the relationship between individuals and communities is the essential building block of moral and political thought. Communitarians from a variety of political traditions, from conservative to Marxist, argue that human rights thinking encourages selfish *egoism*, by placing the concerns of isolated individuals above the collective good. Alasdair MacIntyre rejects the idea of human rights completely and, in a famous phrase that rivals Bentham's reference to rights as 'nonsense upon stilts', has argued that human rights are 'as real as unicorns' (cited in Etzioni 2012). Other communitarians reject liberal individualism while retaining some commitment to the idea of human rights, advocating moral dialogue to resolve conflicts between individual rights and collective goods, which will lead to different emphases and outcomes in different socio-political contexts (Etzioni 2012).

It is true that individuals may sometimes use human rights instruments for reasons that others consider to be trivial or motivated by narrow self-interest. Rights talk is also frequently used in a disingenuous fashion by governments and other powerful groups to justify agendas that are exploitative or harmful. However, human rights advocates assert that most of the time human rights principles are used to defend members of vulnerable groups – such as refugees,

---

Box 1.2   Most codified human rights norms are not absolute

Excerpt from Article 19, International Covenant on Civil and Political Rights:

2. Everyone shall have the right to freedom of expression …
3. The exercise of the rights provided for in paragraph 2 of this article carries with it special duties and responsibilities. It may therefore be subject to certain restrictions, but these shall only be such as are provided by law and are necessary:
   (a) For respect of the rights or reputations of others;
   (b) For the protection of national security or of public order (*ordre public*), or of public health or morals.

---

political dissidents, indigenous peoples or cultural minorities – from serious forms of discrimination and harm. For Ignatieff (2001), it is the extent to which members of oppressed groups have *themselves* sought to define their struggles in terms of human rights that has proved the value of individual rights.

An examination of the wording of human rights instruments (see Box 1.2) shows that most are not expressed in absolute terms, but are drafted in a way that provides space for consideration of the common good. In fact, Article 29 of the Universal Declaration of Human Rights (UDHR) states explicitly (though rather vaguely) that individual rights need to be balanced against broader considerations such as the general welfare, the preservation of social order and the rights of others.

The *legal formalism* of human rights, when codified as international law (see Chapter 2), is also a basis for criticism among those who favour political activism and social engagement over legalistic and state-centred approaches. As Kurasawa (2012: 156) explains, 'formalism poorly grasps the cultural processes and forms of social interaction that are at the core of human rights'. Communitarians typically favour informal social controls and community action over appeals to positive law (Etzioni 2012). Anthony Woodiwiss (2005) notes that a resurgence of support for the reciprocity of rights and duties makes human rights more appealing from his sociological perspective, as it accords a central role to interpersonal relations. On the other hand, where a focus on duties manifests within neo-liberal governance as an insistence that individual rights must be earned or deserved, this shifts too much responsibility away from government and ignores significant power differentials that render some people less able to meet their own needs (Hudson 2003). Even some communitarians (notably Michael Walzer) are distancing themselves from the view that communities should be the sole source of moral values, recognizing that this pays too little attention to possible inequalities and injustices in communal practices (Etzioni 2012).

The fact that existing human rights instruments generally specify minimum standards rather than challenging unjust power structures also attracts criticism from those who favour a more progressive politics aimed at achieving equality and social justice. Adherents of what Dembour (2012) describes as the 'protest school' of human rights are also suspicious of the utility of law, including human rights law, to represent the interests of oppressed groups. Fagan (2012: 20, citing J. W. Nickel) has characterized human rights as 'a form of minimal moral perfectionism', which does not 'determine everything that may be considered good and desirable' but rather 'aims to establish a minimal threshold below which a minimally good life is not possible'. Moreover, this minimalist approach is also biased towards strong advocacy of civil and political liberties, alongside much more limited demands in relation to social and economic rights that are usually of most concern to advocates of social justice. Article 2 of the 1966 International Covenant on Economic, Social and Cultural Rights (ICESCR) stipulates that a government should aim to 'achiev[e] progressively' the rights contained in the treaty 'to the maximum of its available resources'. No such 'get out' clause is contained within the International Covenant on Civil and Political Rights (ICCPR), even though the costs of holding democratic elections and maintaining a fair criminal justice system, for example, are considerable.

Despite the objections outlined above, scholars with a commitment to social justice or socialism have sometimes endorsed human rights approaches, opting to focus on human needs, and economic and collective rights, rather than abstract morality (see, for example, Beitz 1979; Campbell 1983). Some scholars also repudiate the view that Marx rejected human rights outright because of scepticism about the existence of a pre-social human nature, while arguing that he rightly viewed the conception and practice of human rights as inscribed into the capitalist economy and thereby tainted by the inequalities it produced (Dembour 2006). The view that a comprehensive realization of human rights can align with socialist goals is reflected in this statement by Nordahl (1992: 184) that a 'society with a full complement of human rights cannot be a class society'. The so-called capabilities approach (see Chapter 3) promoted by political philosopher Martha Nussbaum and development economist Amartya Sen (Nussbaum and Sen 1993) presents an alternative vision that is not entirely antagonistic to human rights but seeks to avoid the abstraction, legal formalism and minimalism that makes human rights unappealing to many critics.

Feminism has provided another source of criticism of human rights. Feminists who, like Carol Smart, are sceptical about the value of law in the pursuit of gender equality, have considered human rights to be of marginal value in addressing systemic problems faced by women, such as discrimination and violence within the home, because of their focus on the relationship between individuals and the state. Freeman responds to this criticism by arguing that 'defending the rights of individual women does not entail denying the structural causes of their violation' (Freeman 2011: 150), and notes that Article 2(e) of the Convention on the Elimination of All Forms of Discrimination against Women (CEDAW) imposes on states the obligation to eliminate discrimination against women by any person, organization or enterprise. By the 1990s, feminist activism within human rights movements had begun to challenge successfully the traditional neglect of the private sphere in domestic law and human rights practice (see also Chapter 4):

> Traditional human rights groups that had long concentrated on human rights abrogations by governments against their citizens began to accept the fact that violations of rights by citizens against each other were equally valid human rights abrogations. The private and public spheres began to merge in human rights theory and practice. (Arvonne 1999: 904)

Moreover, feminist intellectual Nancy Fraser credits the 'women's rights are human rights' movement (see Thomas and Beasley 1993; Peters and Wolper 1995) with defining a new global phase of feminism (Fraser and Naples 2004).

Perhaps one of the most protracted debates about human rights has revolved around the claim of *universality* that underpins orthodox human rights thinking and pervades international human rights instruments. The UDHR grounds international human rights norms in the 'recognition of the inherent dignity and of the equal and inalienable rights of all members of the human family', and states in Article 2 that *everyone* is entitled to the rights set out therein. However, far from being universal or universally accepted, critics argue that the form and content of contemporary human rights norms reflect the liberal-democratic tradition from which these norms emerged. Imposing them on others from different religious and political traditions may therefore amount to a form of cultural imperialism. The debate pits the claims to universalism made within international human rights instruments against the particularist view that social and political relations can only be understood within particular contexts. Opponents of universalism may dispute the foundational assumptions of human rights, such as the inherent equality of all human beings; reject the whole idea of human rights in favour of communitarian, authoritarian or utilitarian modes of rule directed towards the common good; or merely object to particular human rights norms that do not align with their world view.

Accusations that the presumption of universality associated with human rights thinking ignores important cultural, political and religious differences between peoples have particular resonance in today's multicultural and identity-conscious world. It is important for human rights advocates to acknowledge that the contemporary framework of human rights was forged in the particular context of post-war Europe and effectively institutionalized the political values of the liberal democracies of Europe and North America at that time. While many other governments have subsequently agreed to be bound by various treaties arising from this system, it is an empirical reality that many groups do not accept the fundamental premises of human rights thinking. But the extreme opposite to universalism – cultural relativism – can be equally problematic, potentially leaving individuals at the mercy of unjust practices justified on cultural grounds. In an increasingly interconnected world, practices that do not treat all people as deserving of equal concern and respect, such as discriminating against women or sexual minorities, or inflicting cruel, inhuman and degrading punishments, will be objectionable to large numbers of people. Of course, the rights-violating practices of advanced liberal democracies in which the rights of workers or the homeless are not protected adequately, or the elderly are not cared for appropriately, are equally open to criticism. A middle ground can be found based on respectful cross-cultural dialogue in which all participants need to acknowledge that their moral judgements are influenced by culturally conditioned norms and values (Etzioni 2012). For example, Mookherjee (2009) has proposed that universal human rights should not necessarily 'trump' cultural considerations (as argued, for example, by Donders 2010) provided that women from minority groups are able to contest what may be male-dominated interpretations of their culture.

It is possible to acknowledge the validity of many of the criticisms discussed above without abandoning the idea of human rights completely. If the idea has strategic value in promoting accountable government, and as a vehicle for expressing human solidarity and achieving practical benefits for humankind, then it might be hoped that understandings of human rights can be reconceived to meet the needs and expectations of a rapidly changing and diverse world. In fact, the preamble to the UDHR refers to the principles contained in that foundational document as a 'common standard of achievement' and exhorts governments to 'strive by teaching and education to promote respect for these rights and freedoms'. This seems to convey the aspirational nature of the document, while undoubtedly overstating the extent to which its content reflects the shared aspirations of all humanity. This interpretation seems to align with the 'deliberative school' described by Dembour (see above). While the 'natural school' takes universality as a given, and 'protest scholars' infer from the ubiquity of injustice that human rights are universally relevant, 'deliberative scholars' advocate that universality should be achieved by building on areas of 'overlapping consensus'. Only discourse scholars reject claims of universality completely and are suspicious of consensus-based approaches that ignore or underestimate inequalities in power relations.

Despite the reference to 'discourse' in his formulation of 'discourse ethics', German philosopher Jürgen Habermas (1996) is perhaps the best-known human rights scholar from the deliberative school. He advocates resolving conflict over the content and meaning of human rights via respectful dialogue, starting with the basic premise that 'only those norms and normative institutional arrangements are valid which can be agreed to by all concerned under special argumentation situations named discourses' (cited in Benhabib 2004: 13). It has been objected that this approach provides an idealized process, but not a definitive answer to the problem of disputes over the meaning and content of rights. Some commentators have suggested that opportunities for agreement could be maximized by sorting human rights norms into hierarchies, noting that agreement is more likely where the field of discussion is narrowed to core concerns (Koji 2001). Ignatieff (2001) has made a similar point, arguing that promoting a 'thin' conception of human rights (which in his view contains only negative rights or liberties) is essential if their usefulness and value is to be universally acknowledged.

1.5 Core human rights concepts

The contemporary human rights framework is premised on three core assumptions about the universality, inalienability and indivisibility of human rights. Each of these principles, in turn, has been the subject of criticism and controversy. The claim of universality and the main objections to it have already been considered. The claim that human rights are indivisible – that is, that all the rights contained in the UDHR and subsequent treaties are interrelated so that none can be taken away without damaging the overall framework – is challenged seriously by proposals about 'core values' and 'hierarchies of human rights' (Koji 2001). Ironically, these challenges to the indivisibility of human rights often arise from attempts to establish universality, as discussed above. The legal concept of derogation (discussed further in Chapter 2) also creates hierarchies within positive rights, since non-derogable rights, such as freedom from torture, slavery or arbitrary deprivation of life, freedom of conscience and recognition as a person under the law, are given a more secure status than rights that can be breached legitimately under emergency conditions. Moreover, the framing of many social, cultural and economic rights also designates them explicitly as aspirational, as already discussed. The recognition that the content of human rights law is not fixed for all time, but should be subject to change and ongoing negotiation, also challenges any straightforward doctrine of indivisibility.

The concept of inalienability asserts that human rights are inherent to the human person and therefore cannot be lost or taken away. The realm of criminal justice is one of the main arenas in which the inalienability of human rights is put to the test. The belief that individuals forfeit their human rights when they commit criminal offences is often expressed in popular discourse. This view is compatible with the emphasis placed on individual responsibility and moral character within contemporary neo-liberal governance, such that rights are commonly conceived of as being 'earned'. In contrast, the doctrine of inalienability asserts that human rights protections are not conditional on good behaviour, on membership of a favoured group in society, or on any other indicator of personal merit; they derive from our shared humanity and apply always to everyone. Comments made by Australian High Court Justice Michael Kirby in *Muir v The Queen* at paragraph 25 illustrate very clearly the inalienability doctrine:

> Prisoners are human beings. In most cases, they are also citizens in this country, 'subjects of the Queen' and 'electors' under the Constitution. They should, as far as the law can allow, ordinarily have the same rights as all other persons before this Court. They have lost their liberty whilst they are in prison. However, so far as I am concerned, they have not lost their human dignity or their right to equality before the law. (*Muir v The Queen* [2004] HCA 21, at paragraph 25)

The breach of an individual's right to liberty for a reason allowed within human rights frameworks – for example, in order to imprison those who have been convicted of criminal acts under fair and reliable legal procedures – is not the same thing as a wholesale denial of that individual's human rights. Put another way, human rights commitments require that individuals retain the right to be free from torture even when they are a convicted prisoner; are ensured the right to a fair trial even when they are a suspected terrorist; and have rights to privacy and social assistance on release even when they are a known paedophile. These are propositions that may attract considerable opposition even within liberal democracies. For this reason, human rights advocates often argue that human rights are most needed in a climate of 'popular punitivism' or generalized social conflict.

Arguably related to the idea of inalienability is Hannah Arendt's famous exposition of 'the right to have rights' (Arendt 1968; see also Benhabib 2004).

To comprehensively deny an individual the right to have rights is to place him or her outside the boundaries of legal protection and moral concern. For Arendt, a German Jew, this was more than a theoretical possibility. Having experienced the failure of the 'rights of man' to protect minorities in Nazi Germany, Arendt was critical of the fragility of human rights that are based on a universalist foundation of human dignity. She asserted that: 'Although human rights were to attach to humans simply in their being human, the truth was that without membership as citizens of a polity, human rights proved to be powerless' (Berkowitz 2012: 62). After the Second World War, the importance of universal protection under the law was recognized in Article 26 of the ICCPR, which states that 'All people are equal before the law and are entitled without any discrimination to the equal protection of the law', and rights to nationality were also established. However, according to Berkowitz, Arendt's project was aimed at putting the philosophical foundations of human rights on a more secure footing that makes them independent of state sovereignty. Since there is no 'sphere of humanity' that could underwrite human rights independently, Arendt's solution was to ground them in the idea of 'the right to have rights', which she interpreted as the right to belong to some kind of community and/or polity.

1.6 Conclusion

It seems that the only option for supporters of human rights – other than adherents of the 'natural school' – is to accept that the overall concept and specific content of human rights will remain contested, since our understanding of human rights is unavoidably embedded within variable cultural, social and political contexts. Nevertheless, an international legal framework exists that sets out the human rights principles that various governments have agreed to uphold. Since no world government has yet emerged, the translation of purportedly universal human rights norms into international human rights law has proceeded through the apparatus of the United Nations. Far from bypassing state sovereignty according to Arendt's vision, this framework operates within a system of independent sovereign nations, creating an ongoing tension between individual and group rights and the rights of states. Chapter 2 provides a basic overview of the current system of international human rights law.

Additional readings and materials

Universal Declaration of Human Rights
    Available at: http://www1.umn.edu/humanrts/instree/b1udhr.htm.

Constitution of the United States of America

    Available at: http://www.archives.gov/exhibits/charters/constitution.html

International Covenant on Economic, Social and Cultural Rights

    Available at: http://www1.umn.edu/humanrts/instree/b2esc.htm.

International Covenant on Civil and Political Rights

    Available at: http://www1.umn.edu/humanrts/instree/b3ccpr.htm.

Cushman, T. (2012) *Handbook of Human Rights*, Abingdon: Routledge.

Dembour, M. (2006), *Who Believes in Human Rights? Reflections on the European Convention*, Cambridge, Cambridge University Press.

Donnelly, J. (2002) *Universal Rights in Theory and Practice*, Ithaca, NY: Cornell University Press.

Douzinas, C. (2000) *The End of Human Rights: Critical Legal Thought at the Turn of the Century*, Oxford: Hart Publishing.

Kalin, W. (2013) 'Late modernity: human rights under pressure?' *Punishment and Society* 15(4): 397–411.

Locke, J., *The Second Treatise of Government* (first published 1689). Available as a free download from Project Gutenberg at http://www.gutenberg.org/ebooks/7370.

Neier, A. (2012) *The International Human Rights Movement: A History*, Princeton, NJ: Princeton University Press.

Nickel, J.W. (1987) *Making Sense of Human Rights: Philosophical Reflections on the Universal Declaration of Human Rights*, Berkeley, CA: University of California Press.

Osiatynski, W. (2009) *Human Rights and Their Limits*, Cambridge: Cambridge University Press.

Court case cited

Muir v The Queen [2004] HCA 21 (Australia).

References

Arendt, H. (1968) *The Origins of Totalitarianism*, New York: Harcourt Brace Jovanovich.

Arvonne, S. (1999) 'Becoming Human: The Origins and Development of Women's Human Rights', *Human Rights Quarterly*, 21(4): 853–906.

Beitz, C.R. (1979) 'Human Rights and Social Justice', in P. Brown and D. MacLean (eds), *Human Rights and US Foreign Policy*, Lexington, KY: Lexington Books.

Benhabib, S. (2004) *The Rights of Others*, Cambridge: Cambridge University Press.

Berkowitz, R. (2012) 'Hannah Arendt on Human Rights', in T. Cushman (ed.), *Handbook of Human Rights*, Abingdon: Routledge.

Bufacchi, V. (2008) 'The Truth about Rights', *Journal of Human Rights*, 7(4): 311–26.

Campbell, T. (1983) *The Left and Rights: A Conceptual Analysis of the Idea of Socialist Rights*, London: Routledge & Kegan Paul.

Caranti, L. (2012) 'Kant's Theory of Human Rights', in T. Cushman (ed.), *Handbook of Human Rights*, Abingdon: Routledge.

Dembour, M. (2006) *Who Believes in Human Rights? Reflections on the European Convention*, Cambridge: Cambridge University Press.

Dembour, M. (2012) 'What Are Human Rights? Four Schools of Thought', in T. Cushman (ed.), *Handbook of Human Rights*, Abingdon: Routledge.

Donders, Y. (2010) 'Do Cultural Diversity and Human Rights Make a Good Match?', *International Social Science Journal*, 61(199): 15—35.

Dworkin, R. (1984) *Theories of Rights,* London: Duckworth.

Etzioni, A. (2012) 'A Communitarian Critique of Human Rights', in T. Cushman (ed.), *Handbook of Human Rights*, Abingdon: Routledge.

Fagan, A. (2012) 'Philosophical Foundations of Human Rights', in T. Cushman (ed.), *Handbook of Human Rights*, Abingdon: Routledge.

Feser, E. (2012) 'The Metaphysical Foundations of Natural Rights', in T. Cushman (ed.), *Handbook of Human Rights*, Abingdon: Routledge.

Fraser, N. and Naples, N. (2004) 'To Interpret the World and Change It: An Interview with Nancy Fraser', *Signs*, 29(4): 1103—24.

Freeman, M. (2011) *Human Rights*, Cambridge: Polity Press.

Gearty, C. (2006) *Can Human Rights Survive? The Hamlyn Lectures 2005*, Cambridge: Cambridge University Press.

Haas, M. (2008) *International Human Rights: A Comprehensive Introduction*, Abingdon: Routledge.

Habermas, J. (1996) *Between Facts and Norms: Contributions to a Discourse Theory of Law and Democracy*, Cambridge, MA: MIT Press.

Hudson, B. (2003) *Justice in the Risk Society: Challenging and Re-affirming Justice in Late Modernity*, London: Sage.

Ignatieff, M. (2001) *Human Rights as Politics and Idolatry*, Princeton, NJ: Princeton University Press.

Koji, T. (2001) 'Emerging Hierarchy in International Human Rights Law and Beyond: From the Perspective of Non-derogable Rights', *European Journal of International Law*, 12(5): 917—41.

Kurasawa, F. (2012) 'Human Rights as Cultural Practices', in T. Cushman (ed.), *Handbook of Human Rights*, Abingdon: Routledge.

Mookherjee, M. (2009) *Women's Rights as Multicultural Claims: Reconfiguring Gender and Diversity in Political Philosophy*, Edinburgh: Edinburgh University Press.

Nordahl, R. (1992) 'A Marxian Approach to Human Rights', in A. An-Na'im (ed.), *Human Rights in Cross Cultural Perspectives*, Philadelphia, PA: University of Pennsylvania Press.

Nussbaum, M. and Sen, A. (eds) (1993) *The Quality of Life*, Oxford: Clarendon Press.

Peters, J. and Wolper, A. (1995) *Women's Rights, Human Rights: International Feminist Perspectives*, New York/London: Routledge.

Rorty, R. (1993) 'Human Rights, Rationality and Sentimentality', in S. Shute and S. Hurley (eds), *On Human Rights*, New York: Basic Books.

Smart, C. (1989) *Feminism and the Power of Law,* New York: Routledge.

Thomas, D. and Beasley, M. (1993) 'Domestic Violence as a Human Rights Issue', *Human Rights Quarterly*, 15(1): 36—62.

Woodiwiss, A. (2005) *Human Rights: Key Ideas*, London: Taylor & Francis.

CHAPTER 2

International Human Rights Law

Key concepts

Treaties — Sovereignty — Legal positivism — Monitoring mechanisms — Margin of appreciation

2.1 Introduction

Amid all the debate about what human rights are, what they are for, and whether they will endure, human rights remain significant largely because they have been translated into a body of international law underpinned by United Nations (UN) institutions. For legal positivists and other adherents of the 'natural school' of human rights (see Dembour in Chapter 1), the question 'What are human rights?' is answered definitively by referring to this body of law. In this view, human rights are simply the rights that have been agreed formally by governments in treaties and covenants under the auspices of the UN. For those who take a broader view of human rights as moral, political or socio-economic claims, or as a platform from which to address structural inequality, international human rights instruments may not encapsulate everything that human rights are or could be. Nevertheless, they remain highly significant records of the norms and standards that have been agreed formally by governments, if not always observed in practice. In this chapter we provide a brief overview of the global human rights framework articulated in international, regional and domestic legislation.

2.2 The UN and international human rights treaties

Human rights do not constitute the primary *raison d'être* of the UN. The main purpose of the UN is to regulate economic and political relations between nations in pursuit of peace and prosperity. The UN operates as a system of co-operation between autonomous states – not as an independent authority standing over them. It provides an authoritative forum in which representatives of Member States discuss issues of mutual interest, resolve conflicts and sometimes co-operate, without significantly sacrificing their sovereignty – that is, their right to control events and policies within their own territory. In turn, human rights law represents only a small proportion of the international treaties negotiated through UN processes, which include agreements on trade, the law of the sea, the conduct of war and the maintenance of security, and humanitarian obligations to refugees and others affected by conflict. The content of treaties agreed by Member States is generally quite deferential to state sovereignty and within this system states are conceived of as the primary bearers of rights. Article 2 of the UN Charter 1945 specifies that the organization is 'based on the principle of sovereign equality of all its Members'. Of course, as with all political institutions, some members are more able to pursue their interests through the UN than others. And the structure of the UN is also far from democratic. All Member States can participate in the General Assembly. However, the Security Council exercises considerable executive power and retains 'primary responsibility' for maintaining international peace and security. Ten members are elected for a temporary term of office by the General Assembly, while the five permanent members – China, France, Russia, the United Kingdom and the United States (USA) (reflecting the concentration of global power after the Second World War) – each hold a power of veto and therefore wield immense and disproportionate influence.

International human rights law promotes and protects human rights at the international, regional and local levels. Human rights law is contained in international treaties that have been debated and drafted through UN processes, and formally ratified by Member States. It also consists of customary international law, which is a body of binding rules derived from consistent application of human rights norms by nation-states. The mechanisms by which international human rights norms are incorporated into domestic legal systems are discussed in Chapter 6.

Treaties, conventions and covenants are generally considered to be legally binding on states that agree to ratify them. Declarations or statements of principles are merely statements of intent and are usually the starting point for debating and formulating more specific, enforceable treaties. It is not easy to reach agreement about the wording of human rights instruments, and the process of creating a binding agreement can be very lengthy. For example, the finalization of the Declaration on the Rights of Indigenous People in 2007 followed many years of campaigning and diplomacy, and is only the first step towards adopting legally binding guarantees to protect the special interests of indigenous peoples.

Signatories to a treaty may enter *reservations*, indicating their refusal to be bound by certain provisions, but not so many as to undermine the purpose of the treaty. This enables governments to tailor their support for human rights agreements in light of their particular political and cultural circumstances. The deference accorded to state sovereignty is also reflected in the principle of *derogation*, which recognizes the right of states to set aside the binding agreements they have previously made during a declared emergency. Derogation is a comprehensive but temporary measure that is governed by explicit procedures. Article 4 of the International Covenant on Civil and Political Rights (ICCPR) places limitations on the circumstances in which states may withdraw from their human rights obligations under the Covenant, and specifies that no derogation is permissible for core rights such as the prohibition against arbitrary loss of life (Article 6), torture (Article 7) and slavery (Article 8), and guarantees of recognition as a person under the law (Article 16), non-retrospectivity of the law (Article 15), non-discrimination (Article 2) and freedom of thought, conscience and religion (Article 18).

The Universal Declaration of Human Rights (UDHR), adopted in 1948, is the blueprint for the modern human rights system. The preamble grounds the Declaration in the context of the 'disregard and contempt for human rights [that] have resulted in barbarous acts which have outraged the conscience of mankind'. This locates the historical and social context for this foundational document firmly within post-war Europe, though its aspirations are conspicuously universal. While it is classified as a declaration, which might suggest that it holds little authority, legal commentators agree widely that the document has attained the status of *jus cogens* – or customary international law – meaning that it is considered binding on all governments even without a formal process of ratification. This interpretation may not be accepted, of course, by all of the world's governments, nor the many millions of people who know nothing of its existence. In any case, most of the principles set out in the UDHR have been translated into the two major human rights conventions that make up the 'International Bill of Rights': namely, the International Covenant on Economic, Social and Cultural Rights (ICESCR) and the ICCPR, which were adopted in 1966 and entered into force 10 years later.

The division of the rights contained in the UDHR into two separate treaties reflects the fundamental distinction between civil liberties and welfare entitlements, as discussed in Chapter 1. The ICCPR is concerned primarily with freedom from undue interference by the state in relation to life, liberty, privacy, security of the person, and freedom of conscience and association. The ICESCR articulates the rights to earn a living and enjoy fair working conditions, and supports family life, access to health care services and education, and the right to participate freely in cultural life. Unlike the ICCPR, the ICESCR allows that signatory states may recognize the rights contained in the document only to the extent that their economic situation allows. As discussed in Chapter 1, this reveals a bias in favour of civil and political rights within the international human rights system, which are often described as *first generation* rights. While the two major covenants came into force in 1966, the rights contained in the ICCPR can be traced to the Rights of Man that were articulated in revolutionary France and America in the eighteenth century. They reflect the emphasis placed at the time on securing freedom from tyranny. *Second generation* rights embody a more recent political focus on equality, the positive role of government in securing the wellbeing of citizens, and the rise of the welfare state. *Third generation* rights – sometimes described as 'soft' or unofficial rights – are contained in various declarations and resolutions, such as the Vienna Declaration and Programme of Action (VDPA), and do not have the formal and binding status of treaties. These more aspirational statements incorporate newly recognized and emerging rights such as the right to a healthy environment, economic and social development, and various collective rights. Some commentators refer to an emerging *fourth generation* of rights concerning indigenous peoples. As discussed in Chapter 1, the relative weight attached to these different bodies of rights reveals ideological divisions and entrenched power relations within the UN, but also demonstrates the possibility of introducing new candidates for incorporation into international human rights law in response to changing global priorities and conditions.

Beyond these foundational documents that set out the broad contours of human rights protection, hundreds of treaties and declarations have since been agreed on very specific topics ranging from racial discrimination to the prevention of torture, women's rights, children's rights, minority rights and indigenous rights. The Minnesota Human Rights Library provides an easy-to-use gateway to the full range of human rights instruments, indexed both alphabetically and by subject matter (see the web address at the end of this chapter). More recently concluded treaties such as the Convention on the Rights of the Child (CROC), adopted in 1989, and the Convention on the Elimination of All Forms of Discrimination against Women (CEDAW), adopted in 1979, are notable for their emphasis on the indivisibility of rights, including the argument that fulfilment of second generation rights, such as effective participation in social and economic life, is necessary in order to realize an individual's first generation rights. In addition, a myriad of codes of practice relating to the conduct of business, the provision of human rights education and the administration of justice have emanated from various committees, conferences and other standard-setting bodies within the UN system. Box 2.1 identifies some key human rights instruments that are relevant to the prevention of crime and the administration of criminal justice.

Box 2.1   Selected UN treaties, standards and guidelines relevant to crime prevention and criminal justice

Convention Against Transnational Organized Crime (2003)

Convention Against Torture and Other Cruel, Inhuman or Degrading Treatment or Punishment (1987)

Code of Conduct for Law Enforcement Officials (1979)

Basic Principles on the Use of Force and Firearms by Law Enforcement Officials (1990)

Standard Minimum Rules for the Administration of Juvenile Justice (Beijing Rules) (1985)

Declaration of Basic Principles of Justice for Victims of Crime and Abuse of Power (1985)

Basic Principles on the Independence of the Judiciary (1985)

Basic Principles on the Role of Lawyers (1990)

Guidelines on the Role of Prosecutors (1990)

Basic Principles on the Use of Restorative Justice Programmes in Criminal Matters (2000)

Standard Minimum Rules for Non-Custodial Measures (Tokyo Rules) (1990)

Standard Minimum Rules for the Treatment of Prisoners (1977)

Body of Principles for the Protection of all Persons under Any Form of Detention or Imprisonment (1988)

These less formal documents are intended to set standards and provide guidelines for voluntary adoption by Member States.

The body of international criminal law that was consolidated in the Rome Statute (1998) is also attracting the interest of criminologists with a transnational perspective (for example, Parmentier and Weitekamp 2007; Braithwaite *et al.* 2010; Savelsberg 2010). International criminal law covers large-scale, systematic human rights abuses that are generally committed during times of political unrest or armed conflict. This includes war crimes, crimes of aggression, genocide and crimes against humanity. International criminal law has a separate history from the body of human rights law that has developed from the UDHR. War crimes have their origin in the Geneva Conventions that govern the conduct of war. Genocide and crimes against humanity were also originally defined in conventions that were drafted independently from the UDHR. As with many other UN systems, the jurisdiction of the International Criminal Court (ICC) reflects a view of core international crimes that is an artefact of the Second World War. Despite the progress in this area and its close link to international human rights obligations, international criminal law has not been endorsed and codified with the same rate of success.

While it is of great interest to a globally aware criminology, international criminal law is of marginal relevance to the topics covered in this book. Because our focus is on 'everyday criminology' as practised in advanced liberal democracies (see About this Book on pages 1–2), the most relevant body of international human rights law for our discussion is the 'everyday human rights law', which was summarized earlier in the chapter and includes the International Bill of Rights and subsequent third- and fourth-generation rights. Future references to international human rights law should be read as referring to this body of 'everyday' human rights instruments that mediate the legal relations between the individual and the state.

2.3 Monitoring and enforcing human rights

Since human rights law is concerned primarily with relations between individuals and the state, it has always taken a back seat to the major geo-political issues that occupy the attention of UN Member States. The profile of human rights within the UN was raised in 1993 when the General Assembly passed a resolution to create a High Commissioner for Human Rights. The Office of the High Commissioner for Human Rights (OHCHR) has a core mandate to promote and protect 'the enjoyment and full realization, by all people, of all rights established in the Charter of the United Nations and in international human rights laws and treaties'. This includes supporting other human rights monitoring mechanisms, taking a lead in human rights education, engaging with civil society and promoting human rights across the UN. This function was performed previously by the UN Centre for Human Rights, which was formed in the 1980s.

Though the profile of human rights has only been raised in recent decades, human rights have been represented within the UN system since the organization's inception. Two significant human rights institutions were created directly by the UN Charter following sustained activism: the Commission on the Status of Women, and the Human Rights Commission, both formed in 1946. The Human Rights Commission operated under the auspices of the Economic and Social Council (ECOSOC) Committee, which monitored the ICESCR, and its members were elected by ECOSOC members. In contrast to the OHCHR, which is staffed by human rights 'experts' (indicating a measure of independence from governments), the Human Rights Commission was an inter-governmental body. According to most reports, the Commission initially adopted a non-interventionist stance that was highly respectful of state sovereignty. From around the 1960s, during which time decolonization processes and the struggle against apartheid and occupation were high on the UN agenda, the Commission became more interventionist and more deeply politicized. Over time, it developed a reputation for allowing members with dubious human rights records to influence its operation, and was seen by many observers to have lost its legitimacy.

The Human Rights Commission was eventually replaced in 2006 by the UN Human Rights Council, which was formed by a resolution of the UN General Assembly. Like the Commission, it is an inter-governmental body but its members are elected by and report directly to the General Assembly. The Council works closely with the OHCHR on thematic issues including non-discrimination and the rights of indigenous peoples and minorities. The Council has not escaped its own controversies, including accusations of political bias (Lepard 2012). The Human Rights Council is still developing new accountability mechanisms such as a process of Universal Periodic Reviews (UPRs), to which all Member States are subject. Smith (2013) has summarized the performance of the five Permanent Member States of the UN Security Council in the first round of this new process, revealing a mixed human rights record among these prominent nations. The Human Rights Council also hosts an advisory committee of independent experts (the Sub-Commission on the Promotion and Protection of Human Rights), an extensive entourage of Special Rapporteurs, and independent experts and working groups on topics that span the full gamut of civil, political, social, cultural and economic rights.

As with other bodies of law, the purpose in codifying human rights norms is to encourage voluntary compliance with the minimum standards they articulate, and provide a means of redress for violations. The ICC, created by the Rome Statute, deals with large-scale breaches of human rights that have been designated as international crimes, rather than individual cases of human rights violations, as discussed in the previous section. The ICC has the power to convict and punish individual perpetrators, while the less punitive treaty monitoring processes associated with 'everyday' human rights treaties are directed towards governments rather than named individuals. Because of the difficulties of accessing human rights remedies through UN procedures, and the deference shown to the sovereignty of Member States, enforcement is still relatively weak. However, this is not to discount completely the impact of international human rights law.

Nine major human rights treaties have an associated monitoring committee to which signatory states are required to report on a regular basis (see Box 2.2). These are the ICCPR, ICESCR, the Convention on the Eradication of Racial Discrimination (CERD), CEDAW, the International Convention against Torture and other Cruel, Inhuman or Degrading Treatment or Punishment (CAT), CROC, the International Convention for the Protection of All Persons from Enforced Disappearance (ICCPED) and the International Convention on

---

Box 2.2   Human rights monitoring bodies within the UN

Charter-based bodies

These bodies are established directly under the UN Charter and therefore have a wide-ranging jurisdiction over all UN Member States:

- Human Rights Council
- Universal Periodic Review

Treaty-based bodies

These committees are established by particular treaties and are only authorized to monitor compliance by ratifying states with the undertakings contained in that treaty.

Monitoring committee	Treaty
Human Rights Committee	ICCPR
Committee on Economic, Social and Cultural Rights	ICESCR
Committee on the Elimination of Racial Discrimination	CERD
Committee on the Elimination of Discrimination Against Women	CEDAW
Committee Against Torture	CAT
Subcommittee on Prevention of Torture	SPT
Committee on the Rights of the Child	CROC
Committee on the Rights of Persons with Disabilities	CRPD
Committee on Enforced Disappearances	ICCPED
Committee on Migrant Workers	Migrant Workers' Convention

Source: http://www.ohchr.org/EN/HRBodies/Pages/HumanRightsBodies.aspx.

---

the Protection of the Rights of All Migrant Workers and Members of their Families (or the Migrant Workers' Convention). Unlike the universal monitoring processes authorized under the UN Charter, only states that have ratified a particular treaty are subject to scrutiny by the corresponding committee. These compliance procedures are set out in the administration sections of each treaty. The ICESCR has a particularly well-established monitoring regime overseen by ECOSOC, with the regular reporting requirements on states set out in Articles 16–25. States are expected to indicate in their reports 'factors and difficulties affecting the degree of fulfilment of obligations under the Covenant' (Article 17.2), and the monitoring body may, in response, issue recommendations for changes to state practice and can provide technical assistance to this end (Article 23). The intention is clearly educational and non-adversarial, and the system ultimately relies on the co-operation of signatory states in reporting truthfully and responding positively to criticism. Periodic country reports under the main treaties are open to public scrutiny. They can readily be located using the Universal Human Rights Index research tool (see web address at the end of this chapter).

Reporting requirements are supplemented by visits to signatory countries made by Special Rapporteurs and inspection delegations. This enables monitoring bodies to collect information and make observations independently of government, and to collaborate with local human rights non-governmental organizations (NGOs), who are able to offer a different perspective on human rights compliance in that country. For example, a Special Rapporteur on the situation and rights of indigenous people visited Australia in August 2009 under the auspices of the OHCHR to consider the human rights implications of the Northern Territory Emergency Response (NTER) (see Chapter 4). In addition to meeting government representatives, the Special Rapporteur liaised closely with indigenous groups, the Australian Human Rights Commission and other human rights NGOs. Another example is the Committee against Torture, which is empowered under Article 20.3 of the CAT to visit countries in which serious allegations about the systemic use of torture have been made, but may only do so with the agreement of the State Party concerned. The European Committee for the Prevention of Torture (CPT), formed to investigate and prevent torture in Europe under the European Convention on Human Rights, takes a more proactive stance and regularly visits signatory countries to inspect institutions where individuals are detained, again with the permission and co-operation of the country concerned (see web address at the end of this chapter).

Some human rights treaties provide mechanisms for state-to-state complaints that are generally resolved through mediation and/or rights of individual petition, through which individuals may lodge specific complaints about violations of their rights for adjudication by the UN committee associated with that treaty. The Human Rights Committee (HRC) established to monitor compliance with the ICCPR is by far the most developed example of this quasi-judicial function at the UN level. It can make findings about whether governments have breached any of the rights contained in that treaty in a particular case before it, make specific recommendations to states with regard to recompense, and propose more general changes to law or practice to prevent further occurrences. As with the other functions of these committees, there is no formal mechanism to enforce compliance with committee rulings, and the system relies on voluntary compliance, diplomatic pressure and a concern by states to be viewed as a good 'global citizen'.

Governments also control whether or not their citizens have access to these mechanisms for individual complaint. In the case of the ICCPR, states must sign the Optional Protocol to that treaty in order to recognize the competence of the HRC to 'receive and consider communications from individuals subject to its jurisdiction who claim to be victims of a violation by that State Party of any of the rights set forth in the Covenant' (Article 1). It is possible for a country to be a signatory to the main convention without allowing its citizens the right to take individual complaints to the UN. For example, the US ratified the ICCPR (rather belatedly) in 1992, but not the Optional Protocol, arguing that its citizens have effective redress against human rights violations through the US Constitution. Even when access to individual complaint mechanisms is available to individuals, these UN bodies are geographically remote and highly bureaucratic, so that considerable barriers exist in getting cases to adjudication. Individuals must also exhaust any domestic remedies available to them before lodging complaints with UN bodies.

The response to recommendations or adverse findings from UN monitoring bodies and individual complaints mechanisms varies according to the attitude of governments and the degree to which human rights principles are embedded within domestic law, civil society and political culture. It is something of a paradox that human rights are often considered to be a 'bulwark against the state', while individuals have little choice but to rely on states to protect their rights and provide access to means of redress if their rights are violated. Despite widespread cynicism that the ratification of UN treaties is largely 'symbolic' and most states have no intention of complying with their provisions, Haas (2008) claims that research has demonstrated positive effects on human rights compliance following the ratification of human rights treaties, which varies according to mode of governance. The 'halo effect' has been found to be least pronounced in repressive dictatorships, moderate in stable democracies that already have a reasonably good human rights record, and most pronounced in intermediate or unstable regimes. This rather surprising result is said to arise because it is common in unstable countries for one political party to be a staunch supporter of the international human rights system and therefore to engage enthusiastically in order to create human rights infrastructure while it has the opportunity to do so.

2.4 Human rights law beyond the UN

To supplement the UN treaty monitoring and enforcement system, and bring human rights closer to home, several regional inter-governmental bodies have emerged to set human rights standards and monitor, promote and enforce human rights in their region. These are the African Union (formerly the Organization of African Unity), the Organization of American States (incorporating the Inter-American Commission on Human Rights), and the Council of Europe. Asia and the Middle East are yet to develop a formal human rights framework. The Association of Southeast Asian Nations (ASEAN) established the Intergovernmental Commission on Human Rights in 2009, with a remit to promote human rights in the region in response to the Vienna Declaration (Muntarbhorn 2012). To date, it has not established any mechanisms for adjudicating complaints or enforcing human rights obligations. The Asia Pacific Forum (APF) was established earlier in 1996 as an initiative of the national human rights agencies of Australia, India, Indonesia and New Zealand (of which only Indonesia is a full ASEAN member) with a view to supporting governments in the region. The organization is hosted by the Australian Human Rights Commission, and its membership has continued to grow, but it lacks the authority of an inter-governmental entity and its status is in some ways closer to that of a government-funded NGO. An Arab Charter on Human Rights was adopted in 2004 by the Council of the League of Arab States (LAS) and soon attracted controversy because of the inclusion of a highly political statement condemning Zionism. The Arab Human Rights Committee was established five years later to monitor compliance with the Charter.

With the exception of the APF, each of these regional bodies has developed its own agreements about human rights that reflect the cultural and political priorities within the region. For example, the foundational statement on human rights by the former Organization of African Unity (OAU) is the African [Banjul] Charter on Human and Peoples' Rights, which emphasizes the priority placed on collective rights within African traditions. The ASEAN Human Rights Declaration agreed in Phnom Penh at the 2012 ASEAN meeting has been met with widespread criticism, including from the UN High Commissioner for Human Rights, for the precedence the statement grants to domestic law over human rights principles, and for ASEAN's failure to consult with civil society in the region in developing the declaration. Similar accusations of failure to consult have been levelled at the LAS in relation to their human rights charter. A recent proposal spearheaded by Australia, the United Kingdom and Canada for a Commonwealth Commissioner to monitor human rights among Commonwealth nations has so far gained little support. Box 2.3 contains a summary of regional human rights mechanisms; web addresses for key bodies are provided at the end of the chapter.

Of the existing regional bodies, the European system is by far the most developed in terms of its enforcement mechanisms. The European Convention on Human Rights (ECHR) was the first of the regional treaties to

---

Box 2.3   Regional intergovernmental human rights mechanisms

Regional organization	Treaty or declaration	Judicial body
African Commission on Human and Peoples' Rights	Banjul Charter on Human and Peoples' Rights	African Court on Human and Peoples' Rights
Inter-American Commission on Human Rights	American Convention on Human Rights	Inter-American Court of Human Rights
Council of Europe	European Convention on Human Rights	European Court of Human Rights
League of Arab States	Arab Charter on Human Rights	Arab Human Rights Committee
ASEAN Intergovernmental Commission on Human Rights (limited members)	ASEAN Human Rights Declaration	n/a
Proposed Commonwealth Commissioner for Democracy, the Rule of Law and Human Rights	Proposed Charter for the Commonwealth	n/a

---

be ratified by individual European governments, coming into force in 1953. More recently, the European Union (EU) as a collective entity has ratified the EU Charter of Fundamental Rights. Further steps were taken under the Lisbon Treaty to unify the two regimes by initiating proceedings for the EU to accede to the ECHR. The ECHR encompasses most of the Articles of the ICCPR and ICESCR and is interpreted by a fully fledged court, the European Court of Human Rights (ECtHR). The tight drafting of ECHR rights indicates that they were intended to be 'justiceable' (that is, subject to interpretation in court), and the jurisprudence of the court is well developed and influential.

The court initially will determine whether the events described in the complaint constitute a *prima facie* breach of any of the rights set out in the Convention, and if so, consider whether the violation is justified on one of the permissible public interest criteria. For example, Article 11 of the European Convention on Human Rights establishes a right to freedom of peaceful assembly and association with others, but allows restrictions on the exercise of these rights 'such as are prescribed by law and are necessary in a democratic society in the interests of national security or public safety, for the prevention of disorder or crime, for the protection of health or morals or for the protection of the rights or freedoms of others'. This incursion of utilitarian thinking into international human rights law provides some leeway to governments to breach individual rights in the public interest. This discretionary space accorded to governments is known as a 'margin of appreciation' (Harris *et al.* 2009). The task of the court is to decide whether a particular rights violation is both justified and proportionate under the circumstances. Many cases turn on the size of the margin of appreciation adopted by the court.

While it is inevitable that many of the court's findings will be controversial, Harris *et al.* (2009) report that the ECtHR has been influential in prompting policy change, sometimes in signatory countries other than the country against which a finding is made. This indicates the high level of legitimacy accorded to the court. On the other hand, a detailed review of ECtHR jurisprudence carried out by Dembour (2006) led her to five conclusions about the effectiveness of the court as a champion for universal human rights. She found that state interests played a major role in court decisions, human rights considerations were regularly traded off against other concerns, privileged applicants, and men, were more likely to be heard, and the tension between respecting social diversity and attempting to establish common standards meant that the court was destined to be mired in controversy.

Individual complaints are only taken to UN and regional human rights bodies where attempts to seek redress in the country of origin either have failed or are not available. It is generally in the interest of states to provide mechanisms for the enforcement of human rights law within their domestic legal systems if they wish to reduce the number of cases brought against them in these international forums. Incorporation of international human rights treaties into domestic law gives local courts jurisdiction to hear complaints of human rights violations, but the record of such incorporation is patchy. The legal implications of the different methods for translating international human rights norms into domestic settings are discussed from a more theoretical perspective in Chapter 6. In the remainder of this chapter, we consider briefly three examples taken from the Anglophone world that illustrate the very different relationships that are possible between international human rights law and domestic legal systems.

In the USA, the Bill of Rights pre-dates contemporary human rights treaties by several centuries and has inculcated a political philosophy that privileges a negative civil liberties agenda over positive human rights intervention. In addition, suspicion of 'big government' and widespread rejection of the validity of economic and group rights have been barriers to the acceptance of the 'foreign' idea of human rights that are often seen as being only applicable abroad. International human rights obligations are 'non-self-executing', meaning that treaties do not automatically enter into force on US territory on ratification (Hertel and Libal 2011; Lepard 2012). Much of the struggle to introduce international human rights norms into US courts has involved the pursuit of human rights claims concerning events that have taken place beyond America's borders (Davis 2008). Cases involving human rights abusers who are temporarily resident within the USA can be heard by federal courts under the Alien Tort Statute (ATS). However, Davis (2008) reports that these cases are frequently derailed by arguments based on US foreign policy considerations. This has also applied to cases brought against US corporations relating to their actions outside the USA, particularly where the host country has been complicit in the alleged events (such as crimes against humanity, and environmental destruction). Finally, Davis (2008) reports that ATS cases involving allegations against the US Government (for example, in relation to wrongful imprisonment in Guantanamo Bay) have been obstructed by the doctrine of sovereign immunity, and references to national secrets and other defensive arguments concerning the competence of domestic courts to hear these cases. While US citizens can pursue civil rights cases in domestic courts, the engagement with international human rights norms in these wholly domestic cases has been characterized as 'exceptionalism' (Hertel and Libal 2011). However, Hertel and Libal argue that NGOs and lower courts are beginning to lead the way in casting domestic issues within a broader human rights framework.

In Europe, signatories to the ECHR have incorporated its provisions into domestic law in a variety of ways. Britain was almost the last EU country to take legislative action to give direct effect to ECHR rights in domestic courts (just ahead of Ireland), which it did through the introduction of the Human Rights Act 1998 (HRA). Under the HRA, courts may issue declarations of incompatibility where legislation is at odds with ECHR norms, but do not have the power to strike down non-compliant legislation. Gearty (2006) argues that, in comparison with bills of rights elsewhere, the British model has reserved a generous amount of space for political manoeuvring. The heightened security environment of recent years has tested the limits of the courts' powers to enforce human rights standards in the face of patently illiberal laws. The capacity to derogate selectively from the ECHR has allowed the British Government to avoid some potential legal impasses. But it is the non-derogable right to protection from torture that has brought the tensions between parliamentary sovereignty and the rule of law to breaking point. The repeated rulings of British courts preventing the deportation of radical Islamist leader Abu Qatada, on the grounds that evidence obtained through torture could be used against him on his return to Jordan, have infuriated the government, leading Conservative backbenchers to call for Britain to withdraw from the ECHR (discussed in Chapter 6). Writing in 2006, before these events had unfolded, Gearty (2006: 97) concluded, somewhat prophetically, that the legislative framework in the United Kingdom appeared to promote the significance of human rights, while at the same time retaining the supremacy of Parliament to override judicial findings:

> In other words it reflects the human rights mask that the United Kingdom has chosen to wear. Those of us who believe in human rights all hope that it stays put and argue that it should ... But this human rights mask does not necessarily reflect any deep supra-political truths. It can be torn away should the British people through their elected representatives so decide.

While two jurisdictions in Australia (Victoria and the Australian Capital Territory) have enacted human rights charters, the country remains the only advanced liberal democracy without an integrated legal human rights framework or regional human rights treaty. This leaves Australia in an anomalous position in relation to domestic recognition of human rights treaty obligations, particularly considering its current membership of the UN Security Council. A leading commentator on human rights law has concluded that the country 'is a party to all major human rights treaties and yet reluctant to make them work at a domestic level' (Charlesworth 2006: 2). With no bill of rights incorporated into the Australian Constitution, Australian courts have been reluctant to refer directly to human rights norms, but it has been argued that a 'common law bill of rights' has been constructed via disparate decisions of the High Court (Gans *et al.* 2011). Recently, the courts have made some bold decisions overturning harsh border protection policies that would potentially breach Australia's human rights obligations towards asylum seekers (Pickering and Weber 2012). The Australian Human Rights Commission oversees a range of anti-discrimination legislation and is empowered to respond to individual complaints of human rights breaches. It also supports a fully-fledged bill of rights for Australia. A national consultation in 2009 recommended the adoption of a bill of rights. However, the Labor government seized instead on the recommendation for an 'educative' framework aimed at building a 'human rights culture', and decided against legislation for fully enforceable rights, on the grounds that it would be 'contentious' (see Lynch 2013). This was despite the fact that 87 per cent of submissions to the national consultation supported a legislative framework, and independent polling indicated that only 14 per cent of the population was opposed to this course of action. A Human Rights and Anti-Discrimination Bill has since been introduced to the Australian Parliament, but its purpose is merely to consolidate the existing raft of anti-discrimination legislation. The introduction of a bill of rights remains on the agenda, possibly to resurface if and when Australia takes steps to sever its remaining constitutional ties with Britain.

2.5 Conclusion

The codification of human rights principles into binding treaties is a significant step in promoting the protection of human rights, but does not translate seamlessly into human rights compliance. The attitudes taken by governments and populations to the domestic incorporation of human rights agreements reveal the ongoing dialectic between law, politics and civil society. While an intricate web of complaints mechanisms and monitoring systems has been constructed around major treaties, the principle of independent state sovereignty significantly limits the action that can be taken to enforce human rights compliance or ensure redress in individual cases. As Lepard (2012: 595) concludes: 'The effectiveness of international human rights law ultimately depends on the determination of governments to strengthen and uphold it.'

Additional readings and materials

Charter of the United Nations
  Available at: http://www1.umn.edu/humanrts/instree/aunchart.htm.
United Nations — Office of the High Commissioner for Human Rights
  Available at: http://www.ohchr.org/EN/Pages/WelcomePage.aspx.
United Nations — Human Rights Council
  Available at: http://www.ohchr.org/EN/HRBodies/HRC/Pages/HRCIndex.aspx.
United Nations Human Rights Documents library
  Available at: http://research.un.org/en/docs/humanrights.
Universal Human Rights Index (UN research tool)
  Available at: http://www.universalhumanrightsindex.org/.
University of Minnesota Human Rights Library (easy to use)
  Available at: http://www1.umn.edu/humanrts/.
Direct link to Minnesota Human Rights Library treaty ratifications
  Available at: http://www1.umn.edu/humanrts/research/ratification-index.html.
African [Banjul] Charter on Human and Peoples' Rights
  Available at: http://www1.umn.edu/humanrts/instree/z1afchar.htm.
Official site of the African Commission on Human and Peoples' Rights
  Available at: http://www.achpr.org/.
American Convention on Human Rights
  http://www1.umn.edu/humanrts/oasinstr/zoas3con.htm.
Inter-American Commission on Human Rights
  Available at: http://www1.umn.edu/humanrts/iachr/iachr-index.html.

European Convention for the Protection of Fundamental Rights and Freedoms
Available at: http://www1.umn.edu/humanrts/instree/z17euroco.html.
European Court of Human Rights
Available at: http://www.echr.coe.int/Pages/home.aspx?p=home.
European Committee for the Prevention of Torture
Available at: http://www.cpt.coe.int/en/.
ASEAN Human Rights Declaration
Available at: http://www.asean.org/resources/publications/asean-publications/
item/asean-human-rights-declaration-ahrd3.
Arab Human Rights Charter/Committee
Available at: http://www.ijrcenter.org/ihr-reading-room/regional/middle-east-
and-north-africa/.
Alston, P. and Megret, F. (2013) *The United Nations and Human Rights: A Critical Appraisal*, 2nd edn, Oxford: Oxford University Press.
Campbell, T., Ewing, K. and Tomkins, A. (2011) *The Legal Protection of Human Rights, Sceptical Essays*, Oxford: Oxford University Press.
Hannum, H. (2004) *Guide to International Human Rights Practice*, 4th edn, Ardsley, NY: Transnational Publishers.

References

Braithwaite, J., Braithwaite, V., Cookson, M. and Dunn, L. (2010) *Anomie and Violence: Non-truth and Reconciliation in Indonesian Peacebuilding,* Canberra: ANU E Press.
Charlesworth, H. (2006) 'Human Rights: Australia Versus the UN, Democratic Audit of Australia' (Discussion Paper 22/6, Australian National University). Available at: http://apo.org.au/research/human-rights-australia-versus-un (accessed 7 July 2011).
Davis, J. (2008) *Justice across Borders: The Struggle for Human Rights in US Courts*, Cambridge: Cambridge University Press.
Dembour, M. (2006) *Who Believes in Human Rights? Reflections on the European Convention*, Cambridge: Cambridge University Press.
Gans, J., Henning, T., Hunter, J. and Warner, K. (2011) *Criminal Process and Human Rights*, Sydney: Federation Press.
Gearty, C. (2006) *Can Human Rights Survive? The Hamlyn Lectures 2005*, Cambridge: Cambridge University Press.
Haas, M. (2008) *International Human Rights: A Comprehensive Introduction*, Abingdon: Routledge.
Harris, D. J., O'Boyle, M., Warbrick, C. and Bates, E. (2009) *Law of the European Convention on Human Rights*, 2nd edn, New York: Oxford University Press.
Hertel, S. and Libal, K. (2011) 'Paradoxes and Possibilities: Domestic Human Rights Policy in Context', in S. Hertel and K. Libal (eds), *Human Rights in the United States: Beyond Exceptionalism*, Cambridge: Cambridge University Press.

Lepard, B. (2012) 'International Law and Human Rights', in T. Cushman (ed.), *Handbook of Human Rights*, Abingdon: Routledge.

Lynch, P. (2013) 'Australia's Human Rights Framework: Can There Be Action without Accountability?', in P. Gerber and M. Castan (eds), *Contemporary Perspectives on Human Rights Law in Australia*, Sydney: Lawbook Co.

Muntarbhorn, V. (2012) *Briefing Paper: Development of the ASEAN Human Rights Mechanism*, Report No. EXPO/B/DROI/2012/05, Directorate-General for External Policies of the Union, European Parliament. Available at: http://www.europarl.europa.eu/committees/en/droi/studiesdownload.html?language Document=EN&file=76531.

Parmentier, S. and Weitekamp, E. (eds) (2007) *Crime and Human Rights*, Amsterdam: Elsevier.

Pickering, S. and Weber, L. (2012) 'Hardening the Rule of Law and Asylum Seekers: Exporting Risk and the Judicial Censure of State Illegality', in E. Stanley and J. McCulloch (eds), *Resistance and State Crime*, London: Palgrave Macmillan.

Savelsberg, J. (2010) *Crime and Human Rights*, London: Sage.

Smith, R. (2013) 'To See Themselves as Others See Them: The Five Permanent Members of the Security Council and the Human Rights Council's Universal Periodic Review', *Human Rights Quarterly*, 35(1): 1—32.

CHAPTER 3

Human Rights and Civil Society

Key concepts
Capabilities — Civil society — Non-governmental organizations — Human rights culture — Denial

3.1 Introduction

In this chapter we move from thinking about human rights as abstract ideas or bodies of international law, and consider the social, political and economic context in which rights claims are made. This perspective acknowledges the practical realities of people's lives that affect the realization of their human rights, and recognizes the crucial role played by civil society, particularly non-governmental organizations (NGOs).

3.2 Human rights in a social context

In Chapter 1 we heard from communitarians, cultural relativists and other human rights sceptics who reject the idea of universal human rights completely. For these critics, community standards and cultural values have priority over metaphysical abstractions such as human nature or human dignity, and constitute the only viable reference point for the regulation of society. For others, the language of human rights might express important goals, such as equality and the alleviation of human suffering, but has nothing practical to say about how to achieve them. These sceptics are doubtful about the progressive potential of the law in general, and argue that improving people's lives requires a broader engagement with social attitudes, economic circumstances and power relations. They believe that the international human rights regime concentrates too much on relations between individuals and states, and too little on the role of civil society. We argue that it is possible to approach human rights practice with an awareness of the limitations outlined above, but still see value in human rights as ethical and legal norms to be 'agreed', 'fought for' or at least 'talked about' (see Dembour 2012 in Chapter 1). Each of these positions gives qualified support for human rights without necessarily presuming their universality to be self-evident and without equating human rights solely with the content of international human rights treaties. To put it succinctly: 'People may not agree why we have rights, but they can agree that we need them' (Ignatieff 2001: 55).

Viewed from a socially and politically engaged perspective it becomes apparent that 'human rights can only be realized in social arrangements, communities, and society' (Blau and Moncada 2009: 17). In fact, Blau and Moncada argue that extreme individualism and the commitment to neo-liberal capitalism in the USA is a barrier to realizing the full range of human rights and thereby to reducing inequality. They express their commitment to a form of human rights practice that casts the relationship between individuals and collectives as follows: 'People are oppressed as individuals, but they are liberated through, with, and in solidarity with others' (Blau and Moncada 2009: 58). Social, political and economic conditions are therefore relevant to human rights in at least two ways: first, because human rights are *understood* through the lens of pre-existing social and cultural norms; and second, because social, economic and political conditions, as well as law, influence the extent to which human rights aspirations may or may not be *realized* in practice.

The capabilities approach (see Chapter 1) takes as its starting point the observation made above that 'human rights can only be realized in social arrangements, communities, and society'. While drawing on human rights ideas, this perspective moves beyond abstract principles to articulate what individuals can and should be able to achieve in the situated realities of their lives. As Nussbaum explains: 'The common ground between the Capabilities Approach and human rights approaches lies in the idea that all people have some core entitlements just by virtue of their humanity, and that it is a basic duty of society to respect and support those entitlements' (Nussbaum 2011: 62). The aspirations expressed in these frameworks support a politics that Nussbaum describes as 'minimal social justice'. Nussbaum claims that her formulation supplements and clarifies human rights approaches and focuses on duties to support individuals, which may be assigned not only to governments (including foreign governments through development aid), but also to corporations, international agencies and other individuals.

3.3 Building human rights cultures?

The relationship between human rights and societies tends to be given a different ordering when viewed from a socio-legal perspective. Lawyers and human rights advocates often see human rights law and education as leading social and cultural change. Rather than seeing culture as either a barrier to the acceptance of human rights, or a lens through which to understand the meaning of human rights in particular contexts, they talk about actively building a human rights culture. For example, Castan and Gerber (2013) claim: 'If Australia starts taking concrete steps towards embedding human rights within our laws, cultural change will follow.' Similarly, in the US context, Lord and Stein have argued that ratification of human rights treaties can play a broader, transformative role, since 'domestic internalization of human rights norms cause micro-processes of acculturation that form the backbone of lasting social change' (Lord and Stein 2008: 455). These are, of course, empirical claims that may or may not be supported by evidence. But it is notable that national and international human rights bodies invest considerable resources in educating populations about human rights in order to promote a 'human rights culture'. The Office of the High Commissioner for Human Rights, for example, cites public education and engagement with civil society among its key objectives.

The importance of public education in Australia about the meaning of human rights, particularly the principle of inalienability, was brought home in a recent national consultation on the proposed introduction of a bill of rights in ways that are highly relevant to the observance of human rights within criminal justice. While the Human Rights Consultation Committee found widespread support for human rights values, it also expressed its concern that many people polled independently of the consultation considered human rights to be contingent on good individual and group behaviour. The committee reported that 57 per cent of Australians surveyed agreed that it was reasonable to reduce or take away an individual's own rights if he or she did not respect the wider community's rights, while only 17 per cent disagreed with this statement. Moreover, 41 per cent shared the view that, if some members of a group abuse the wider community's rights then it is reasonable to restrict the entire group's rights. Only 26 per cent of those surveyed disagreed with this statement outright and the remainder were undecided (Commonwealth of Australia 2009). In a separate survey commissioned by the Australian Red Cross, 40 per cent of the 1,000 people polled reportedly agreed that it is acceptable to torture enemy soldiers in some circumstances (ABC 2009). While the Consultation Committee noted that many Australians seem unconcerned about possible breaches of their own rights, submissions to the inquiry from organizations working with marginalized groups, such as the poor and homeless, prisoners and ex-prisoners, people with disabilities and indigenous people, were overwhelmingly in favour of improved human rights observance with a view to achieving greater equality.

A view often expressed was that a greater willingness to engage in human rights dialogue at the community level will help with creating a culture in which human rights offer a legitimate way for people to speak out about disadvantage, discrimination and marginalisation and will clarify the community's thinking in this regard. (Commonwealth of Australia 2009: 140)

Importantly, the Consultation Committee reported that support for 'an improved human rights culture' came both from those who supported and those who opposed the codification of human rights through a Human Rights Act. Human rights lawyer Philip Lynch takes a different view, concluding that 'the effectiveness of [educative] measures will be substantially reduced without a robust enabling framework in the form of a comprehensive, judicially enforceable Human Rights Act ... Evidence clearly establishes that human rights legislation and human rights education are complementary and mutually reinforcing' (Lynch 2013: 35). This view has been supported through painstaking statistical research suggesting that ratification of human rights treaties had indeed translated into improved human rights observance in much of the world (Simmons 2009). This was thought to be not only a result of ratification per se, but also of the purchase that legal recognition of human rights gives campaigning groups to hold governments to their promises. Sociologist Darren O'Byrne has theorized the relationship between NGO activism and human rights law as follows: 'They make their demands not merely against an abstract principle, and not solely against a legally enforceable document of international law, but against the language-structure of human rights as a legitimate framework within which demands are made and upheld' (O'Byrne 2012: 834).

Critical legal theorist Marie-Bénédicte Dembour (2006) is less enthusiastic about the social and political value of human rights. Describing herself as a human rights 'nihilist', she argues that human rights often do not deliver on their promise and in fact may stand in the way of more progressive solutions to problems of oppression and inequality. But, despite her significant misgivings, she admits to being 'afraid' to dispense with human rights completely, out of concern for what would fill the space. There are many examples of governments citing their adherence to human rights as a façade to mask their repressive practices. For example, in response to terrorist attacks many liberal democracies have dismantled long-standing due process protections, allowed indefinite administrative detention and even condoned torture, in the name of a broad and ill-defined 'right to security' (Zedner 2007). Moreover, Woodiwiss (2009) has argued that the failure of neo-liberal governments to control corporations and regulate the economy in ways that could enhance human well-being has been justified on the grounds of respect for fundamental economic freedoms. The problem with rights for Woodiwiss is that their codification in law can entrench existing social and economic inequality. It is the task of sociologists, in his view, to give them alternative, potentially radical readings that are more cognizant of the relationship between individuals and collectives, and are capable of imposing limits and responsibilities on the powerful.

On the other hand, it is often the case that groups who are excluded from the full benefits of participation in society are the strongest supporters of human rights. In the post–Second World War period, even as the momentum for establishing an international human rights system was beginning to wane, it was the subjugated populations of colonized countries who used the newly emerging human rights institutions to advance their political agendas for decolonization (Haas 2008). In contemporary times, it is often the most marginalized groups, such as undocumented migrants, indigenous peoples, people with disabilities, women, and sexual and cultural minorities, who find in the language and concepts of human rights a platform for expressing their aspirations. This 'take up from the bottom, from the powerless' is, according to Ignatieff (2001: 71), the ultimate 'test of human rights legitimacy'. Ignatieff sees human rights struggles as unavoidably political, as evidenced by the frequent resistance from cultural and economic elites whose authority is challenged by these claims. He agrees that human rights education is an important way to broaden access to this political tool, but must be implemented in response to genuine demand rather than imposed from above, particularly when working across diverse cultures.

Simmons (2011) takes the human rights project in relation to the 'marginalized other' still further, arguing that interpreting human rights requirements from the perspective of marginalized groups can underpin a more activist politics of social justice and justify positive discrimination (see Chapter 4). Interestingly, Hertel and Libal (2011) note that groups campaigning for the rights of non-citizens in the USA – possibly the segment of society with the least access to constitutional protections – have been the most likely to frame their political demands in the language of human rights. However, Hertel and Libal observe that established civil liberties organizations are also broadening their frame of reference. They conclude:

US-based scholars, activists, lawyers, and policy makers are shifting towards a fuller engagement with international human rights norms and their application to US policy dilemmas. This signals a growing recognition of economic and social rights and their implications for addressing historic patterns of discrimination and inequality within the United States. (Hertel and Libal 2011: 6)

This brings us to the important role of NGOs in the bottom-up promotion of human rights.

3.4 The role of NGOs

The 1993 Vienna Declaration and Programme of Action recognized, in Article 31, the important role of NGOs in promoting human rights at the local, national and international levels. The Declaration also asserted that human rights workers are themselves entitled to protections under the Universal Declaration of Human Rights (UDHR), drawing attention to the risks that activists may face in themselves becoming victims of human rights violations.

NGOs can form a bridge between the international human rights system and particular societies: 'Today, many observers believe that the most effective stimuli for action on behalf of human rights are NGOs. According to one formulation, economic globalization is globalization from above, which can be tamed by the globalization from below that NGOs provide' (Haas 2008: 99). NGOs lobby their own governments, making reference to their human rights undertakings, engage with United Nations (UN) institutions, and may even provide alternative avenues of redress for human rights violations. In Britain, the Equality and Human Rights Commission (EHRC) has developed a Human Rights Measurement Framework (HRMF) to enable NGOs as well as government agencies to assess government compliance with human rights obligations (see web address at the end of this chapter). Haas (2008: 94) argues that NGOs are able to mobilize shame by the 'use of world public opinion to condemn violations and to demand redress for the aggrieved'. According to this commentator, the number of these groups has 'skyrocketed' and the internet provides them with a means of mobilizing mass participation in direct communication with world leaders.

Similarly, Beth Simmons has argued that the ratification of treaties by governments is highly important, but that the most effective stimulus to improving human rights observance is 'local ownership'. She concludes: 'One of the lessons that follows from the research in this book is the crucial role that domestic actors play in their own human rights fate. Rights stakeholders around the world have actively made decisions about when and how to employ the norms contained in human rights treaties to influence practices on the ground in their countries' (Simmons 2009: 371). In the USA, human rights NGOs are faced with a situation in which their own government is prominent in condemning foreign governments for human rights violations, but does not apply the international framework in its own backyard (Sok and Neubeck 2011). The USA has still not ratified several key human rights instruments, notably the Convention on the Elimination of

All Forms of Discrimination against Women (CEDAW) and the Convention on the Rights of the Child (CROC). Sok and Neubeck describe one successful NGO initiative in San Francisco that is aimed at educating populations about CEDAW with a view to implementing its provisions at the local government level, even in the absence of formal ratification by government. Initiatives such as this contribute to building a human rights culture 'from the ground up'.

NGOs have also played a crucial role historically in the development of UN institutions and the adoption of the UDHR,

Box 3.1 Participation of NGOs at the United Nations
Number of NGOs attending annual sessions of the Commission on the Status of Women since 2001

Year	Number
2011	346
2010	447
2009	309
2008	322
2007	267
2006	261
2005	499
2004	201
2003	167
2002	144
2001	196

Source: http://esango.un.org/civilsociety/ (accessed 16 September 2013).

and they continue to engage with UN mechanisms. The International Committee of the Red Cross (ICRC) was formed in 1864 and has a special status within the international system as the official inspector of detention facilities under the Geneva Conventions. According to the UN Department of Economic and Social Affairs NGO Branch, NGOs first played a role in UN deliberations through the Economic and Social Council (ECOSOC), the treaty monitoring body of the International Covenant on Economic, Social and Cultural Rights (ICESCR). Their participation in UN processes is governed by Article 71 of the UN Charter. NGOs that have attained official consultative status are able to provide a valuable independent perspective through their contribution to UN treaty monitoring processes. Box 3.1 indicates the large number of NGOs that have participated in sessions of the Commission on the Status of Women since 2001, many of them pursuing important criminological issues such as violence against women (see Chapter 4).

Less formal consultations involving local NGOs are often a crucial aspect of country visits by Special Rapporteurs. Haas (2008) identifies Amnesty International and Human Rights Watch as key human rights NGOs that have well-developed research, campaigning and publicity functions (see web addresses at the end of this chapter). He credits Amnesty International for pursuing the adoption by the UN of the Convention against Torture and other Cruel, Inhuman or Degrading Treatment or Punishment in 1984. Haas also argues that NGOs may fill the void in countries and regions that have no inter-governmental human rights bodies. One example is the Arab Organization for Human Rights, which formed in 1963 in Cairo and hears complaints of human rights violations, publishes reports, and campaigns for both individual redress and general reforms. The Asian Human Rights Commission, headquartered in Hong Kong since 1998, is another NGO that performs state-like functions, focusing on poverty eradication, gender equality, and the rights of indigenous people and minorities. Hodson (2013) has pointed to the important role that NGOs also play in bringing cases to the attention of international forums, such as the European Court of Human Rights (ECtHR). After a comprehensive examination of ECtHR cases, he concluded that the role of NGOs is most significant in relation to serious violations of the right to life, and systematic torture by state agents. These activities have typically not been subject to sustained examination by local authorities and are unlikely to be pursued by individual complainants.

NGOs may focus on local human rights situations, or may be more international in their outlook and modus operandi. Bell (2012) makes the strong claim in relation to international human rights NGOs that they 'are generating a new type of political power, the purpose of which is to secure the vital interests of human beings on an international scale, regardless of state boundaries'. Bell notes that NGOs working on the ground need to balance abstract principles with real-world constraints in situations that are not faced by lawyers, policy-makers or philosophers, and that this raises a raft of ethical issues. While this rule of thumb may not resolve all the dilemmas encountered by international human rights workers, Ignatieff holds that it is incumbent on human rights activists to give precedence to the wishes of those who are the apparent 'victims' of human rights abuses.

NGOs are also significant as repositories of information about specific human rights abuses, and more general conditions in particular countries. Alston and Gillespie (2012) have argued that, given the advent of new information technologies and the emergence of interconnected online communities, information held by NGOs should be shared more democratically. They have suggested the establishment of an open access 'human rights wiki' that could act as a direct reporting mechanism for all interested members of the international community. The creation of such a global human rights monitoring system, though not without practical and ethical difficulties, could take the role of civil society in relation to human rights into a new dimension, create new lines of accountability (including of NGOs themselves), and promote the bottom-up development of a human rights culture on a global level.

3.5 Indifference and denial

Just as it can promote human rights through NGO activism and the spread of a 'human rights culture', civil society can also play a part in sustaining human rights violations. As O'Byrne (2012: 838) has pointed out, '[t]he sociologist is interested in the processes and conditions which make possible not only the institutionalization of dignified, respectful treatment towards all people in some societies, but also denial of this in others'. Sociologist Stanley Cohen has made a unique contribution to understanding how systemic abuses can be facilitated through the indifference of populations and strategies of denial employed by governments in order to avoid responsibility (Cohen 2001). Cohen observes that, faced with reports of atrocities or suffering, and allegations of state responsibility for them, governments often resort to *literal denial*, by claiming that the reported events simply did not happen; *interpretive denial*, by acknowledging the events but seeking an interpretation that absolves them of blame; or *implicatory denial*, which plays down the significance of the reported events, or subordinates them to higher imperatives (see Box 3.2). The resistance of the former US administration to assertions that

---

Box 3.2   Strategies of denial of human rights abuses

Literal denial	In authoritarian regimes, denial is effected through direct suppression of information. Democratic regimes with an interest in appearing to adhere to human rights norms may use less direct methods, such as attacking the credibility of the observer.
Interpretive denial	A rhetorical strategy whereby raw facts are admitted, but the interpretation adopted by complainants is rejected in favour of terminology that is less pejorative to governments.
Implicatory denial	Applies where governments actively seek to justify harmful actions, or at least deny moral responsibility for them. Events may be attributed to natural forces beyond any human control, or responsibility displaced on to non-state actors, on to the victims themselves or on to those who support them. Alternatively, harm can be presented as an unfortunate but necessary outcome of the pursuit of a higher goal such as national security or border control.

Source: Cohen (2001).

officially sanctioned practices such as waterboarding used by US military and security forces constitute torture is a case in point. Instead, the US authorities referred to the techniques as 'enhanced interrogation techniques' (interpretive denial), argued they were necessary in the so-called war against terror, and at times attributed them to third parties (implicatory denial). Moreover, elements of each of these official strategies are likely to coexist, even when they are seemingly contradictory.

To the extent that these rhetorical devices are effective, Cohen argues that they make it possible for populations to simultaneously 'know-and-yet-not-know' about human rights abuses. This undermines greatly the potential of populations to hold governments accountable, particularly where the abuses relate to unpopular minorities. The level of 'plausible deniability' is magnified where states are able to distance themselves from abuses committed by third parties, such as private corporations (Jamieson and McEvoy 2005), or where the connection between state action or inaction and the resulting harm is indirect, as in the case of avoidable deaths arising from harsh border controls (Weber and Pickering 2011). Excluding the targets of human rights violations from the moral community through processes of neutralization and dehumanization makes it easier to justify rights violations against them. For example, Malloch and Stanley (2005) have argued that the sustained demonization of asylum seekers by governments impairs the capacity of populations to recognize them as rights-bearers (see also Pickering 2001). This argument could be applied more broadly to account for the acceptance of highly punitive criminal justice practices in relation to unpopular and marginalized groups.

O'Byrne (2012: 840) concludes that the sociological study of human rights 'enables us to focus on the language-structure of human rights and how this is constructed and manipulated in social institutions such as the state, the law and the media, such that it makes possible, indeed authorizes, the continuing abuses of such rights'. Operating at the coalface, NGOs often see their task as 'humanizing' denigrated groups and reconstituting them as the bearers of human rights, so that the abuses perpetrated against them can be recognized as human rights violations.

3.6 Conclusion

If the promise of human rights is to be realized in practice, human rights must be grounded in the political, cultural, economic and legal practices of particular societies. It has been argued that the translation of international human rights norms into domestic legislation and the development of a human rights culture from the bottom up can work together in support of this goal, though some commentators may prefer one pathway over the other. From the inception of the UN system, NGOs have proved to be crucial in building bridges between populations, governments and UN bodies, to support compliance with existing human rights norms and lobby for new agreements. With the advent of electronic information technologies, NGOs continue to find new ways to communicate with populations and governments about human rights abuses and how to prevent them.

Additional reading and resources

International Council on Human Rights Policy (Geneva based think tank) Available at: http://www.ichrp.org/.

International Service for Human Rights (based in Geneva) Available at: http://www.ishr.ch/human-rights-defenders.

Human Rights Watch (New York-based international human rights NGO) Available at: http://www.hrw.org/.

Amnesty International (London-based international human rights NGO) Available at: http://www.amnesty.org/.

UN Department of Economic and Social Affairs NGO Branch Available at: http://esango.un.org/paperless/Web.

Equality and Human Rights Commission (UK) — Human Rights Measurement Framework Available at: http://www.equalityhumanrights.com/human-rights/our-human-rights-work/human-rights-measurement-framework/.

Armaline, W., Glasberg, D. and Purkayastha, B. (2011) *Human Rights in Our Own Backyard: Injustice and Resistance in the United States*, Philadelphia, PA: University of Pennsylvania Press.

Goodale, M. (ed.) (2009) *Human Rights: An Anthropological Reader*, Chichester, Wiley-Blackwell.

Madsen, M. and Verschraegen, G. (eds) (2013) *Making Human Rights Intelligible: Towards a Sociology of Human Rights*, Oxford/Portland, OR: Hart Publishing.

Morgan, R. and Turner, B. (eds) (2009) *Interpreting Human Rights: Social Science Perspectives*, Abingdon: Routledge.

References

ABC News (2009) '40pc Think Torturing Enemy Soldiers OK', *ABC News Online*, 12 August 2009. Available at: http://www.abc.net.au/news/2009-08-12/40pc-think-torturing-enemy-soldiers-ok/1388050.

Alston, P. and Gillespie, C. (2012) 'Global Human Rights Monitoring, New Technologies, and the Politics of Information', *European Journal of International Law*, 23(4): 1089—123.

Bell, D. (2012) 'The Ethics of International Human Rights Non-Governmental Organizations', in T. Cushman (ed.), *Handbook of Human Rights*, Abingdon: Routledge.

Blau, J. and Moncada, A. (2009) *Human Rights: A Prrimer*, Boulder, CO: Paradigm Publishers.

Castan, M. and Gerber, P. (2013) 'Human Rights Landscape in Australia', in P. Gerber and M. Castan (eds), *Contemporary Perspectives on Human Rights Law in Australia*, Sydney: Lawbook Co.

Cohen, S. (2001) *States of Denial: Knowing about Atrocities and Suffering*, Cambridge: Polity Press.

Commonwealth of Australia (2009) *National Human Rights Consultation Report*, September, Canberra: Commonwealth of Australia. Available at: http://www.ag.gov.au/RightsAndProtections/HumanRights/TreatyBodyReporting/Pages/HumanRightsconsultationreport.aspx.

Dembour, M. (2006) *Who Believes in Human Rights? Reflections on the European Convention*, Cambridge: Cambridge University Press.

Haas, M. (2008) *International Human Rights: A Comprehensive Introduction*, Abingdon: Routledge.

Hertel, S. and Libal, K. (2011) *Human Rights in the United States: Beyond Exceptionalism*, Cambridge: Cambridge University Press.

Hodson, L. (2013) 'Activating the Law: Exploring the Legal Responses of NGOs to Gross Rights Violations', in M. Madsen and G. Verschraegen (eds), *Making Human Rights Intelligible: Towards a Sociology of Human Rights*, Oxford/Portland, OR: Hart Publishing.

Ignatieff, M. (2001) *Human Rights as Politics and Idolatry*, Princeton, NJ: Princeton University Press.

Jamieson, R. and McEvoy, K. (2005), 'State Crime by Proxy and Juridical Othering', *British Journal of Criminology, Special Issue on State Crime*, 45(4): 504—27.

Lord, J. and Stein, M. (2008) 'The Domestic Incorporation of Human Rights Law and the United Nations Convention on the Rights of Persons with Disabilities', *Washington Law Review*, 83(4): 449—79.

Lynch, P. (2013) 'Australia's Human Rights Framework: Can There Be Action without Accountability?', in P. Gerber and M. Castan (eds), *Contemporary Perspectives on Human Rights Law in Australia*, Sydney: Lawbook Co.

Malloch, M. and Stanley, E. (2005) 'The Detention of Asylum Seekers in the UK: Representing Risk, Managing the Dangerous', *Punishment and Society*, 7(1): 53—71.

Nussbaum, M. (2011) *Creating Capabilities: The Human Development Approach*, Cambridge, MA: Harvard University Press.

O'Byrne, D. (2012) 'On the Sociology of Human Rights: Theorising the Language-Structure of Rights', *Sociology*, 46(5): 829—43.

Pickering, S. (2001) 'Common Sense and Original Deviancy: News Discourses and Asylum Seekers in Australia', *Journal of Refugee Studies*, 14(2): 169—86.

Simmons, B. (2009) *Mobilizing for Human Rights: International Law and Domestic Politics*, New York: Cambridge University Press.

Simmons, W. (2011) *Human Rights Law and the Marginalized Other*, New York: Cambridge University Press.

Sok, C. and Neubeck, K. (2011) 'Building US Human Rights Culture from the Ground Up: International Human Rights Implementation at the Local Level', in W. Armaline, D. Glasberg and B. Purkayastha (eds), *Human Rights in Our Own Backyard: Injustice and Resistance in the United States*, Philadelphia, PA: University of Pennsylvania Press.

Weber, L. and Pickering, S. (2011) *Globalization and Borders: Death at the Global Frontier*, Basingstoke: Palgrave Macmillan.

Woodiwiss, A. (2009) 'Taking the Sociology of Human Rights Seriously', in R. Morgan and B. Turner (eds), *Interpreting Human Rights: Social Science Perspectives*, Abingdon: Routledge.

Zedner, L. (2007) 'Seeking Security by Eroding Rights: The Side Stepping of Due Process', in B. Goold and L. Lazarus (eds), *Security and Human Rights*, Oxford: Hart Publishing.

CHAPTER 4

Collective Rights and Discrimination

Key concepts
Collective rights — Self-determination — Direct/indirect discrimination — Formal/substantive equality — Systemic discrimination

4.1 Introduction

In this chapter we shift our focus from human rights as legal and moral norms that operate in the space between individuals and the state, and consider how human rights can also be applied to socially and culturally defined groups. Collective rights present a challenge to the liberal conception of the individual as the subject of law and governance. None the less, the idea of rights as exercised collectively can be incorporated into human rights frameworks, and there are numerous examples of such to be found in human rights instruments. The importance of collective identities within human rights thinking is underscored by the central place accorded to the principle of non-discrimination within human rights frameworks, a right that only has meaning in the context of social and cultural differences.

4.2 From individual to group rights

Article 29 of the Universal Declaration of Human Rights (UDHR) recognizes the importance to individuals of membership in collectivities, asserting that '[e]veryone has duties to the community in which alone the free and full development of his personality is possible'. This is not a claim about the rights of collectives per se, but emphasizes the importance to human beings of participation within a group. The right to citizenship, a fundamental tenet of liberal-democratic thinking, is also a collective right which recognizes the importance of the state as a guarantor of other basic rights. The rights of sub-state groups such as religious and cultural minorities, indigenous people, migrant workers, women and children were reiterated in the Vienna Declaration, adopted in 1993 at the World Conference on Human Rights. But what is the relationship between individual and group rights?

According to Ingram (2012: 277), collective rights can be thought of as the 'rights that individuals possess only because they belong to a particular group'. Whereas historically group rights might have preserved social and economic advantages deriving from rank and privilege based on birth, contemporary human rights frameworks more often deploy collective rights in relation to vulnerable minorities. Ingram distinguishes two primary categories of group rights: *instrumentalist* rights guard against discrimination with respect to basic human rights possessed by individuals, while *collectivist* rights preserve group identity and support some degree of collective self-determination. In practice, minority groups threatened with a loss of cultural identity may claim both types of group rights, seeking protection from discrimination in their engagement with mainstream institutions while also lobbying to retain some special zones of religious or cultural protection.

Instrumentalist rights might not even be considered to be true group rights at all, but rather as individual rights that are given meaning in relation to group membership. Instrumentalist rights tend to converge with principles of non-discrimination, which will be discussed later in this chapter. According to Ingram (2012: 277), '[b]ecause these individual rights are exercised collectively (as a social practice) and exclusively (by members of a particular group only), they ensure that individual members of a particular group have the freedom to act (worship, associate, express themselves culturally) unhindered by outsiders'. In contrast, collectivist rights are held by groups and can potentially be exercised in ways that violate the recognized human rights of their own members. For example, collectivist norms could be used to justify reduced access to education for girls, inhuman and degrading punishments, or forced marriage. Liberal human rights advocates raise a number of other objections to collectivist rights, such as the difficulty of identifying group boundaries, whether groups are morally entitled to special consideration, and questions about the capacity of groups to be rights-bearers.

Ingram argues that collectivist rights exercised in ways that violate individual rights are comparable to the practice of allowing states a margin of appreciation to breach the rights of individuals in order to achieve some greater social good (see Chapter 2). How far cultural groups can go in violating the individual rights of their members and still remain within the ambit of international human rights standards depends, in Ingram's view, on what value can be placed on the preservation of cultural identity in a particular context as an essential foundation for human flourishing, and on what provisions exist to allow dissenters to exit the group. He concludes that collectivist rights that violate human rights principles are easiest to defend when they protect vulnerable minorities from assimilation by the majority.

Freeman (2011: 135) accepts that some restrictions on individual rights may be justified to preserve what he calls a 'rights-supporting community'. However, he rejects the stronger view that self-determination at the sub-state level can be justified in order to sustain cultural minorities (see Kymlicka 1995). Freeman recognizes this special collective right only in relation to indigenous peoples, who have generally been subjected to colonization – a circumstance that adds considerable weight, in his view, to demands for self-determination:

> In claiming various forms of autonomy, indigenous groups challenge the concept of the liberal-democratic nation-state with a homogeneous concept of citizens' rights. They do so partly because they have been conquered and exploited by the states of which they are supposed to be citizens, and partly because their experience of liberal-democratic citizens' rights has not been positive. (Freeman 2011: 142)

This is not to say that the pursuit of self-determination by indigenous groups is necessarily a threat to individual rights. On the contrary, Freeman observes that indigenous groups have often couched their political claims in the language of human rights. A Draft Declaration on the Rights of Indigenous Peoples was adopted by the UN General Assembly on 13 September 2007 after a long period of consultation and activism by indigenous groups, and despite resistance from many governments. Freeman notes, however, that it is difficult to 'implement the right of *peoples* to self-determination in a world of *states*' (2011: 146). Therefore, the right to cultural and economic self-determination within the Declaration is usually equated to a degree of self-government within a state, rather than an entitlement to secede from it.

Also in the face of considerable resistance, women's rights activists succeeded in 1945 in having the equal rights of men and women written into the UN Charter and UDHR. A Commission on the Status of Women was established, which produced the Convention on the Elimination of Discrimination Against Women (CEDAW) in 1979. CEDAW has been weakened by numerous reservations and, according to Freeman (2011), the associated treaty monitoring committee remains under-resourced and inaccessible to non-governmental organizations (NGOs). However, during the 1990s, increasing numbers of feminist scholars and activists began to frame women's political concerns in terms of human rights, and to engage with UN mechanisms (Fraser 1999; Bergoffen *et al.* 2010). Wonders and Danner (2006: 109) note that women's NGOs that 'both challenge and collaborate with the

United Nations' represent a major source of 'collective power and representation in a globalized world'.

While early human rights instruments were silent on the rights of children as an identifiable social group, the Convention on the Rights of the Child was finally adopted by the UN in 1989. According to Freeman (2011), this convention contains the most complete integration of civil and political rights with social, cultural and economic rights of any UN treaty. However, its impact has been diminished by many reservations, and a weak enforcement system that is overly reliant on NGO activism and does not include a right of individual petition. In practice, children's rights are qualified rights, since they are often dependent on the actions of adults to bring them into being and are at the same time linked to the emerging citizenship capacity of children as they develop (see Chapter 11). At the time of writing, the convention had been ratified by all UN Member States apart from the USA and Somalia.

In the pantheon of collective rights, the rights of sexual minorities have been particularly controversial because of differences in religious and cultural attitudes towards alternative sexualities. Freeman (2011) notes that even liberal-democratic states continue to appeal to 'public morals' provisions in order to deny substantive rights to individuals with alternative sexual orientations. One step towards the recognition of group rights on this basis came in 2004, when the UN Special Rapporteur on the Right to Health declared that this fundamental right included the right of all persons to express their sexual orientation. Another important step was the 2007 adoption of the Yogyakarta Principles on the Application of International Human Rights Law in relation to Sexual Orientation and Gender Identity (the Yogyakarta Principles), which is more a statement of non-discrimination than a manifesto of positive rights. Also important is the granting of consultative status to an increasing number of NGOs representing sexual minorities, and the growing prominence within human rights activism of the flagship issue of same-sex marriage.

Social groups identified by physical or intellectual disability have also experienced many obstacles in the recognition of their collective rights. The UN Convention on the Rights of Persons with Disabilities came into force in 2008. The emphasis throughout this treaty is on achieving equality with mainstream populations. The purpose of the treaty is to 'promote, protect and ensure the full and equal enjoyment of all human rights and fundamental freedoms by all persons with disabilities, and to promote respect for their inherent dignity', and to remove barriers that 'may hinder their full and effective participation in society on an equal basis with others' (Article 1). Resistance to disability rights has generally been based on economic rather than moral grounds, with governments fearing that recognition of the equal rights of this group would impose a major financial burden. The ongoing claims of the disability rights movement concern access to education, jobs and independent living and, more controversially, the right to 'death with dignity', which is also relevant to the wider population (Fleischer 2012).

4.3 Applying collective rights in criminology and criminal justice

Some groups within society, such as victims, offenders, young offenders, terror suspects and prisoners, are defined, at least temporarily, in terms of their contact with the criminal justice system. The application of human rights principles to the protection of these groups will be explored in Section 2 of this book. In this chapter we focus more broadly on the needs and vulnerabilities of specific social groups, such as women, children, cultural minorities, asylum seekers and indigenous people, when they encounter the criminal justice process as either victims or suspects. The potential examples are so numerous that the discussion is of necessity highly selective, but serves to illustrate the importance of group rights and equality within criminal justice.

The rights of child suspects may be expressed through the provision of an 'appropriate adult' to act as a support person during questioning, diversionary programmes, specialist courts and detention facilities (see Chapter 11). Child, and sometimes adult, victims of sexual assault may be provided with alternative means to present evidence in court, in recognition of their particular vulnerability to further traumatization through their involvement in the criminal justice process (see Chapters 9 and 12). The right to an interpreter during criminal proceedings recognizes the particular needs of cultural and linguistic minorities. And advocates for prisoner rights have called for reforms that address the particular needs of women in prison (Hannah-Moffat 2010), and prisoners with mental illness or intellectual disabilities (Dowseand *et al.* 2009). The criminal law itself can also express the special duty on states to protect certain groups – for example, through the prohibition of hate crimes against religious, cultural and sexual minorities (Mason 2005) or the enactment of statutory rape offences (where consent is irrelevant) that recognize the particular vulnerability of children.

Despite the misgivings expressed by many feminists about the capacity of human rights frameworks to address violence in family settings (see Chapter 1), violence against women has been the flagship human rights issue for many of these groups. In 1994, the UN Commission on Human Rights appointed a Special Rapporteur on Violence against Women, and the next step in raising the profile of violence against women through UN auspices came at the Fourth World Conference on Women held in Beijing in 1995.

More recently, a historic agreement on preventing violence against women and girls was reached at the 57th Session of the UN Commission on the Status of Women, which took place in New York and included the recognition that 'custom, tradition or religious consideration should play no part in denying women equal rights or justifying violence against them' (AHRC 2013). Other feminist scholars have called for a broader conception that sees violence against women not merely as being culturally determined, but also as a more broadly based human rights issue stemming from systemic discrimination in relation to the full range of political and economic rights (True 2012).

Workers as an identifiable social group are often overlooked in discussions of collective rights, and many of the international agreements that protect them, including conventions that outlaw forced labour, enshrine the right to form unions and protect the rights of migrant workers, have been negotiated by the International Labour Organization, rather than by mainstream human rights bodies. In a global age in which much of the threat to the well-being of workers comes from transnational corporations, human rights principles are referred to increasingly in criminological scholarship on state-corporate crime (Michalowski and Kramer 2006; Whyte 2009). At a domestic level, corporate manslaughter legislation, coupled with the statutory regulation of occupational health and safety, has an important role to play in protecting workers' rights (Tombs and Whyte 2010). More than 150 lawsuits alleging human rights abuses perpetrated by US and foreign corporations (often oil companies) in more than 60 foreign countries have been filed by American citizens in US courts since the early 1990s (Stempel 2012; see also Leveille 2012).

Perhaps the most fundamental failure to protect the rights of an identifiable group occurs when group membership is itself criminalized. Homosexuality (whether as an act or a status) remains a criminal offence in some countries, or is being reintroduced into their criminal codes. One well-publicized example is the proposed introduction of the death penalty in Uganda for consensual sexual acts between same-sex couples. Anti-homosexuality laws have been debated in that country for several years, with the aim being to 'prohibit and penalize homosexual behaviour and related practices' on the grounds that they 'constitute a threat to the traditional family'. After an international outcry from human rights campaigners (see for example http://www.amnesty.org.au/features/comments/30655/) the provisions for capital punishment were dropped. However, later versions have still provided 'victims' of homosexuality with a defence to murder if they kill their 'attacker', leaving same-sex-attracted people extremely vulnerable to private violence. Several other countries, in Asia, Africa and the Middle East, apply the death penalty for homosexuality.

Well-intentioned approaches to crime prevention that focus on the unique characteristics and vulnerabilities of a particular group may also present their own problems. One example is the Protocol to Prevent, Suppress and Punish Trafficking in Persons, especially Women and Children (UN TIP Protocol), which is attached to the Convention against Transnational Organized Crime (UNTOC). While the importance of addressing exploitation and violence in this context is not in dispute, feminist criminologists have argued that the stress placed on gendered vulnerability to victimization can deny women's agency in relation both to their border crossing and involvement in sex work, and at the same time play down serious labour exploitation that involves men (Segrave *et al.* 2009). This suggests that a poorly formulated collectivist approach can inadvertently formalize stereotypical representations within UN mechanisms that do not apply in all cases.

Similar difficulties have been identified in the use of 'cultural defences' within criminal courts, whereby defendants from minority cultural groups cite cultural practices and beliefs in mitigation, as a defence against criminal charges, or as factors relevant to sentencing. Opponents of these measures often argue simply that one law should apply to all. After reviewing the complexities arising from this growing practice within US courts, Renteln (2010, no page) concludes that: 'It is evident that to guarantee the right to a fair trial, equal justice for all, adequate protection of the free exercise of religion for members of all faiths, and key international human rights, courts should develop appropriate ways to take cultural differences into account.' However, even where this principle is accepted, the manner in which this accommodation of cultural difference plays out in individual cases may be subject to considerable dispute, including over the authenticity of cultural interpretations presented in court.

Fully fledged collectivist rights require that a considerable level of autonomy is granted at the sub-state level to preserve the identity and practices of a threatened minority. Within crime and criminal justice settings, the clearest example of this is seen in the adoption of indigenous justice practices. Indigenous peoples survive within modern nation-states with varying degrees of autonomy and recognition of the harms of colonization (Cunneen 2007a). A seemingly universal outcome of the colonization process is the disproportionately high level of involvement of indigenous people with criminal justice systems in a range of countries (see Box 4.1). Positive initiatives such as community self-policing (Wakeling *et al.* 2001; Blagg and Valuri 2004; Cunneen 2007b; Lithopolous 2007), full or partial recognition of indigenous customary law (ALRC 1986; Law Commission – Te Aka Matua O Te Tura 2001), and alternative justice practices (Tauri 1999; Marchetti and Daly 2004; Mirsky 2004a; Mirsky 2004b) are justified because of the special claims of colonized people to some measure of self-determination.

Box 4.1   Worldwide patterns of indigenous over-imprisonment

- In New Zealand, the Maori population represents 14 per cent of the total population but 51 per cent of the prison population.
- In Canada, the Aboriginal population represents 3 per cent of the total population but 17 per cent of the prison population.
- In the USA, the rate of confinement in local jails for First Nation peoples is estimated to be four times the national average.
- In Australia, Aboriginal people account for less than 2 per cent of the total population but around 22 per cent of the prison population.

(Figures quoted in Cunneen 2006, which is also the data source for the chart below.)

- In Australia, Aboriginal juveniles are 20 times more likely to be in juvenile detention on average than non-Aboriginal young people.

(Quoted in Taylor 2007)

Estimated overimprisonment rates for indigenous peoples

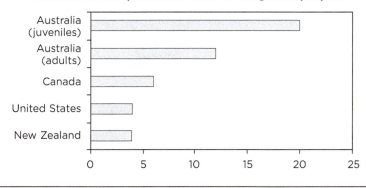

Circle Sentencing was introduced in the Australian state of New South Wales (NSW) in 2002, with the intention of providing a more culturally appropriate response to criminal offending by Aboriginal people. The process takes place in an informal setting and includes the input of respected community elders, but ultimate legal authority rests with the sentencing magistrate. Because of its positioning within the mainstream legal process, which in turn defines the offences with which the defendants have been charged, at best Circle Sentencing can be seen as a hybrid practice that falls short of full self-determination. Moreover, Blagg (2008) argues that, while the restorative justice principles on which the court processes are based may have their origins in indigenous practices from elsewhere in the world, they are not characteristic of traditional practice among Australian Aboriginal groups. An evaluation conducted by the NSW Bureau of Crime Statistics and Research found that Circle Sentencing had no measurable impact on recidivism compared with appearances at mainstream courts (Fitzgerald 2008). However, this quantitative assessment considered only one of the eight programme objectives shown in Box 4.2 (indicated in **bold**), which reflects the mainstream cultural and economic values that shaped the research.

At the other extreme, the Northern Territory Emergency Response (NTER) intervention stands as an example of complete disregard for the principles of indigenous self-determination (Maddison 2008). In response to persistent child physical and sexual abuse within many remote Aboriginal communities in Australia, the former Liberal government introduced wide-ranging emergency legislation into the Northern Territory in 2007, including the elements shown in Box 4.2. While some people welcomed the swift action, the pre-election measures were implemented without community consultation; applied only to traditional Aboriginal communities rather than to Australians

---

Box 4.2   Self-determination in indigenous criminal justice

NSW Circle Sentencing objectives	NTER main elements
Include communities in sentencing	Run compulsory health checks for children
Increase confidence in sentencing	Quarantine welfare payments
Reduce cultural barriers in courts	Ban X-rated pornography
Provide better options for offenders	Improve housing (through market solutions)
Provide better support for victims	Implement Work for Dole clean-up schemes
Ensure participation of victims and offenders	Increase mainstream policing
Increase offender awareness of consequences for victims and community	Scrap permits on Aboriginal-owned land
Reduce recidivism	Take control of town camps
	Implement alcohol restrictions
	Appoint managers of government business
	Use army to deliver some services
	Suspend Racial Discrimination Act

Notes: NSW = New South Wales; NTER = Northern Territory Emergency Response.

living elsewhere; and wound back many hard-fought gains in self-governance for remote communities. The UN Human Rights Committee monitoring the International Covenant on Civil and Political Rights (ICCPR) sent a Special Rapporteur to Australia, who found the measures to be racially discriminatory and incompatible with Australia's international human rights obligations (Anaya 2010). The Australian Human Rights Commission (AHRC) produced reports indicating how the legitimate crime prevention objectives of the intervention could be pursued without violating individual and collective human rights (Social Justice Commissioner 2007), but the incoming Labor government continued many of the measures.

4.4 The many faces of discrimination

While failure to observe the collective rights of particular groups sustains inequality, failure to protect the instrumental rights of individual group members can also be expressed in terms of discrimination. The prohibition against discrimination that appears within all major human rights instruments follows logically from the recognition of the equal moral worth of all human beings that underpins human rights thinking. Article 26 of the ICCPR states that:

> All people are equal before the law and are entitled without any discrimination to the equal protection of the law. In this respect, the law shall prohibit any discrimination and guarantee to all persons equal and effective protection against discrimination on any grounds such as race, colour, sex, language, religion, political or other opinion, national or social origin, property, birth or other status.

The International Covenant on Economic, Social and Cultural Rights (ICESCR) (Article 2.2) and the European Convention on Human Rights (ECHR) (Article 14) express their non-discrimination provisions in narrower terms, asserting that the rights set out in those particular instruments must be exercised without discrimination on any of the same grounds. The inclusion of the category 'other status' leaves space for contestation over the claims of unspecified groups, such as those defined by disability, sexual orientation or immigration status. The 1966 Convention on the Eradication of Racial Discrimination (CERD) was the first specialized instrument prohibiting a particular form of discrimination, followed by the introduction of CEDAW in 1979.

Interpretations regarding which actions or inactions are discriminatory may be hotly contested. Such debates often turn on differing conceptions of the meaning of equality. Those who advocate *formal* equality focus on equality of *process*, and believe that all differential treatment is discriminatory. In this view, non-discrimination amounts to ensuring that everyone is treated in an identical fashion. Advocates of *substantive* equality, however, focus more on equality of *outcomes* and acknowledge that some groups experience pre-existing disadvantages. This justifies differential treatment if it is necessary to achieve an equivalent enjoyment of rights, and requires that only similarly placed individuals be treated alike.

Advocates of formal equality often deny or overlook the fact that social systems are geared inherently towards the needs of dominant social groups. Supporters of substantive equality are likely to point out that there are far fewer women prisoners (and prison governors) than men, so that prison regimes are often not suited to women's needs; that courts can be intimidating, but more so for juvenile offenders and child victims; and that while police interrogation can be unnerving for anyone, these problems are magnified for those with an intellectual disability or language barrier. The differential treatment of people in a way that is intended to overcome a disadvantage is generally called *positive* discrimination. While advocates of substantive equality accept positive discrimination but reject negative discrimination that creates disadvantage, those who support formal equality make no such distinction and tend to see any differential treatment as unjustified.

Beliefs about formal and substantive equality, and interpretations of what is and is not discriminatory, are associated to some extent with political orientations. Formal equality often aligns with classic liberal or conservative views that downplay the influence of social factors and see people as isolated individuals who are fully responsible for their own actions and social conditions. Substantive equality is more compatible with critical ideologies (and social science disciplines) that take structural and historical factors into account. Perhaps surprisingly, given their liberal underpinnings, international human rights instruments support a substantive equality view that recognizes the need for positive discrimination in some carefully delimited contexts. For example, Article 1.4 of CERD asserts that:

Special measures taken for the sole purpose of securing adequate advancement of certain racial or ethnic groups or individuals requiring such protection as may be necessary in order to ensure such groups or individuals equal enjoyment or exercise of human rights and fundamental freedoms shall not be deemed racial discrimination, provided, however, that such measures do not, as a consequence, lead to the maintenance of separate rights for different racial groups and that they shall not be continued after the objectives for which they were taken have been achieved.

Article 4 of CEDAW also stipulates that any temporary measures required to achieve substantive equality for women must not violate non-discrimination principles, and singles out the unique status of maternity as justifying ongoing special treatment. Article 1 confirms that the purpose of the treaty is to outlaw negative discrimination, not differential treatment that may be positive in intent. It further clarifies that the term 'discrimination against women' applies only to differential treatment that 'has the effect or purpose of impairing or nullifying' women's enjoyment of their human rights on an equal basis with men. A 2012 report prepared by the Equality and Human Rights Commission for the visit of the CEDAW monitoring committee to the UK recommended that the committee should ask the government what actions it was taking 'to ensure that decision makers understand the concept of substantive rather than formal gender equality, and are aware of both the lawfulness and legitimacy of women-only services' (Equality and Human Rights Commission 2012: 4). This suggests that the commitment of governments to substantive equality is still fragile and contested.

Not all discrimination is about individual prejudice or explicitly unfair laws. Indeed, a great deal of discrimination is embedded within social or institutional practice, and may be far more difficult to identify and eradicate than is overt discrimination. *Direct* discrimination occurs where a particular group is targeted openly for less favourable treatment, and may take the form of racism, sexism, ageism or homophobia. *Indirect* discrimination occurs where practices that may not be discriminatory in intent (although this may be difficult to determine), but nevertheless result in outcomes that unfairly disadvantage a particular group. A related concept is that of *systemic* discrimination, which is built unwittingly into the processes and working assumptions of an organization or wider social practice. Everyday discrimination may be normalized so that its damaging consequences are largely undetected. Patriarchy is an example of systemic discrimination against women that is supported widely by social, cultural and religious beliefs, and so deeply entrenched in everyday practices that it often goes unnoticed.

Systemic discrimination also arises within criminal justice institutions. The idea of institutional racism within policing came to prominence in Britain in 1993 after the failure of the London Metropolitan Police to prosecute the killers of black teenager Stephen Lawrence, who was stabbed to death by a group of racist white youths while waiting at a bus stop with a friend. The official inquiry into the handling of the case (Macpherson 1999) found that investigating officers responded to the two victims as if they were suspects, based on racial stereotypes, thus delaying the gathering of vital evidence. It took 20 years of persistent campaigning by Stephen's family and supporters to finally achieve the convictions of two of the killers. British policing was shaken to the core and forced to address the accusation of 'institutional racism', defined by the Macpherson Inquiry as:

> The collective failure of an organisation to provide an appropriate and professional service to people because of their colour, culture, or ethnic origin. It can be seen or detected in processes, attitudes and behaviour which amount to discrimination through unwitting prejudice, ignorance, thoughtlessness and racist stereotyping which disadvantage minority ethnic people. (Macpherson 1999: para. 6.34)

This definition extended the understanding of police racism beyond the idea of individual 'bad apples' who were openly and intentionally racist (though this may also apply). It acknowledged that discrimination was also subtly and deeply embedded in shared understandings about 'how things are done', which in this case were reinforced on a day-to-day basis by police occupational culture (discussed in Chapter 8).

4.5 Discrimination in crime prevention and criminal justice

Within criminology there is a long-standing tradition of empirical studies aimed at detecting discrimination. For example, Hood (1992) found disparities in sentencing practices for different ethnic groups in England once legally relevant factors had been taken into account; prison ethnographers have explored racialized prison practices (Bosworth 2004); and Gale and Wundersitz (1989) identified 'hidden prejudice' in a young offender system in South Australia even though it was geared explicitly towards diverting young Aboriginal offenders away from court processes. One US study found that the racial identity of both the offender and the victim was relevant in sentencing practices in the state of Georgia, so that murder convictions involving a white victim and black perpetrator were 11 times more likely to result in the imposition of a death sentence than in cases where the victim was black and the perpetrator was white (Baldus *et al.* 1990). Other studies have investigated gender discrimination in criminal justice practices and institutions, or have adopted an intersectionality framework to research multiple identities and compounding forms of disadvantage embedded in criminal justice institutions and practices (see Heidensohn 1986 and Daly 1989 as leading examples of each genre).

The form of discrimination that is aligned most intimately with the criminal justice process, and yet is frequently overlooked, is discrimination on the grounds of criminal record. As discussed in Chapter 10, the rehabilitative ideal is enshrined within international human rights law; however, criminal justice practices are driven increasingly by paradigms of aggregate risk and punitivism

(Pratt *et al.* 2005; Simon 2007). In this socio-political climate, the label of 'sex offender' or 'recidivist' can operate as if it were a fixed social category and can have an impact on an individual's life opportunities on an ongoing basis. In Australia, this form of discrimination has been recognized as a human rights violation. The Human Rights Commission has conducted a campaign against discrimination in employment on the grounds of criminal record (see http://www.humanrights.gov.au/human_rights/criminalrecord/index.html), and has upheld several individual complaints on this basis (see, for example, AHRC 2012a, 2012b).

Policing is one of the most highly researched areas of criminal justice in relation to discrimination. Social inequalities can influence who is most under suspicion as an offender and who is most valued as a victim, resulting in both 'over-policing' (the disproportionate targeting and/or use of heavy-handed tactics against a particular population group) and 'under-policing' (in which police fail to respond adequately to the victimization of particular groups because of entrenched attitudes that identify these groups as undeserving).

In relation to over-policing, the means by which police form suspicions about who should be the subject of their intrusive powers and the social designation of some population groups as 'suspect populations' combine to create a high likelihood that systematic discrimination will be a feature of operational policing. Box 4.3 illustrates the high levels of disproportionality in several different countries in police use of stop-and-search powers in relation to suspect populations defined by race or ethnicity.

One of the most comprehensively documented examples of over-policing within criminology is the disproportionate targeting of stop-and-search powers in Britain. The stopping of pedestrians and drivers in public places to ask questions and sometimes conduct a search of the person or vehicle is a controversial policing tactic that has been linked to major disturbances such as the Brixton race riots (Scarman 1982) and the more recent uprisings in other parts of London. Historical powers to stop members of the public based on reasonable suspicion that they are committing or intending to commit a crime – the so-called 'suss laws' – were supplemented in recent years with special pre-emptive powers to stop individuals in the absence of suspicion. These powers, under Section 44 of the Terrorism Act 2000, have been found to promote unfair policing directed towards Muslim communities (Parmar 2011). The European Court of Human Rights found that Section 44 stops contravene the right to privacy under the ECHR (*Gillan and Quinton v The United Kingdom* Application no. 4158/05 12 January 2010). Separate powers under Section 60 of the Criminal Justice and Public Order Act 1994 to stop individuals in designated areas, originally introduced to combat football hooliganism, also raise human rights concerns. Research conducted by the

---

Box 4.3   Discriminatory use of police stop-and-search powers

- Although they represent only 4.7 per cent of the city's population, black and Latino males between the ages of 14 and 24 accounted for 41.6 per cent of stops conducted by the New York Police Department (NYPD) in 2011. The number of stops of young black men exceeded the size of the entire city population of young black men (168,126 as compared to 158,406).

Source: NYCLU (2011).

- The UK Equality and Human Rights Commission calculated that, across England and Wales, black people were stopped by police at an average rate of 129 per 1,000 residents, Asian people at a rate of 40 per 1,000, and white people at a rate of 17 per 1,000.

Source: EHRC (2010).

- No data is collected on stop-and-search practices in Australia, but Aboriginal people are on average 17 times more likely to be taken into police custody than non-Aboriginal people, and much more likely to be taken into custody for victimless public order offences.

Source: AIC (2002).

EHRC (2012) found that black and Asian minorities were also disproportionately impacted by Section 60 stops, and that police agencies sometimes admitted explicitly targeting particular ethnic groups in designated areas.

Long-standing powers under the Police and Criminal Evidence Act 1984 to stop and search *with* suspicion have been monitored for many years, and this monitoring has consistently revealed a disproportionate targeting of minority youths, as shown in Box 4.3. On 24 August 2012, the British *Guardian* newspaper reported that a black teenager claimed to have been stopped 50 times by the London Metropolitan Police (Taylor 2012). Political and academic debates centre around the extent to which the official statistics demonstrate discriminatory policing rather than disproportionate criminality among minority groups (see Bowling and Phillips 2007 for a review of these arguments). The UK Equality and Human Rights Commission concluded that disproportionate stops of black and Asian people constituted an unjustifiable breach of human rights:

In seeking to protect the rights of the majority, the police at times infringe certain individual rights, such as the right to privacy or to freedom of movement and association. However, they are only permitted to do so if the infringement is rational, proportionate and lawful. Yet the evidence shows that, on the contrary, some police forces are using their powers disproportionately suggesting they are stopping and searching individuals in a way that is discriminatory, inefficient, and a waste of public money. (EHRC 2010: 3)

Systemic discrimination can also arise through the under-policing of offences against vulnerable or marginalized groups. At the time of writing, outrage across India at the brutal rape and murder of a university student in Delhi has catalysed demands for more comprehensive laws concerning gendered violence and better handling of women's complaints by police, who often ignore or even penalize women who report violent crimes against them. This has prompted campaigns by international human rights groups, as the case has come to symbolize the widespread failure to protect women from violence and to respond decisively when violence occurs. Building on CEDAW, the Declaration on the Elimination of all Forms of Violence against Women was adopted in 1993, which requires governments to exercise due diligence to prevent and punish violence against women committed by state agents or private persons (Article 4(c)). The Vienna Declaration also clarified that violence against women and sexual harassment were to be defined as forms of discrimination under CEDAW. Though violence against women also needs to be confronted on a broader front, Larsen and Guggisberg (2009) identify the police as pivotal in providing a first response to victims of intimate partner violence in ways that can either recognize or undermine the victim's status as a rights-bearer.

4.6 Conclusion

While human rights are most often expressed at an individual level, human rights frameworks also recognize that identification with groups is an essential feature of the human condition. True collective rights such as self-determination are generally associated with indigenous groups. However, many individual rights also recognize the need for individuals to participate in cultural and political life or to express their sexual identity. This framework of positive rights is reinforced by an overarching principle of non-discrimination on a discrete, and expanding, range of grounds.

Additional readings and materials

Declaration on the Elimination of all Forms of Violence Against Women, A/RES/48/104 adopted 20 December 1993
Available at: http://www.un.org/documents/ga/res/48/a48r104.htm.

Declaration on the Rights of Indigenous Peoples 61/295 adopted 13 September 2007 Available at: http://www.un.org/esa/socdev/unpfii/documents/DRIPS_en.pdf.

Protocol to Prevent, Suppress and Punish Trafficking in Persons, Especially Women and Children, Supplementing the United Nations Convention against Transnational Organized Crime, G.A. Res. 25, annex II, U.N. GAOR, 55th Sess., Supp. No. 49, at 60, U.N. Doc. A/55/49 (Vol. I) (2001), entered into force 25 December 2003 Available at: http://www1.umn.edu/humanrts/instree/trafficking.html.

Vienna Declaration and Programme of Action, World Conference on Human Rights Vienna, 14—25 June 1993 A/CONG. 157/23 Available at: http://www.unhchr.ch/huridocda/huridoca.nsf/(Symbol)/a.conf. 157.23.en.

Anaya, S.J. (2004) *Indigenous Peoples in International Law*, 2nd edn, Oxford: Oxford University Press.

Anaya, S.J. (2009) *International Human Rights and Indigenous Peoples*, New York: Wolters Kluwer.

Cook, R. (2011) *Human Rights of Women: National and International Perspectives*, Pennsylvania, PA: University of Pennsylvania Press.

References

AHRC (Australian Human Rights Commission) (2012a) *Campbell v Black and White Cabs Pty Ltd and Tighe: Report into Discrimination in Employment on the Basis of Criminal Record [2012] AusHRC 50*, Sydney: Australian Human Rights Commission.

AHRC (2012b) *Mr CG v State of NSW (Railcorp NSW [2012] AusHRC 48*, Sydney: Australian Human Rights Commission.

AHRC (2013) 'Historic International Violence Agreement Reached', Sydney: Australian Human Rights Commission Available at: https://www.humanrights. gov.au/news/stories/historic-international-violence-agreement-reached, accessed 6 November 2013.

AIC (Australian Institute of Criminology) (2002) *2002 National Police Custody Survey*, Canberra: AIC.

ALRC (Australian Law Reform Commission) (1986) *Recognition of Aboriginal Customary Laws*, ALRC Report 31, Sydney: Australian Law Reform Commission.

Anaya, J. (2010) *Report by the Special Rapporteur on the Situation of Human Rights and Fundamental Freedoms of Indigenous People: The Situation of Indigenous Peoples in Australia*, Geneva: United Nations General Assembly.

Baldus, D., Woodworth, G. and Pulaski, C. (1990) *Equal Justice and the Death Penalty: A Legal and Empirical Analysis*, Boston, MA: Northeastern University Press.

Bergoffen, D., Gilbert:, Harvey, T. and McNeely, C. (2010) *Confronting Global Gender Justice: Women's Lives, Human Rights*, Hoboken, NJ: Taylor & Francis.

Blagg, H. (2008) *Crime, Aboriginality and the Decolonisation of Justice*, Sydney: Hawkins Press.

Blagg, H. and Valuri, G. (2004) 'Self-policing and Community Safety: The Work of Aboriginal Community Patrols in Australia', *Current Issues in Criminal Justice*, 15(3): 205–19.

Bosworth, M. (2004) 'Theorizing Race and Imprisonment: Towards a New Penality', *Critical Criminology*, 12(2): 221.

Bowling, B. and Phillips, C. (2007) 'Disproportionate and Discriminatory: Reviewing the Evidence on Police Stop and Search', *The Modern Law Review*, 70(6): 936–61.

Cunneen, C. (2006) 'Aboriginal Deaths in Custody: A Continuing Abuse', *Social Justice*, 33(4): 37–51.

Cunneen, C. (2007a) 'Criminology, Human Rights and Indigenous Peoples', in S. Parmentier and E. Weitekamp (eds), *Crime and Human Rights*, Oxford: Elsevier.

Cunneen, C. (2007b) 'Justice Agreements, Strategic Plans and Indigenous/Police Relations', *Indigenous Law Bulletin*, 6(28): 19–21.

Daly, K. (1989) 'Neither Conflict Nor Labeling Nor Paternalism Will Suffice: Intersections of Race, Ethnicity, Gender, and Family in Criminal Court Decisions', *Crime and Delinquency*, 35(1): 136–68.

Dowse, L., Baldry, E. and Snoyman, P. (2009) 'Disabling Criminology: Conceptualizing the Intersections of Critical Disability Studies and Critical Criminology for People with Mental Health and Cognitive Disabilities in the Criminal Justice System', *Australian Journal of Human Rights*, 15(1): 29–46.

EHRC (Equality and Human Rights Commission) (2010) *Stop and Think: A Critical Review of the Use of Stop and Search Powers in England and Wales*, London: EHRC.

EHRC (2012) 'Submission of the Equality and Human Rights Commission: A status National Human Rights Institution for the United Kingdom of Great Britain and Northern Ireland on the list of issues for the Convention on the Elimination of Discrimination against Women (CEDAW) Committee pre-sessional working group meeting', London: Equality and Human Rights Commission.

Fitzgerald, J. (2008) 'Does Circle Sentencing Reduce Aboriginal Offending?', *Criminal Justice Bulletin No. 115*, Sydney: NSW Bureau of Crime Statistics and Research.

Fleischer, D. (2012) 'The Rights of the Disabled', in T. Cushman (ed.), *Handbook of Human Rights*, Abingdon: Routledge.

Fraser, A. (1999) 'Becoming Human: The Origins and Development of Women's Human Rights', *Human Rights Quarterly*, 21(4): 853–906.

Freeman, M. (2011) *Human Rights*, Cambridge: Polity Press.

Gale, F. and Wundersitz, J. (1989) 'The Operation of Hidden Prejudice in Pre-Court Procedures: The Case of Australian Aboriginal Youth', *ANZ Journal of Criminology*, 22(1): 1–21.

Hannah-Moffat, K. (2010) 'Sacrosanct or Flawed: Risk, Accountability and Gender-Responsive Penal Politics', *Current Issues in Criminal Justice*, 22(2): 193–215.

Heidensohn, F. (1986) 'Models of Justice: Portia or Persephone? Some Thoughts on Equality, Fairness and Gender in the Field of Criminal Justice', *International Journal of the Sociology of Law*, 14(3—4): 287—98.

Hood, R. (1992) *Race and Sentencing*, Oxford: Clarendon Press.

Ingram, D. (2012) 'Group Rights: A Defense', in T. Cushman (ed.), *Handbook of Human Rights*, Abingdon: Routledge.

Kymlicka, W. (1995) *Multicultural Citizenship: A Liberal Theory of Group Rights*, Oxford: Clarendon Press.

Larsen, A.C. and Guggisberg, M. (2009) 'Police Officers, Women and Intimate Partner Violence: Giving Primacy to Social Context', *Australian Journal of Gender and Law*, 1. Available at: https://genderandlaw.murdoch.edu.au/index.php/sisterinlaw/issue/view/6.

Law Commission — Te Aka Matua O Te Tura (2001) *Maori Custom and Values in New Zealand Law*, Wellington: Law Commission.

Leveille, K. (2012) 'A Debate Two Hundred Years in The Making: Corporate Liability and the Presumption Against Extraterritoriality Under the Alien Tort Statute', *Houston Law Review*, 50(2): 654—85.

Lithopolous, S. (2007) *International Comparison of Indigenous Policing Models*, Ottawa, ON: Public Safety Canada.

Macpherson, W. (1999) *The Stephen Lawrence Inquiry: Report of an Inquiry by Sir William Macpherson of Cluny*, London: The Stationery Office.

Maddison, S. (2008) 'Indigenous Autonomy Matters: What's Wrong With the Australian Government's "Intervention" in Aboriginal Communities', *Australian Journal of Human Rights*, 14(1): 41—61.

Marchetti, E. and Daly, K. (2004) 'Indigenous Courts and Justice Practices in Australia', *Trends and Issues in Crime and Criminal Justice*, No. 277, Canberra: Australian Institute of Criminology.

Mason, G. (2005) 'Hate Crime and the Image of the Stranger', *British Journal of Criminology*, 45(6): 837—59.

Michalowski, R. and Kramer, R. (2006) *State-Corporate Crime: Wrongdoing at the Intersection of Business and Government*, New Brunswick, NJ: Rutgers University Press.

Mirsky, L. (2004a) *Restorative Justice Practices of Native American, First Nation and Other Indigenous People of North America: Part One*, Bethlehem, PA: International Institute for Restorative Practices (IIRP).

Mirsky, L. (2004b) *Restorative Justice Practices of Native American, First Nation and Other Indigenous People of North America: Part Two*, Bethlehem, PA: International Institute for Restorative Practices (IIRP).

NYCLU (New York Civil Liberties Union) (2011) *Stop-and-Frisk: 2011 NYCLU Briefing*, New York: NYCLU.

Parmar, A. (2011) 'Stop and Search in London: Counter-terrorist or Counter-productive?', *Policing and Society*, 21(4): 369—82.

Pratt, J., Brown, D., Brown, M., Hallsworth, S. and Morrison, J. (2005) *The New Punitiveness: Trends, Theories, Perspectives*, Uffculme, Devon: Willan Publishing.

Renteln, A. (2010) 'Making Room for Culture in the Court', *The Judges' Journal*, 49(2). Available at: http://www.americanbar.org/content/dam/aba/migrated/sections/criminaljustice/PublicDocuments/Unit_9_Renteln.authcheckdam.pdf.

Scarman, L.G. (1982) *The Scarman Report: The Brixton Disorders 10—12 April 1981*, London: Pelican Books.

Segrave, M., Milivojevic, S. and Pickering, S. (2009) *Sex Trafficking: International Context and Response*, Uffculme, Devon: Willan Publishing.

Simon, J. (2007) *Governing through Crime: How the War on Crime Transformed American Democracy and Created a Culture of Fear*, New York: Oxford University Press.

Social Justice Commissioner (2007) 'Chapter 3: The Northern Territory "Emergency Response" Intervention — A Human Rights Analysis', *Social Justice Report 2007*, Sydney: Australian Human Rights Commission.

Stempel, J. (2012) 'Supreme Court May Narrow Law in Human Rights Cases', 1 October, Reuters, Washington. Available at: http://www.reuters.com/article/2012/10/01/us-usa-court-human-rights-idUSBRE89006B20121001.

Tauri, J. (1999) 'Explaining Recent Innovations in New Zealand's Criminal Justice System: Empowering Maori or Biculturalising the State?, *Australian and New Zealand Journal of Criminology*, 32(2): 153—67.

Taylor, D. (2012) 'Black Teenager "Stopped 50 Times" Plans to Sue Met Police for Harassment', 24 August, *The Guardian*. Available at: http://www.guardian.co.uk/uk/2012/aug/24/black-teenager-met-police.

Taylor, M. (2007) 'Juveniles in Detention in Australia, 1981—2006', Technical and Background Paper No. 26, Canberra: Australian Instutute of Criminology.

Thomas, D. and Beasley, M. (1993) 'Domestic Violence as a Human Rights Issue', *Human Rights Quarterly*, 15(1): 36—62.

Tombs, S. and Whyte, D. (2010) 'A Deadly Consensus: Worker Safety and Regulatory Degradation Under New Labour', *British Journal of Criminology*, 50(1): 46—65.

True, J. (2012) *The Political Economy of Violence against Women*, Oxford: Oxford University Press.

Wakeling, S., Jorgensen, M., Michaelson, S. and Begay, M. (2001) *Policing on American Indian Reservations*, Washington, DC: National Institute of Justice.

Whyte, D. (2009) *Crimes of the Powerful: A Reader*, Maidenhead: Open University Press.

Wonders, N. and Danner, M. (2006) 'Globalization, State-Corporate Crime, Women', in R. Michalowski and R. Kramer (eds), *State-Corporate Crime: Wrongdoing at the Intersection of Business and Government*, New Brunswick, NJ: Rutgers University Press.

CHAPTER 5

Integrating Criminology and Human Rights

Key concepts
Natural school — Deliberative school — Protest school — Discursive school

---

5.1 Introduction

Having outlined in the previous chapters how human rights can be understood from a philosophical, socio-political and legal perspective, we now consider how human rights thinking is being applied within criminology. In this chapter we review some contemporary and classic contributions towards what has been described as a 'criminology for human rights' (Stanley 2007). No doubt there are many significant omissions. But the publications considered here span a range of criminological approaches and vary with respect to the explicitness and level of conviction with which human rights law, language and philosophy are invoked. The discussion is organized around Dembour's four ideal types of human rights thinking (Dembour 2012), which were introduced in Chapter 1.

5.2 Reviewing the criminological record

Despite the clear relevance of human rights to crime and criminal justice, criminologists have been slow to apply human rights concepts in their work. This may be for ideological reasons, such as objections among critical scholars about false universalism or legal formalism (see Chapter 1); while less critical colleagues may simply maintain a primary focus on effectiveness and efficiency rather than normative concerns. For many criminologists without a legal background, human rights may be considered to be the exclusive domain of lawyers. Moreover, criminologists working in jurisdictions in which human rights are not foregrounded in public life – such as Australia, which has limited domestic incorporation of human rights, and the USA, in which constitutionally guaranteed civil liberties are often considered more relevant – may have limited incentives to appeal to human rights principles in their analysis or activism. In the United Kingdom, the introduction of the Human Rights Act in 1998 prompted a raft of criminological writing that explored the application of human rights standards to policing (Neyroud and Beckley 2001), prisons (Coyle 2003), victims (Doak 2008) and criminal justice as a whole (Cheney 1999).

While they note that academic criminology is engaging with human rights more than ever before, Murphy and Whitty (2013: 571) claim that very little is known about the role human rights have played within criminology:

> So far as we can see, there is *no* work that traces human rights within academic criminology: no systematic accounts of the historical sites, forms, dynamics and extent of criminological engagements. How and why academic criminology has moved towards, or away from, human rights – its concepts, forms, actors, institutions, cultures, practices and discourses – in particular contexts and eras is unknown.

Dembour's four ideal types of human rights thinking, introduced in Chapter 1, are helpful in making sense of the various ways in which human rights thinking has been applied within criminology (Dembour 2012). The key features of the four idealized schools of thought Dembour has proposed are summarized in Box 5.1. In tentatively identifying criminological work that appears to embody each of these approaches, there is no intention to infer that criminologists remain rigidly associated with one particular ideal type. As Dembour herself has stressed, any one of us may align ourselves strategically – whether consciously or inadvertently – with more than one of the ideal types listed in the box, depending on the issues under consideration. In particular, many of the criminologists whose work appears in the 'natural' category would disavow vigorously any belief in natural law. Some of the work referred to in that category shares with the natural school only the characteristic that human rights principles are referred to as specific legal and political entitlements. The intention with the classifications in Box 5.1 is merely to illustrate the range of criminological work that has engaged with human rights thinking, and to attempt to organize it in a coherent way.

5.2.1 Natural human rights criminology

Criminological work that exemplifies the natural or legalistic approach to human rights seeks to use human rights law and concepts as standards against which to judge the operation of criminal justice programmes and systems. This

Box 5.1   Four 'schools' of human rights thinking within criminology

	Key features*	Exemplars within criminology
Natural	Human rights as given; primarily negative entitlements; embodied in law; justified by nature/god/reason; universal, though may be differently translated	Applying specific human rights norms to criminal justice practices, e.g. policing, courts, probation, prisons Legal perspectives Possibly 'crime science'
Deliberative	Human rights as agreed upon; operate as principles; embodied in law; based on consensus; potentially universal	Methodological similarities with peacekeeping criminology, e.g. transitional justice, restorative justice
Protest	Human rights as fought for; as claims or aspirations; should be embodied in law but the law often falls short; based on perpetual social struggle; universal in the sense that human suffering is universal	Crimes of the powerful State-corporate crime Critical criminology with a focus on fairness and substantive equality
Discursive	Human rights as talked about; based on language; can be whatever you want them to be; exist as law but law is irrelevant; their supposed universality is a pretence	Post-structuralist, e.g. Foucauldian, Radical Feminist or Marxist

Note: * This column is adapted from Dembour 2012.

approach holds promise for the mainstreaming of human rights within criminology, adding a powerful normative perspective that distinguishes this form of engaged scholarship from the uncritical approach of some administrative criminology. A disparate literature making reference to human rights either as broad principles or specific legal obligations, in relation to policing, is beginning to emerge (Vaughan and Kilcommins 2007; Bullock and Johnson 2012); courts and sentencing (Henham 1998; Naughton 2005; Burnard 2008); victims (Anderson 1995; Edwards 2004); prisons (Bo 2002; Zinger 2006; Murphy and

Whitty 2007); probation (Hudson 2001; Canton 2013; Zinger 2012; Fenton 2013); and state crime (Cohen 1993). Other examples include the work of Alison Liebling on moral performance in prisons (Liebling 2011) and Lucia Zedner on the erosion of due process rights (Zedner 2007). The approach (although not necessarily the scholars themselves) could be classified broadly as liberal, placing a high value on the normative power of human rights and other ethical standards, and seeking to preserve their protective function against the onslaught of popular punitivism (Pratt *et al.* 2005), securitization (Goold and Lazarus 2007) and the emergence of a risk society (Hudson 2003).

Writing from the perspective of a legally influenced criminology, Lucia Zedner's analysis of the erosion of due process rights in the name of security is a prime example of this genre. Her chapter in the *Security and Human Rights* collection by Goold and Lazarus (2007) 'examines recent security measures, broadly defined, that have particular implications for individual liberties because they circumvent the procedural requirements of the criminal law to impose prospective constraints in respect of remote harms' (Zedner 2007: 257). The chapter engages directly with human rights instruments, discussing derogation from the European Convention on Human Rights prohibition against arbitrary detention (Article 5). It concludes that an absence of human rights protections in relation to certain security practices designated as 'preventive' is 'unsafe', particularly in a context where the burdens of these policies fall mainly on minorities who cannot necessarily expect to be protected via political processes.

Human rights frameworks can potentially be accommodated within any criminological approach that eschews empiricism and the purely technical approaches to criminal justice and crime control associated with much of mainstream criminology. For example, proponents of 'crime science' and 'evidence-based criminology' often claim to incorporate questions of ethics and justice alongside their focus on 'what works'. This is seen in the work on third party policing by Lorraine Mazerolle and Janet Ransley (Mazerolle and Ransley 2006). While the term 'human rights' does not appear in their index, the book concludes with a consideration of the ethical challenges of third party policing and calls for accountability and efforts to ensure that 'all groups, including young people, are treated with dignity and respect' (ibid.: 198). However, Loader and Sparks argue that normative considerations are generally limited to 'an acknowledgement amongst crime scientists of the settled side-constraints – such as human rights (Laycock 2005: 9) – that delimit what can be done in the name of effective crime detection and prevention' (Loader and Sparks 2011: 108). This assessment suggests that human rights thinking is expanding its support base within empirical criminology, but often remains secondary to the core focus on crime control.

5.2.2 Deliberative human rights criminology

Work within peacemaking criminology that emphasizes discussion, mediation and the reaching of consensus appears to fall within the deliberative category, most notably because of its methodological congruence with this position. McEvoy argues that using both the machinery and rhetoric of human rights can transform peacemaking criminology into a practical tool for conflict resolution (McEvoy 2003). Examples include the important work being done by criminologists in transitional justice following armed conflict (Jamieson and McEvoy 2007; Stanley 2009; Braithwaite *et al.* 2010) and on a more domestic level, in restorative justice (Braithwaite 2002a). This category could stretch perhaps to include Loader and Sparks' general advocacy of a public criminology that is actively engaged with the democratic process, though their position is more sceptical of the value of individual human rights than this classification might suggest.

Criminologists concerned with transitional justice have argued that human rights have a particular resonance in post-conflict societies, where they can be employed as a 'lingua franca', potentially cutting across long-established social divisions (Jamieson and McEvoy 2007; see also Mageen 1997). The value of human rights within the political realm is endorsed similarly by Michael Ignatieff, who suggests that human rights 'has become the lingua franca of global moral thought, as English has become the lingua franca of the global economy' (Ignatieff 2001: 52). In a 2011 article, McEvoy describes a presentation delivered by John Braithwaite on human rights and restorative justice within transitional justice settings, in which Braithwaite's responsiveness to concerns raised by other speakers at the international conference exemplifies the deliberative approach:

> On the night before he was due to present, he decided to write a different paper than the one he had prepared. He didn't shy away from the need to have enforceable human rights standards to ensure good practice, but he did much more ... [he stressed] the importance of recognizing agency and leadership coming from unlikely sources and the fact that transitional societies need to be given the space to develop their own indigenous forms of peacemaking that suit local circumstances, rather than accepting off-the-shelf models ... John Braithwaite showed himself capable of navigating the most shark infested political waters, sticking to principles concerning human rights and justice, 'getting it right' about the capacity for people and societies to change and yet doing so in a humble way which did not patronize his local audience. (McEvoy 2011: 311)

Braithwaite has also been a leading supporter of the application of restorative justice outside post-conflict settings, arguing that a criminal justice system that produces injustice (which he frames as 'institutional collapse') needs to reconceptualize its foundations, both procedurally and substantively, through the lens of human rights. In an article on setting standards for restorative justice, Braithwaite once again reveals his preference for local consensus-building within a framework influenced, but not wholly determined, by international human rights standards:

> Ultimately, such top down lists motivated by UN instruments or the ruminations of intellectuals are only important for supplying a provisional, revisable agenda for bottom up deliberation on restorative justice standards appropriate to distinctively local anxieties about injustice. A method is outlined for moving bottom up from standards citizens settle for evaluating their local programme to aggregating these into national and international standards. (Braithwaite 2002b: 563)

5.2.3 Protest human rights criminology

Criminologists who label themselves as 'critical' are the most likely to approach human rights from a protest perspective. This category includes criminologists from Julia and Hermann Schwendinger to Stanley Cohen, numerous contemporary scholars of state-corporate crime, and other critical criminologists who use human rights concepts to pursue research with a focus on social justice and equality. Criminologists with a commitment to representing the most marginalized groups in society, such as indigenous people, have often found in human rights a vehicle to express their political aspirations (Cunneen 2007, 2011). Murphy and Whitty (2013) suggest that some strands of cultural criminology may also have an affinity with human rights approaches because of their emphasis on representing spectacles of human suffering.

It is now more than 40 years since the Schwendingers noted that legalistic definitions of crime make criminologists 'subservient to the state', and argued that '[i]n the process of redefining crime, criminologists will redefine themselves, no longer to be the defenders of order but rather the guardians of human rights' (Schwendinger and Schwendinger 1970: 149). Hermann and Julia Schwendinger saw the core rights of personal security, freedom of speech and assembly, but above all the right to equality, as being fundamental to human flourishing, and argued that individuals *and systems* that denied those basic rights should be labelled criminal.

This agenda has been pursued most actively by critical criminologists alert to the potential for states and global corporations to misuse their political and economic power. These scholars have incorporated the idea of human rights violations into definitions and discussions of state crime (Barak 1991; Cohen 1993; Green and Ward 2000; Ross 2000; Kauzlarich *et al.* 2003; Chambliss and Michalowski 2010; Stanley and McCulloch 2012); state-corporate crime (Michalowski and Kramer 2006b); crimes of globalization (Friedrichs and Friedrichs 2002); and serious harm (Hillyard *et al.* 2004). While they do not always accept the Schwendingers' labelling of *whole systems* of inequitable governance as being criminal, theorists of state-corporate crime have focused their critiques on the forms of individual, corporate and institutional behaviour that lead to the most egregious suffering (Whyte 2009). No criminologist has pursued the project of aligning critical criminology with human rights activism with such effectiveness and vigour as the late Stanley Cohen (see Downes *et al.* 2007). His contributions include seminal works on state crime (Cohen 1993) and the sociology of denial (Cohen 2001), a period of time spent 'doing human rights' with a non-governmental organization (NGO), and active engagement with UN human rights mechanisms, including a consultative role on a report that analysed the human rights implications of contemporary patterns of social control (ICHRP 2010).

Despite this substantial scholarly engagement, the relationship between critical criminologists and human rights is not always an easy one. Critical scholars whose commitment to progressive politics stems from radical feminism, Marxism or post-colonialism may find the liberal origins and overtones of human rights to be a poor fit with their ideology, and might prefer to place themselves with the human rights 'nihilists' in the discursive category. Scholars working from radical perspectives often advocate fundamental structural change that goes beyond the enforcement of the minimum standards set out in human rights instruments, reject the abstraction and assertions of universalism of orthodox conceptions of human rights, and consider that existing human rights institutions are incapable of delivering on social justice goals in the face of state imperialism and growing corporate power. For example, Michalowski and Kramer (2006a: 13) point out that, '[u]nder the current United Nations structure, powerful states – particularly the permanent members of the Security Council – enjoy significant advantages in determining the substantive content of international law and practice interpretations of what constitutes human rights'. Elsewhere, Michalowski (2012) has queried whether supranational law – described as 'the master's tools' – is even capable of confronting the crimes of the powerful. Bowling and Sheptycki (2012) have criticized the fact that UN mechanisms to combat transnational organized crime have focused almost entirely on the suppression of psychotropic drugs and terrorism, while ignoring large-scale economic crimes committed by corporate elites. And Stanley (2007: 171) has pointed out that mainstream human rights approaches overlook 'the seemingly endless, everyday violations and human insecurities' that arise from the normal workings of the global capitalist system.

Despite these reservations, critical criminologists from a range of ideological positions have been drawn to human rights frameworks to pursue their progressive agendas. It is possible to harbour doubts about the limits of the international human rights machinery without abandoning completely the idea, and ideals, of human rights. Citing the work of Stan Cohen, Pat Carlen and Nikolas Rose, Murphy and Whitty (2013: 574) note that '[r]adical criminology, for example, denounced rights as "mere ideology"; yet, in later streams of critical criminology, rights were recognized as potential tools'. This resembles the pragmatic stance advocated by sociologist Anthony Woodiwiss (2005) in his 'sceptic's defence of human rights'. Cohen has argued that a commitment to human rights is compatible with a broader politics of social justice, warning that 'intellectual skepticism [about human rights] cannot become an excuse for political nonengagement' (cited in Jamieson and McEvoy 2007: 435). Barbara Hudson has made a similar argument, claiming that human rights can be brought into alignment with both social justice and feminist agendas (Hudson 2000). In fact, she asserts that critical criminologists have a moral obligation to incorporate social justice and human rights into their theorizing and research methodologies (Hudson 2002). Other critical criminologists have advocated solidarity with the human rights movement as a foundation for activism. For example, Welch (2012: 369) proposes that 'critical criminology should align itself with other human rights organizations to advance protections against state crime while holding perpetrators accountable for their violations', while Barak (1990: 25) argues that 'to confront state criminality as a legitimate enemy of civil society is to join the struggle for universal human rights and social justice'.

British criminologist Phil Scraton supports criminological practice that endorses a human rights approach but also recognizes the need for broader social change. For example, he has argued that '[d]espite well-rehearsed and important critiques of human rights legislation, a positive rights discourse and agenda which recognizes the determining contexts of social injustice and the realities and consequences of personal suffering can provide a starting-point; a processual and procedural alternative to the administration of law and justice' (Scraton 2002: 36). David Scott (2013), an avowed abolitionist, has taken up this challenge, advocating a radical rearticulation of human rights in relation to prisoners that extends beyond the narrow confines of procedural justice to pursue wider objectives of social justice and legitimacy. Australian criminologist, Dave Brown, a veteran campaigner for leftist political causes within law and criminal justice, is also a cautious human rights convert:

> There is a need also to become more adept at using human rights arguments and to be able to give them a practical and specific operation, embodied in actual standards of practice, for example in how to actually run a prison system (Wilkie and Brown, 2002). There is a tendency for many on the left, myself included, to retain a residual hostility to what are seen as 'rhetorical' and 'abstract' human rights arguments, rather than to enter more constructively into debates around how human rights concepts might be made more concrete and operationalised. (Brown 2002: 96)

Brown made good on this commitment in the same year he wrote these words, by co-editing a collection on human rights in Australian prisons (Brown and Wilkie 2002).

Practitioners of the protest variant of human rights criminology have also struggled with the abstract legal formalism of human rights, given their preference for pursuing social transformation through political action. For example, Hogg has argued that large-scale problems 'will not be addressed through the establishment of formal human rights machinery but only through political solutions that are centrally concerned with a redistribution of resources' (Hogg 2002: 211). Even so, he claims that '[m]any see hopeful signs in the international human rights movement', adding that '[h]uman rights practice has in some important ways begun to catch up with the sort of human rights agenda set by Julia and Herman Schwendinger' (Hogg 2002: 209). The biggest dilemma, in Hogg's view, arises when deciding whether to work to alleviate inequality on a global scale or to retain a focus on social justice at home.

5.2.4 Discursive human rights criminology

It is debatable whether it makes sense to speak of a discursive human rights criminology at all, since scholars of this persuasion are described by Dembour (2012) as human rights 'nihilists'. Criminologists who operate from a post-structuralist, feminist, Foucauldian or Marxist perspective may reject human rights and other bodies of law as being irrelevant to the pursuit of radical deconstruction and alternative discursive practices. Carol Smart's devastating critique of rights places her firmly within the category of criminologists who consider human rights to be merely a discursive practice. Smart famously issued a warning to feminists to avoid the 'siren call of the law', claiming that the feminist movement was 'too easily "seduced" by law and even where it is critical of law it too often attempts to use law pragmatically in the hope that new law or more law might be better than old law' (Smart 1989: 160). Her approach to legal rights is said to have been a 'forerunner of the governmentality perspectives on human rights' (Murphy and Whitty 2013: 574), suggesting that the growing contingent of Foucauldian scholars within criminology will also have little interest in engaging in human rights discourse. Indeed, it has been argued that human rights are 'impossible' within 'a postmodern account of law and justice' (Salter 1996).

However, it is possible to find criminologists working from a Foucauldian perspective, such as Michael Welch (2004, 2009, 2012), who readily incorporate the language of rights into their scholarship. In fact, it has been argued that a distinction can be found in the work of Foucault between his earlier 'rejectionist' stance on human rights and a more liberal position amounting to a 'critical affirmation' of rights that emerged in his later writing (Golder 2011). Golder concludes: 'Neither a full embrace nor a total rejection of human rights, the Foucauldian politics of human rights developed here elaborates (and attempts to connect) several disparate figures in his thought: rights as ungrounded and illimitable, rights as the strategic instrument-effect of political struggle, and rights as a performative mechanism of community' (Golder 2011: 283).

In a similar fashion, some commentators have challenged the orthodox reading of Marx, which casts human rights as irredeemably bourgeois and egoistic. For example, having set out the well-known objections expressed by Marx, Freeden concludes:

> All this is not to argue that Marx was a crude objector to human rights or that he would have rejected all the substantive values they aim to encapsulate. Rather, he saw human nature as solely realizable through a transformation of human and material relationships. The protective aspect of rights, directed against other individuals or human agencies, which is so important to the liberal tradition, was unnecessary in his vision of society because the eradication of class conflict would remove what he saw as the only source of threat to human development and expression ... Contemporary socialist views of rights still occasionally exhibit these tensions and reservations but they are reluctant to do away with the idea of rights altogether. (Freeden 1991: 22)

Finally, Hudson has argued that human rights can be reconciled with postmodern positions as long as sweeping claims of universalism are abandoned. In her influential book *Justice in the Risk Society*, after reviewing a range of philosophical approaches and giving her qualified support to discursive and communitarian conceptions of human rights, she concludes that a minimalist commitment to universalism is the only guarantee of achieving justice in a world of strangers:

> [I]t is this book's conclusion that some rights must be regarded as inalienable, while others may be suspended only in extreme circumstances and with properly argued justification. Discursive justice, it is argued, reaches its limits at the edge of communities who share the same basic moral principles or who can at least make themselves comprehensible to each other; beyond sympathy and beyond comprehension only rights can guard against injustice. (Hudson 2003: xvii)

These interpretations of key rejectionist thinkers such as Foucault and Marx, and of discursive perspectives more generally, open up some space for human rights. Still, their followers are likely to remain ambivalent and reluctant protagonists of human rights within criminology.

5.3 Human rights, globalization and human suffering

In addition to the conceptual diversity demonstrated in the previous section, the issues researched by criminologists from a range of methodological traditions are taking on an increasingly transnational dimension. It might therefore be argued that globalization is reinforcing the alignment between criminology and human rights in a way that potentially cuts across the four schools of thought discussed above. A perspective that stretches beyond the narrow confines of state-based law and criminal justice institutions is needed to address this extra-territorial research agenda, and criminologists are turning increasingly to human rights to provide a supra-national normative framework. As Ignatieff has observed, international human rights institutions are a powerful way to 'embody a sense of global conscience' (cited in Hogg 2002). Human rights standards can provide an important point of reference in transnational spaces where powerful states wage their wars against drugs (Bowling 2010), terrorism (Welch 2012) or border crossing (Weber and Pickering 2011). For example, while they acknowledge the many failures to enforce human rights standards within specific transnational policing operations, Bowling and Sheptycki (2012) nevertheless conclude that effective human rights regimes are crucial to the accountability of global policing networks:

> As policing moves into the transnational realm, there will likely evolve a supranational system to regulate its power within and beyond national

borders 'from above' and an active globally connected civil society to engage police accountability 'from below' ... Such an ethos would be imbued with notions and principles such as responsiveness to the global commonwealth, adherence to international human rights norms and the values of 'human security'. (Bowling and Sheptycki 2012: 136)

Feminist criminologists Nancy Wonders and Mona Danner also advocate a qualified engagement with UN mechanisms to curb abuses against women, arguing that these are the only institutions with the capacity to oppose state and corporate harms:

Women's NGOs both challenge and collaborate with the United Nations, which represents the single most important arena for forming and enforcing international agreements that may mediate the effects of globalization. The policies, conventions and treaties that emerge from the United Nations, however, provide one of the only standards by which state-corporate crimes can be identified and responded to (Michalowski and Kramer 1987). For this reason, we also argue that women's NGOs will continue to have a strategic role to play in the future if women are to have collective power and representation in a globalized world. (Wonders and Danner 2006: 109)

5.4 Conclusion

Criminologists who engage actively with human rights, while they may vary in many other respects, all see the pursuit of human wellbeing rather than the smooth functioning of state institutions as the key objective of criminological enquiry. As Jamieson and McEvoy point out, '[c]riminologists and sociologists in particular who take an interest in suffering normally regard it as axiomatic that the institutions of the state are themselves a source of considerable suffering' (2007: 426). This emphasis on the human condition and the suspect role of states as both protectors and abusers of human rights was central to the agenda articulated by Herman and Julia Schwendinger 40 years ago. They concluded that '[t]o defend human rights, criminologists must be able to sufficiently identify the violations of these rights – by whom and against whom; how and why' (Schwendinger and Schwendinger 1970: 146). In the coming chapters we hope to illustrate how criminologists might pursue this vision of a criminology for human rights, through both critique of human rights breaches and the articulation of a positive, rights-enhancing agenda.

Additional reading and resources

Cohen, S. (2001) *States of Denial: Knowing about Atrocities and Suffering*, Cambridge: Polity Press.

Dembour, M. (2012) 'What Are Human Rights? Four Schools of Thought', in T. Cushman (ed.) *Handbook of Human Rights*, Abingdon: Routledge.

Downes, D., Rock, P., Chinkin, C. and Gearty, C. (2007) *Crime, Social Control and Human Rights: From Moral Panics to States of Denial — Essays in Honour of Stanley Cohen*, Uffculme, Devon: Willan Publishing.

Schwendinger, H. and Schwendinger, J. (1970) 'Defenders of order or guardians of human rights?', *Issues in Criminology*, 5: 123—57.

Stanley, E. (2007) 'Towards a Criminology for Human Rights', in A. Barton, K. Corteen, D. Scott and D. Whyte (eds) *Expanding the Criminological Imagination*, Uffculme, Devon: Willan Publishing.

References

Anderson, T. (1995) 'Victims' Rights or Human Rights?' *Current Issues in Criminal Justice*, 6(3): 335—45.

Barak, G. (1990) 'Crime, Criminology and Human Rights: Towards an Understanding of State Criminality', *Journal of Human Justice*, 2(1): 11—28.

Barak, G. (1991) *Crimes by the Capitalist State: An Introduction to State Criminality*, New York: State University of New York Press.

Bo, B.P. (2002) 'Imprisonment of Non-Nationals: Do Recent Amendments to the Norwegian Immigration Act Comply with Human Rights and Moral Standards?', *Current Issues in Criminal Justice*, 14(1): 31—42.

Bowling, B. (2010) *Policing the Caribbean: Transnational Security Cooperation in Practice*, Oxford: Oxford University Press.

Bowling, B. and Sheptycki, J. (2012) *Global Policing*, London: Sage.

Braithwaite, J. (2002a) *Restorative Justice and Responsive Regulation*, New York: Oxford University Press.

Braithwaite, J. (2002b) 'Setting Standards for Restorative Justice', *British Journal of Criminology*, 42(3): 563—77.

Braithwaite, J., Braithwaite, V. Cookson, M. and Dunn, L. (2010) *Anomie and Violence: Non-Truth and Reconciliation in Indonesian Peacebuilding*, Canberra: Australian National University Press.

Brown, D. and Wilkie, M. (2002) *Prisoners as Citizens: Human Rights in Australian Prisons*, Sydney: Federation Press.

Brown, D. (2002) '"Losing my religion": Reflections on Critical Criminology in Australia', in K. Carrington and R. Hogg (eds), *Critical Criminology: Issues, Debates, Challenges*, Uffculme: Willan Publishing.

Bullock, K. and Johnson, P. (2012) 'The Impact of the Human Rights Act 1998 on Policing in England and Wales', *British Journal of Criminology*, 52(3): 630—50.

Burnard, A. (2008) 'Right to a Fair Trial: Young Offenders and the Victorian Charter of Human Rights and Responsibilities', *Current Issues in Criminal Justice*, 20(2): 173—88.

Canton, R. (2013) 'The Point of Probation: On Effectiveness, Human Rights and the Virtues of Obliquity', *Criminology and Criminal Justice*, 13(5): 577—593.

Chambliss, W. and Michalowski, R. (2010) *State Crime in the Global Age*, Uffculme: Willan Publishing.

Cheney, D. (1999) *Criminal Justice and the Human Rights Act 1998*, Bristol: Jordans.

Cohen, S. (1993) 'Human Rights and Crimes of the State: The Culture of Denial', *Australian and New Zealand Journal of Criminology*, 26(2): 97—115.

Cohen, S. (2001) *States of Denial: Knowing about Atrocities and Suffering*, Cambridge: Polity Press.

Coyle, A. (2003) *A Human Rights Approach to Prison Management: Handbook for Prison Staff*, Oxford: Blackwell.

Cunneen, C. (2007) 'Criminology, Human Rights and Indigenous Peoples', in S. Parmentier and E. Weitekamp (eds) *Crime and Human Rights*, Oxford: Elsevier.

Cunneen, C. (2011) 'Postcolonial Perspectives for Criminology', in M. Bosworth and C. Hoyle (eds) *What Is Criminology?*, Oxford: Oxford University Press.

Dembour, M. (2012) 'What Are Human Rights? Four Schools of Thought', in T. Cushman (ed.) *Handbook of Human Rights*, Abingdon: Routledge.

Doak, J. (2008) *Victims' Rights, Human Rights and Criminal Justice: Reconceiving the Role of Third Parties*, Oxford: Hart Publishing.

Downes, D., Rock, P., Chinkin, C. and Gearty, C. (2007) *Crime, Social Control and Human Rights: From Moral Panics to States of Denial — Essays in Honour of Stanley Cohen*, Uffculme, Devon: Willan Publishing.

Edwards, I. (2004) 'An Ambiguous Participant: The Crime Victim and Criminal Justice Decision Making', *British Journal of Criminology*, 44(6): 967—82.

Fenton, J. (2013) 'Risk Aversion and Anxiety In Scottish Criminal Justice Social Work: Can Desistance and Human Rights Agendas Have an Impact?', *Howard Journal of Criminal Justice*, 52(1): 77—90.

Freeden, M. (1991) *Rights*, Oxford: Oxford University Press.

Friedrichs, D. and Friedrichs, J. (2002) 'The World Bank and Crimes of Globalization: A Case Study', *Social Justice*, 29(1—2): 13—36.

Golder, B. (2011) 'Foucault's Critical (Yet Ambivalent) Affirmation: The Three Figures of Rights', *Social and Legal Studies*, 20(3): 283—312.

Goold, B. and Lazarus, L. (2007) *Security and Human Rights*, Oxford: Hart Publishing.

Green, P.J. and Ward, T. (2000) 'State Crime, Human Rights, and the Limits of Criminology', *Social Justice*, 27(1): 101—15.

Henham, R. (1998) 'Human Rights, Due Process and Sentencing', *British Journal of Criminology*, 38(4): 592—610.

Hillyard, P., Pantazis, C., Tombs, S. and Gordon, D. (2004) *Beyond Criminology: Taking Harm Seriously*, London: Pluto Press.

Hogg, R. (2002) 'Criminology Beyond the Nation State: Global Conflicts, Human Rights and the "New World Disorder"', in K. Carrington and R. Hogg (eds), *Critical Criminology: Issues, Debates, Challenges*, Uffculme, Devon: Willan Publishing.

Hudson, B. (2000) 'Criminology, Difference and Justice: Issues for a Critical Criminology', *Australian and New Zealand Journal of Criminology*, 33(2): 168—82.

Hudson, B. (2001) 'Human Rights, Public Safety and the Probation Service: Defending Justice in the Risk Society', *Howard Journal*, 40(2): 103—13.

Hudson, B. (2002) 'Critical Reflection as Research Methodology', in V. Jupp (ed.), *Doing Criminological Research*, London: Sage.

Hudson, B. (2003) *Justice in the Risk Society*, London: Sage.

Ignatieff, M. (2001) *Human Rights as Politics and Idolatry*, Princeton, NJ: Princeton University Press.

ICHRP (International Council on Human Rights Policy) (2010) *Modes and Patterns of Social Control: Implications for Human Rights Policy*, Geneva: ICHRP.

Jamieson, R. and McEvoy, K. (2007) 'Conflict, Suffering and the Promise of Human Rights', in D. Downes, P. Rick, C. Chinkin and C. Gearty (eds), *Crime, Social Control and Human Rights: From Moral Panics to States of Denial — Essays in Honour of Stanley Cohen*, Uffculme, Devon: Willan Publishing.

Kauzlarich, D., Mullins, C. and Matthews, R. (2003) 'A Complicity Continuum of State Crime', *Contemporary Justice Review*, 6(3): 241—54.

Liebling, A. (2011) 'Moral Performance, Inhuman and Degrading Treatment and Prison Pain', *Punishment and Society*, 13(5): 530—50.

Loader, I. and Sparks, R. (2011) *Public Criminology?*, Abingdon: Routledge.

Mageen, P. (1997) 'Human Rights and the Peace Process in Northern Ireland', *Critical Criminology*, 8(1): 31—48.

Mazerolle, L. and Ransley, J. (2006) *Third Party Policing*, Cambridge: Cambridge University Press.

McEvoy, K. (2003) 'Beyond the Metaphor: Political Violence, Human Rights and "New" Peacekeeping Criminology', *Theoretical Criminology*, 7(3): 319—46.

McEvoy, K. (2011) 'Book Review: John Braithwaite, Valerie Braithwaite, Michael Cookson and Leah Dunn, *Anomie and Violence: Non-truth and Reconciliation in Indonesian Peacebuilding*', Canberra: Australian National University Press.

Michalowski, R. (2012) 'The Master's Tools: Can Supranational Law Confront Crimes of Powerful States?', in E. Stanley and J. McCulloch (eds), *State Crime and Resistance*, Abingdon: Routledge.

Michalowski, R. and Kramer, R. (2006a) 'The Critique of Power', in *State-Corporate Crime: Wrongdoing at the Intersection of Business and Government*, New Brunswick, NJ: Rutgers University Press.

Michalowski, R. and Kramer, R. (eds) (2006b) *State–Corporate Crime: Wrongdoing at the Intersection of Business and Government*, New Brunswick, NJ: Rutgers University Press.

Murphy, T. and Whitty, N. (2007) 'Risk and Human Rights in UK Prison Governance', *British Journal of Criminology*, 47(5): 798—816.

Murphy, T. and Whitty, N. (2013) 'Making History: Academic Criminology and Human Rights', *British Journal of Criminology*, 53(4): 568—87.

Naughton, M. (2005) 'Redefining Miscarriages of Justice: A Human Rights Approach to Unearth Subjugated Discourses of Wrongful Criminal Conviction', *British Journal of Criminology*, 45(2): 165—82.

Neyroud: and Beckley, A. (2001) *Policing, Ethics and Human Rights*, Uffculme, Devon: Willan Publishing.

Pratt, J., Brown, D., Brown, M., Hallsworth, S. and Morrison, J. (2005) *The New Punitiveness: Trends, Theories, Perspectives*, Uffculme, Devon: Willan Publishing.

Ross, J. (2000) *Varieties of State Crime and Its Control*, New York: Criminal Justice Press.

Salter, M. (1996) 'The Impossibility of Human Rights within a Postmodern Account of Law and Justice', *Journal of Civil Liberties*, 1: 29—66.

Schwendinger, H. and Schwendinger, J. (1970) 'Defenders of Order or Guardians of Human Rights?', *Issues in Criminology*, 5(2): 123—57.

Scott, D. (2013) 'The Politics of Prisoner Legal Rights', *Howard Journal of Criminal Justice*, 52(3): 233—50.

Scraton: (2002) 'Defining "Power" and Challenging "Knowledge": Critical Analysis as Resistance in the UK', in K. Carrington and R. Hogg (eds), *Critical Criminology: Issues, Debates, Challenges*, Uffculme, Devon: Willan Publishing.

Smart, C. (1989) *Feminism and the Power of Law*, London: Routledge.

Stanley, E. (2007) 'Towards a Criminology for Human Rights', in A. Barton, K. Corteen, D. Scott, and D. Whyte (eds), *Expanding the Criminological Imagination*, Uffculme, Devon: Willan Publishing.

Stanley, E. (2009) *Torture, Truth and Justice*, London: Routledge.

Stanley, E. and McCulloch, J. (eds) (2012) *State Crime and Resistance*, Abingdon: Routledge.

Vaughan, B. and Kilcommins, S. (2007) 'The Europeanization of Human Rights: An Obstacle to Authoritarian Policing in Ireland?', *European Journal of Criminology*, 4(4): 437—60.

Weber, L. and Pickering, S. (2011) *Globalization and Borders: Death at the Global Frontier*, Basingstoke: Palgrave Macmillan.

Welch, M. (2004) 'Trampling Human Rights in The War on Terror: Implications to the Sociology of Denial', *Critical Criminology*, 12(1): 1—20.

Welch, M. (2009) 'Guantanamo Bay as a Foucauldian Phenomenon: An Analysis of Penal Discourse, Technologies, and Resistance', *The Prison Journal*, 89(1): 3—20.

Welch, M. (2012) 'War on Terror, Human Rights and Critical Criminology', in W. DeKeseredy and M. Dragiewicz (eds), *Routledge Handbook of Critical Criminology,* Abingdon: Routledge, pp. 360—71.

Whyte, D. (2009) *Crimes of the Powerful: A Reader*, Maidenhead: Open University Press.

Wonders, N. and Danner, M. (2006) 'Globalization, state-corporate crime, women', in R. Michalowski and R. Kramer (eds) *State-Corporate Crime: Wrongdoing at the Intersection of Business and Government*, New Brunswick, NJ, Rutgers University Press.

Woodiwiss, A. (2005) *Human Rights: Key Ideas*, London: Taylor & Francis.

Zedner, L. (2007) 'Seeking Security by Eroding Rights: The Side-Stepping of Due Process', in B. Goold and L. Lazarus (eds), *Security and Human Rights*, Oxford: Hart Publishing, pp. 257–76.

Zinger, I. (2006) 'Human Rights, Compliance and the Role of External Prison Oversight', *Canadian Journal of Criminology & Criminal Justice*, 48(2): 127–40.

Zinger, I. (2012) 'Conditional Release and Human Rights in Canada: A Commentary', *Canadian Journal of Criminology & Criminal Justice*, 54(1): 117–35.

Applying Human Rights in Criminology

In this section we shift the focus away from human rights as abstract ideas, positive laws or political claims and instead organize the discussion around the subject matter of what we have called 'everyday criminology' (see About this Book).

Each of the chapters in this section concentrates on a particular aspect of criminology or criminal justice, and considers how a human rights perspective can enhance, or in some cases hinder, our analysis and practice.

We do not adopt an explicit stance towards human rights (see Chapter 5), though the tone is generally supportive of the value of bringing human rights perspectives to bear on criminological questions.

In each of the chapters we highlight relevant human rights instruments and discuss the benefits and pitfalls of incorporating human rights concepts into an understanding of crime prevention and criminal justice.

Our emphasis is primarily on Anglophone countries and Europe, in which the bulk of 'everyday criminology' takes place. However, a few examples from elsewhere in the world find their way into the discussion because of their topicality.

Our illustrative examples are of necessity highly selective, and readers will identify many important human rights issues that have been left out of the discussion. This surfeit of possible examples only serves to reinforce the growing relevance of human rights within criminology.

CHAPTER 6

Criminal Law

Key concepts
Legal certainty of law and punishment — Non-retroactivity and proportionality of law and punishment — Shield/sword binary function — Territoriality principle — State of emergency

6.1 Introduction

When Lady Hale, to date the most senior female judge in the history of the United Kingdom, was asked by London School of Economics students whether she would recommend the repeal of the UK Human Rights Act 1998 (HRA), she replied that the country would deeply regret a decision to repeal the Act, as many people have derived great benefit from its introduction (Rozenberg 2013). And yet, arguments backed by the current Home Secretary, Theresa May, would suggest that the government is even considering pulling out of the European Convention on Human Rights (ECHR), to enable it to better promote its interests (BBC 2013).

It is undeniable that, in their relatively short history, international human rights frameworks have had an enormous influence on domestic criminal law, in both amending current criminal law and favouring the conditions for the creation of new legislation (Ashworth 2009). The overarching principle of legal certainty, whereby crimes and punishments must be defined by law, has been incorporated into domestic legislation for many years. And stemming from this principle are the two corollaries of retroactivity and proportionality of law and punishment. The first corollary refers to the point that law cannot be applied retroactively, guaranteeing that no person may be found guilty of any act committed when it did not constitute a criminal offence based on the law at the time. The second corollary suggests that the aims that justify any restriction imposed on an individual by criminal law will have to be measured against the severity of the nature of the prohibited act, according to the principle of proportionality. The basic human rights principle of legal certainty is reflected in Article 11 of the Universal Declaration of Human Rights (UDHR), and in many other regional conventions such as the ECHR (Article 7), the European Union (EU) Charter of Fundamental Rights, the American Convention on Human Rights (Article 9), the African Charter on Human and Peoples' Rights [Banjul Charter] (Article 7), and the Arab Charter on Human Rights (Article 6). Similar international recognition is offered to another all-embracing human right: the principle of presumption of innocence until proven otherwise in a court recognized by the law. And the veto of punishment outside the law also constitutes an embedded principle in many domestic criminal laws. There is, therefore, consensus about the positive influence of international human rights obligations on domestic criminal law. These principles and corollaries have had a massive influence on how certain controversial topics have been legislated through the years, such as the prohibition on torture and the abolishment of the death penalty, the protection of ethnic minorities, and the reinforcement of due process.

Because of their success in shaping domestic criminal law in both direct and indirect ways, human rights frameworks have recently been presented, as seen above in relation to the UK context, as interfering with the natural progression of domestic developments in legal and policy areas, and therefore as working against the national interest. The UK's call for independence from legal obligations deriving from external sources is not unique. Traditionally, domestic criminal law has acted as a tool to protect individuals from violations of their rights by other subjects, with the state standing as the benevolent power to distribute 'justice'. The rapid development of human rights in domestic criminal law has at least challenged, if not in some cases significantly altered, this positivistic view. Is the state doing enough to protect the rights of all the people in its territory? Is the state itself acting in a proper and just manner? It is evident that a human rights perspective on domestic legislation has engendered a degree of questioning of the role of the state, and a new level of awareness of what is fair and just. This innovative approach has highlighted gaps in the legal system – raising questions, for example, about whether women or minority groups are adequately protected, and whether the power held by multinational corporations is monitored closely enough – and led to demands for a more comprehensive scrutiny of the actions or omissions of the state. In turn, the state is questioning the advantages and disadvantages of supporting a human rights lens on the domestic legal system. From the government's standpoint, a patriotic narrative on whether to maintain a human rights perspective goes beyond the justice system and is portrayed as a means of protecting the nation's interests. This approach to human rights principles can also be seen as evidence of executives reflecting on how human rights frameworks have weakened state sovereignty, fragmented state power and turned state policy into action that is visible and open to question by many. This is the underlying approach taken by this chapter: to reflect on the role of human rights and developments in criminal law in the context of the advancement of new configurations of power that are absorbing state sovereignty, and the state's efforts to control or halt this process.

6.2 Human rights in domestic criminal law

The inclusion of human rights bills within domestic legislation, such as the Canadian Human Rights Act 1985, the New Zealand Human Rights Act 1993 and the UK HRA, is one of the ways in which national legislation can incorporate international frameworks in this area. Continental European countries use other instruments, such as their constitutions, to allow for access to outside sources to which they are signatory parties. Similarly, the US 1787 Constitution and its amendments incorporate a number of fundamental rights, including the controversial right to keep and bear arms, introduced with the Second Amendment to the Constitution in 1791, supporting the natural rights of self-defence. Access to international human rights treaties via constitutions often means that there is a self-executing approach, which implies that no further legislative action is required and that domestic courts can interpret international law directly. Yet in recent times the US Supreme Court – with some exceptions, including the 2006 *Hamdam v Rumsfeld* case – has embraced a more restrictive approach to treaty interpretation, reflecting an increasingly deferential attitude towards executive power (Sloss *et al.* 2011). The 1996 Constitution of the Republic of South Africa is unique in that it has also embraced a holistic set of rules for the protection of economic, social and cultural rights with explicit reference to the International Covenant on Economic, Social and Cultural Rights (ICESCR). This approach emerged as a response to discriminatory practices towards the black population during the colonial and apartheid regime (Liebenberg 2007). Addressing the deep structural inequalities within South African society by using the most influential legal document in the country was a decisive step forward, according to former President Nelson Mandela. Mandela was a South African anti-apartheid revolutionary, elected as the first black president during the period 1994 to 1999, after having served 27 years in prison for conspiracy against the government. In his 1991 address to the African National Congress Bill of Rights Conference, Mandela questioned the value of fundamental rights without real power to access them:

> A simple vote, without food, shelter and health care is to use first generation rights as a smokescreen to obscure the deep underlying forces which dehumanise people. It is to create an appearance of equality and justice,

while by implication socioeconomic inequality is entrenched. We do not want freedom without bread, nor do we want bread without freedom. We must provide for all the fundamental rights and freedoms associated with a democratic society. (Cited in Liebenberg 2007)

Some other signatory countries to international conventions do not have ad hoc domestic legislation or a constitution that allows direct access to these instruments, and do not include a section on subjects' rights – for example, for historical reasons. Exemplary here is Australia, where the Constitution came into force in 1901 and to which amendments have never been made (see Box 6.1). In these countries, human rights protective measures arise from a number of laws and court cases.

Box 6.1   Australia: a case of contradiction?

Despite consultation on a federal human rights bill, Australia has yet to reach an agreement on the need for such legislation. The 2009 national human rights consultation saw the former president of the Australian Human Rights Commission, Catherine Branson QC, arguing for a need to implement an instrument to protect the voiceless individuals in Australia. The outcome of this consultation, however, did not change the position of the federal government, which in 2010 rejected the idea of adopting a federal human rights charter (Kirby 2011).

And yet, within Australia, one state and one territory (Victoria and the Australian Capital Territory [ACT]) have adopted charters for the protection of human rights (Victoria in 2006, and ACT in 2004). Former Victorian Attorney-General, Rob Hulls, who embraced the charter in his state, high-lighted the contradiction of Australia positioning itself at the international level as a defender of rights while failing to implement a comprehensive protection for its people at the national level: 'We've made it clear to other countries that we don't agree with their human rights record in some instances. Well, how can you do that on the one hand, and on the other hand be one of the last Western societies in the world not to have a human rights instrument?' (Tomazin 2011).

As far back as 1995, Hilary Charlesworth was referring to the ambivalent attitude of Australia towards international human rights at the domestic level as a case of split personality. Australia acts in the international arena wearing 'shining armour as a guardian of international human rights standards', but this attitude 'looks decidedly tarnished' with regard to domestic matters (Charlesworth, 1995: 129).

Despite differences in the paths by which countries choose to incorporate international sources of human rights, there are a number of civil, economic, cultural and political principles considered to be fundamental values in domestic criminal law and criminal proceedings. Yet sometimes these principles need to be balanced against each other in order to define prevailing standards – a challenging job often left to international and domestic courts. Many recent court cases across different international jurisdictions reflect the ongoing debate around which principle should prevail, and how to balance conflicting values. For example, in 2013, a court of appeal in the UK argued that the right to privacy is a prevailing principle under the ECHR, and takes prominence over the need for disclosure of previous convictions to the police (*R v Greater Manchester Chief Constable*). Another example was a 2012 Canadian Supreme Court case in which the freedom of the witness to wear the Islamic face veil, the *niqab*, was debated against the fairness of the trial and the rights of the defendants (*R v NS*).

6.3 Shield/sword binary function of human rights

The many human rights principles aimed at the protection of people caught in the criminal justice process are used in what is known as the 'shield/sword' binary function of human rights, following the terminology proposed by Christine Van den Wyngaert, a current judge of the International Criminal Court (ICC). The shield function of human rights principles works to neutralize the application of the law against the individual. For example, the several international obligations in the area of anti-discrimination have worked as a shield that has limited or halted completely domestic criminal laws that infringe human rights. This shield function symbolizes a mechanism to remedy the negative effects of criminal laws on people. The decriminalization of homosexual sex in various Western jurisdictions is an example of this shielding of individuals by human rights obligations against domestic criminal laws.

Conversely, the sword function triggers the application of the law when it is beneficial to the individual. This function helps in the application of existing laws, or advances existing laws to the benefit of the individual. An example of the sword function can be found in the area of domestic violence, whereby legislative developments common to many jurisdictions have been influenced by the recognition of women's and children's rights as human rights at an international level. The sword function can also be seen in the ongoing legislative process for improving the protection of victims of domestic violence. For example, in the UK, the Family Act 1996 has been amended by the Domestic Violence, Crime and Victims Act 2004, which extends provisions to combat domestic violence by criminalizing certain actions, such as the death of a child or a vulnerable adult as a result of neglect or abuse.

It has been pointed out, nevertheless, that the binary shield/sword function of human rights obligations represents a paradox of criminal law (Delmas-Marty, cited in Tulkens 2011). The application of criminal law needs to be monitored constantly against human rights standards because it can help to protect (sword function), yet at the same time, such an application may highlight those areas in criminal law that are damaging to the individual, underlining the need for protection against criminal law (shield function). This binary function implies a recognition that criminal law can be harmful. This point has long been discussed in socio-legal debates discourses around the boundaries and limitations of the law. Criminal law, as a social construct produced by the powerful mainstream society, is a tool that can be used to achieve contradictory aims, including the persecution of its people (Packer 1968; Gramsci 1971). The state maintains a monopoly on power, building the legitimacy of its instruments, including criminal law as a tool of control, through a process of hegemony (Gramsci 1971). This includes the power to categorize activities as criminal, since the definition of the content of the law falls under the exclusive control of the state (see, for a general overview, Muncie 2001). Targeting conventional forms of crime, such as street crime, has allowed the state to respond to the needs of its citizens while maintaining mainstream consensus and power. The law, in essence, is a 'bourgeois law', proposed and accepted by the powerful groups within society.

In contrast, the process of reviewing criminal law and categorizing, in a progressive-critical manner, its impact on individuals is more recent. A human rights lens has enabled the interpretation of criminal law and proceedings using its own normative tools. This process has responded to the need for an ethical review of the function and role of criminal law that is anchored to local legal advancements and international commitments. Even if this is still a process of hegemony – of powerful states imposing their interpretation of the human rights narrative – it has allowed for the power configurations to shift. These emerging configurations include agencies other than the nation-state, such as international governmental agencies, supranational courts and non-governmental organizations (NGOs), which have entered the international arena as watchdogs with tools to fight the expansion of the nation-state. Thus the application of the shield/sword binary function of human rights obligations on the nation-state allows domestic criminal law to be scrutinized against a set of values regarded as being superior to state interest in so far as they focus on the individual. This process of scrutiny can either reinforce the application of domestic criminal law or facilitate the questioning of its impact.

Thus both the localization and internationalization of human rights frameworks have changed the central figure of the state, whose power has been fragmented and absorbed at the sub- and supra-national levels. Yet, the sword/shield function still operates within a criminal justice system that is territorially bound, and linked to state sovereignty. Human rights philosophy and mechanisms can influence a number of stakeholders, but ultimately criminal law finds application within the state's territory (with relatively few exceptions in the EU). The gap between what international and transnational human rights frameworks aspire to establish, and the resistance of the state to translate this into domestic legislation allows for the formation of grey areas wherein the state, corporations and other powerful lobby groups continue to implement their hegemonic agendas.

Indeed, at times, powerful states have found a perfect way to reach other nation-states and impose their own vision of domestic criminal law by exploiting the human rights channel. For example, one could consider how the 2000 United Nations Protocol to Prevent, Suppress and Punish Trafficking in Persons, especially Women and Children (hereafter, the UN TIP Protocol) has been linked inescapably to its 'parent', the UN Convention on Transnational Organized Crime (UNTOC). This Convention allows states to adopt an aggressive border protection policy, which produces effects contrary to human rights objectives. Or, to dig further using the same example, we might consider how the USA has added to the UN TIP Protocol its own national instrument, issued by the Department of State, to monitor national legislative efforts in this area across the globe, via annual ratings of other nation-states (the Trafficking in Persons Reports, or TIP Reports), and to impose sanctions on non-compliant states (Van Dijk 2011). Using a tiered system, the Department of State classifies other countries according to their level of compliance with US-based legislation, the Trafficking Victims Protection Act 2000 (TVPA). The TVPA:

> seeks to combat human trafficking by punishing traffickers, protecting victims, and mobilizing U.S. government agencies to wage a global anti-trafficking campaign ... A country that fails to take significant actions to bring itself into compliance with the minimum standards for the elimination of trafficking in persons receives a negative assessment in this report. Such an assessment could trigger the withholding of non-humanitarian, non-trade-related assistance from the United States to that country. (Introduction, US Department of State 2004)

Such an approach to human trafficking has angered other countries and NGOs, since the USA has acted as a superior rather than as a peer (Gallagher

2011). Nevertheless, this has allowed the USA to promote its neo-liberal agenda of prohibitionism aggressively, with controversial results in many developing countries, such as Cambodia (Sandy 2013).

While the shield/sword approach may offer a good paradigm to help in understanding the role and function of human rights in domestic criminal law, it is evident that the tension between the shield and the sword is limited by the boundaries of a normative principle. As such, it suggests a broad-stroke approach and lacks sufficient power to ensure vertical or horizontal 'positive obligation', despite the intentions of international legal practitioners. Further, the examples of the UNTOC and the TIP Reports suggest that the sword function of human rights is exploited to justify criminal justice aims other than humanitarian protection. The sword function may even produce negative externalities whereby supranational and national bodies use human rights policy to monitor and influence criminal law in other jurisdictions to achieve self-serving objectives.

6.4 Counter-terrorism and supreme emergency exception

The shield function of human rights within domestic criminal law has been tested heavily by the counter-terrorist regime that has emerged following the terrorist attack on the USA on 11 September 2001 ('9/11'). In this area, what has been described as a priority of national interest has produced a suspension of fundamental human rights and a situation whereby such rights cannot find domestic application. Anti-terrorist policies have allowed the executive to (re)claim state sovereignty against the fragmentation of its power to a number of other agencies.

If it is accepted that human rights are intended to protect the negative freedom of people (freedom from abuse and torture), then it can be expected that such protection can be accessed at all times by everyone. Anything less would suggest the failure of the shield function of international obligations. The manipulative use of nationally bound criminal law has served to suspend the shield function of human rights, and criminal law is once again being used as a tool of the state to achieve aims identified as priorities, thereby surrendering principles of individual protection. Ignatieff (2001) has tried to resolve this paradox by suggesting a lesser role of human rights within domestic policy, or a scaling down of our commitment to human rights when necessary, allowing space for self-determination and military intervention for the protection of values shared by a group of people in a given territory. Others (Zedner 2007; Pickering *et al.* 2008) point out that the widening gap between national criminal law and international human rights frameworks is producing an increasingly preoccupying suspension of human rights through the securitization of Western society. This gap enables the implementation of executive-led legal initiatives, such as the establishment of the category of pre-crime, which legitimizes and prolongs this state of affairs and silences its human targets (such as predefined terrorists) even further. In this field, it is evident that criminal law is used not only as a reaction to crime, or as a proactive response (for example, for deterrent purposes), but also to criminalize behaviours before they occur, thereby allowing the state to bypass the criminal process to enact an urgent pre-emptive response.

For example, the UK Anti-terrorism, Crime and Security Act 2001 allowed the Home Secretary to detain indefinitely without charge or trial any foreign nationals who were suspected of terrorism, thus antagonizing basic principles of human rights and criminal proceedings. Even though such legislation was replaced by control orders within the Prevention of Terrorism Act 2005 (for a criticism of this, see Zedner 2007), after a December 2004 House of Lords ruling (*A and Others*), the legislation was used between 2001 and the end of 2004. This allowed the state to produce legislation and use it immediately until judicial scrutiny intervened. The enactment of a law to be used immediately (de Lint and Virta 2004) to legitimize state behaviours, even if clearly in contrast with internalized principles of human rights (via the UK HRA and other instruments), reveals the instrumentality and hegemonic aspects of legislation. Box 6.2 presents a case study to illustrate the struggle between prioritizing national interest over individual human rights.

Counter-terrorism laws show the weaknesses of the shield/sword metaphor in so far as it is, in a way, bound to the same problem of the legal definition of crime as established by criminal law. The positivistic nature of such a metaphor determines its limits, the limits of a subject that is not defined in a more scientific, critical manner (Schwendinger and Schwendinger 1970), but inevitably represents a compromise that has been prioritized according to external elements. Positive law and human rights are human constructs that complement and contrast with each other, but also have the power to advance one another. The individualistic nature of human rights reveals how the essence of such a framework has absorbed the essence of the law. This is even more evident in the case of state crime, as discussed in the next section.

Box 6.2   The case of Abu Qatada: 'the government gets what the government wants'

Detention without trial

Abu Qatada, of Jordanian nationality, lived in Britain from 1993 until July 2013. After an extended legal battle, the Home Office forced him to leave the country and at the time of writing he faces terrorist charges in Jordan.

Abu Qatada had been the target of an embargo by the UN Security Council Committee 1267 for his alleged affiliation with al-Qaeda. Soon after that, together with six Algerians, a Jordanian, a Tunisian and seven others, he was imprisoned in Britain from 2002 to 2005 under the Anti-terrorism, Crime and Security Act, which permits indefinite detention without trial. In the 2004 ruling, *A and Others*, Lord Bingham highlighted how the right to a fair trial is the only possible legitimate means of suspending the right to freedom. He also pointed out that being charged under current criminal law is a fundamental point of entry to the criminal justice system, which might eventually lead to imprisonment if found guilty:

> 9. ... a non-national who faces the prospect of torture or inhuman treatment if returned to his own country, and who cannot be deported to any third country, *and is not charged with any crime*, may not ... be detained here even if judged to be a threat to national security [emphasis added].

Four years later, in 2009, the European Court of Human Rights (ECtHR) declared that such a form of detention without trial was against the human rights principles (*A and Others v United Kingdom*).

Deportation and torture

In August 2005, Abu Qatada was served with a notice of intention to deport him to Jordan, which he appealed against. The UK Special Immigration Appeals Commission dismissed his appeal, claiming that an agreement negotiated between the UK and Jordan would protect him against torture. This ruling was overturned by a Court of Appeal but upheld by the House of Lords in February 2009, who questioned whether the risk of using evidence obtained by torture would amount to a flagrant denial of justice. This decision was overturned again by the ECtHR in 2012 (*Othman [Abu Qatada] v The United Kingdom*). The European Court highlighted that Abu Qatada would indeed face a flagrant denial of justice if sent back to Jordan.

In 2013, the British Government signed a bilateral agreement with Jordan with guarantees that Abu Qatada would be able to access a fair trial (Booth and Malik 2013). While negotiating with Jordan, the government was also exploring the option of making use of Article 15 of the European Convention for the Protection of Human Rights which allows a member state to withdraw temporarily from some of its obligations in times of national emergency that threaten the life of the nation (Travis 2013). However, this was revealed to be unnecessary, since 'Abu Qatada's lawyer, Edward Fitzgerald QC, then unexpectedly told the Special Immigration Appeals Commission (SIAC) that his client was prepared to leave if the treaty [bilateral agreement with Jordan] was enshrined in law' (Booth and Malik 2013).

6.5 State crime, criminal law and human rights

The use of criminal law by the state against its own people is an area that has been examined only recently through the human rights lens. Here, the expectation underpinning the shield/sword binary function is that human rights safeguards act as a shield when criminal law is used by the state against its own people. The Nazi Germany regime is a prime example of this. Stricter laws were introduced in the late 1930s to remove political opposition, and to reduce what was defined as deviant behaviour, such as alcoholism, begging, homosexuality and other defined forms of promiscuity. These laws led to the gradual erosion of the civil rights of Jewish Germans and ultimately culminated in acts of genocide after Jews were deprived of their citizenship and deported to extermination camps. Since those dark years of humanity, human rights obligations have been discussed under the 'never again' banner, to limit and monitor the action of the state (see Chapter 1). Now the state is recognized not solely as 'a victim, a punisher or a mediator, but it is also identified as a perpetrator of crime' (Ross 2000: 1).

Yet the state cannot be deemed to be criminally liable (Cohen 1990), and state crime does not exist as an offence in either domestic or international criminal law. On the one hand, human rights frameworks have brought states' actions to light and broadened awareness of the fairness of the conduct of states via the multiplication of judicial and governmental or non-governmental platforms at the international level. On the other hand, the prosecution of state action has become more difficult because of the establishment of principles of international law such as individual criminal responsibility (under Rule 102 of the Geneva Protocols and in the ICC Statute, Article 25). Despite this, a number of activities, such as corruption, corporate or political crime, and forms of collective homicide, genocide and torture, can be linked directly to the actions or omissions of one or more states. States can produce harmful impacts or contravene domestic or international laws to ensure themselves a more powerful position at the local or international level, and the intended and unintended effects of such activities are the 'most devastating and costly types of crime' (Rothe and Ross 2008: 741; see also Green and Ward 2004).

Thus, criminal law does not contain a definition to frame the action of the state as criminal, and existing international laws do not offer an opportunity to approach state harm from a legalist standpoint (Green and Ward 2004). Yet Kramer and Michalowski (2005: 448) suggest that the combination of international and national laws may offer a way towards understanding such behaviour using the instruments given to us by a normative approach to legal settings.

This is echoed by Rothe and Friedrichs (2006: 156) when they highlight that international laws provide a basis that, while constrained legalistically, 'incorporates nearly all the definitions and standards used by criminologists of state crime'. In this context, international human rights frameworks play an important role, as argued by Cohen (1993), albeit indirectly, when considering how human rights tools might be used by supranational government and non-government agencies to reframe geo-political relations whereby socio-political interests and human rights conditions can be explored beyond an individualist or territorially bound perspective. Society networks and the globalization process have undoubtedly enabled a broader and more consistent appreciation of human rights issues and socio-legal responsibilities. For example, the high visibility of the war in the former Yugoslavia, and of the associated genocide and ethnic cleansing that occurred in the 1990s, was a product of globalization. The 'call for action' to redress injustice in response to these war atrocities was unique in its immediacy. The formation of a dedicated UN court, the International Criminal Tribunal for the former Yugoslavia (ICTY), about to be closed down for exhausting its aims and considered as a success of human rights intervention, was accepted by the international community as a proper response. However, the court was not given any precise tasks or sufficient financial means, its creation was an act of *accidental* prosecutorial connection to German police, and its judges were bound to redefine in an aggressively proactive manner international law as it had been interpreted until that time (Box 6.3).

Box 6.3   Extract from the official history of the ICTY

The Prosecutor personally invested much time and energy to build the credibility of the Office of Prosecution and to obtain the cooperation of states. Many commentators in the international and diplomatic community were sceptical that the ICTY could function effectively or achieve results. In some parts of the former Yugoslavia, there was downright refusal to accept the legitimacy of the Tribunal, and clear obstruction of its work ...

It was important for the ICTY to demonstrate that international prosecutions were a reality. The first investigations centered on the reported widespread and horrific attacks on Bosnian Muslims and Croats in the Prijedor area of northwestern Bosnia, and the first case before the ICTY concentrated particularly on the notorious Omarska, Keraterm and Trnopolje Serb-run detention camps. Duško Tadić, the accused in that case, had been in custody in Germany and was being investigated there for similar crimes. The ICTY Prosecutor asserted the Tribunal's primacy over national courts and insisted on the case being transferred to The Hague.

Source: Available at http://www.icty.org/sid/95.

The interplay of NGOs with governmental and judicial bodies, in what has come to be known as the New Law Order (Slaughter 2004), has also been crucial for identifying state conduct as wrongful. For example, Amnesty International has run several campaigns aimed at protecting people from gross violations of human rights perpetrated by states. In one case, its campaigns have underlined the situation in the Democratic Republic of the Congo, where government and paramilitary forces had tortured, raped and killed civilians, and used child soldiers. By the time the international community began to examine this situation more closely at the beginning of the twenty-first century, the country's internal conflicts had led to the deaths of five million people, including from indirectly war-related causes such as malnutrition and disease. The by then newly established ICC opened investigations in 2004 and trials against identified former state members began in 2009 (Chazal 2013). And yet we are still far from any significant investment in rethinking human rights as emergent tools to redress the culture of denial of state-perpetrated harm and to action cases of such dimensions. We have been using this restricted version of human rights to explore the limits of hegemonic criminal law, with some poor results. A human rights approach to identifying the significance and impact of criminal law on individuals and collective groups can be used to redress this imbalance. And a more critical interpretation of human rights principles could act as a lens to (re)consider the criminogenic action of the state. For example, the international legal principle of trans-boundary responsibility could be explored further to develop a closer link between human rights and state responsibility. This principle is invoked to claim that the state bears a responsibility for people that goes beyond its nationality, and that it should protect all human beings. This international normative framework would enable the designation of state responsibility beyond state territorial boundaries.

6.6 Conclusion

The influence of human rights on domestic criminal law is evident in many ways, and important principles that support the protection of the individual have been absorbed at the state level. Yet the anthropocentric approach to criminal law, legal-procedural law directly related to specific physical human needs or rights, has been injected into human rights frameworks. Human rights have been construed with legal formalism, and must compete with a number of concurrent imperialist explanations of power and economic interest (Michalowski 2009). As Woodiwiss (2005) alerts us, as much as it can be used to give a voice to powerless and silent victims, a human rights framework can also be exploited to support the continuation of abuse through the protection of certain state activities. A human rights framework is thus just a tool in the hands of people, a tool of cultural relativism within Western society; therefore, its many functions and roles depend on its application. Douzinas (2007: 10) states that 'real rights are those given by states to their citizens' and that marginalized people have very limited access to rights. The substitution of natural law with human rights has been a significant revelation in proving that human rights are conceived and applied by humans, rather than being an intrinsic characteristic of people. Yet the fragility of human rights is revealed when they are subjected to compromises and negotiations between powerful agencies (Woodiwiss 2005). Nevertheless, human rights settings and agencies would benefit from the lessons to be learnt by reflecting on the expansion, beyond its original purpose, of criminal law under conditions defined by the state as exceptional. The case of anti-terrorist measures is an example of this. Such a strong emergence of the configuration of executive power calls for action to counter it. Human rights, as a discipline and a way of (re)thinking domestic criminal law in contemporary society, offer us a platform from which to challenge and counterbalance state power.

Additional readings and materials

Craven, Z. (2003), *Human Rights and Domestic Violence, Australian Domestic and Family Violence Clearinghouse*, Sydney: University of New South Wales. Available at: http://www.adfvc.unsw.edu.au/PDF%20files/human_rights.pdf.

Emmerson, B., Ashworth, A., Macdonald, A. (2012) *Human Rights and Criminal Justice*, London: Sweet & Maxwell.

Johnson, E.A. (2011) 'Criminal Justice, Coercion and Consent in "Totalitarian" Society: The Case of National Socialist Germany', *British Journal of Criminology*, 51: 599—614.

Lazarus, L. (2012) 'Positive Obligations and Criminal Justice: Duties to Protect or Coerce', in J. Roberts and L. Zedner (eds), *Principled Approaches to Criminal Law and Criminal Justice: Essays in Honour of Professor Andrew Ashworth*, Oxford: Oxford University Press.

Tulkens, F. (2011) 'The Paradoxical Relationship between Criminal Law and Human Rights', *Journal of International Criminal Justice*, 9: 577—95. Available at: http://jicj.oxfordjournals.org/content/9/3/577.full.pdf+html.

The Human Rights Law Centre has an easy-to-access Caselaw Database at http://www.hrlc.org.au/caselaw. On the Caselaw Database front page, there is a summary of key cases worldwide related (mainly) to criminal law and human rights.

Court cases cited

R v NS 2012 SCC 72 (20 December 2012) (Canada).

R (on the application of T) v Greater Manchester Chief Constable & Ors [2013] EWCA Civ 25 (29 January 2013) (UK).

Hamdam v Rumsfeld 548 US 557 (2006) (US).

A and Others [2004] UKHL 56 (UK).

A and Others v United Kingdom, Application no. 3455/05 (2009) (UK).

Othman (Abu Qatada) v The United Kingdom Application no. 8139/09 (2012) (UK).

References

Ashworth, A. (2009) *Principles of Criminal Law*, Oxford: Oxford University Press.

Booth, R. and Malik, S. (2013) 'Abu Qatada Arrives in Jordan after Eight-year Deportation Battle', 7 July 2013. Available at: http://www.theguardian.com/world/2013/jul/07/abu-qatada-jordan-deportation-battle.

BBC (British Broadcasting Corporation) (2013) 'Theresa May: Tories to Consider Leaving European Convention on Human Rights', 9 March 2013. Available at: http://www.bbc.co.uk/news/uk-politics-21726612.

Charlesworth, H. (1995) 'Australia's Split Personality: Implementation of Human Rights Treaty Obligations in Australia', in P. Alston and M. Chiam (eds), *Treaty-Making and Australia: Globalisation Versus Sovereignty?*, Leichhardt, NSW: Federation Press, pp. 129–40.

Chazal, N. (2013) 'Complex and Contradictions: The International Criminal Court and the Construction of International Criminal Justice', PhD thesis, Flinders University.

Cohen, A. (1990) 'Criminal Actors: Natural Persons and Collectivities', in Melvin J. Lerner (ed.), *New Directions in the Study of Justice, Law, and Social Control*, New York: Plenum Press, pp. 101–25.

Cohen, S. (1993) 'Human Rights and Crimes of the State: The Culture of Denial', *Australia and New Zealand Journal of Criminology*, 26: 97–115.

de Lint, W. and Virta, S. (2004) 'Security in Ambiguity: Towards a Radical Security Politics', *Theoretical Criminology*, 8: 465–89.

Douzinas, C. (2007) *Human Rights and Empire: The Political Philosophy of Cosmopolitanism*, Abingdon: Routledge-Cavendish.

Gallagher, A. (2011) 'Improving the Effectiveness of the International Law of Human Trafficking: A Vision for the Future of the US Trafficking in Persons Reports', *Human Rights Review*, 12(3): 381–400.

Gramsci, A. (1971) *Selections from the Prison Notebooks*, New York: International Publishers.

Green, P. and Ward, T. (2004) *State Crime: Governments, Violence and Corruption*, London: Pluto Press.

Ignatieff, M. (2001) *Human Rights as Politics and Idolatry*, Princeton, NJ: Princeton University Press.

Kirby, M. (2011) 'Protecting Human Rights in Australia Without A Charter', *Commonwealth Law Bulletin*, 37(2): 255—80.

Kramer, R. and Michalowski, R. (2005) 'War, Aggression and State Crime', *The British Journal of Criminology*, 45(4): 446—69.

Liebenberg, S. (2007) 'Protecting Economic, Social and Cultural Rights under Bill of Rights: The South African Experience', *Human Rights Defender*, 16(3).

Michalowski, R. (2009) 'Power, Crime and Criminology in the New Imperial Age', *Crime, Law and Social Change*, 51(3—4), 303—25.

Muncie, J. (2001) 'The Construction and Deconstruction of Crime', in J. Muncie and E. McLaughlin (eds), *The Problem of Crime*, London: Sage.

Packer, H.L. (1968) *The Limits of the Criminal Sanction*, Stanford, CA: Stanford University Press.

Pickering, S., McCulloch, J. and Wright-Neville, D. (2008) 'Counter-terrorism Policing: Towards Social Cohesion', *Crime, Law and Social Change: An Interdisciplinary Journal*, 50(1—2), 91—109.

Ross, J. (2000) *Varieties of State Crime and Its Control*, Monsey, NY: Criminal Justice Press.

Rothe, D. and Friedrichs, D. (2006) 'The State of the Criminology of Crimes of the State', *Social Justice*, 33(1): 147—61.

Rothe, D. and Ross, J. (2008) 'The Marginalization of State Crime in Introductory Textbooks on Criminology', *Critical Sociology*, 34(5): 741—52.

Rozenberg, J. (2013) 'Judges Would Regret Human Rights Act Repeal, Warns Lady Hale', *The Guardian*, 14 March. Available at: http://www.guardian.co.uk/law/2013/mar/14/judges-regret-human-rights-act-repeal.

Sandy, L. (2013) 'International Agendas and Sex Worker Rights in Cambodia', in M. Ford (ed.), *Social Activism in Southeast Asia*, New York: Routledge, pp. 154—69.

Schwendinger, H. and Schwendinger, J. (1970) 'Defenders of Order or Guardians of Human Rights?', *Issues in Criminology*, 5: 123—57.

Slaughter, A.-M. (2004) *A New World Order: Government Networks and the Disaggregated State*, Princeton, NJ: Princeton University Press.

Sloss, D., Ramsey, M. and Dodge, W. (2011) 'Continuity and Change Over Two Centuries', in D. Sloss, M. Ramsey and W. Dodge (eds), *International Law in the US Supreme Court*, Cambridge: Cambridge University Press.

Tomazin, F. (2011) 'Do We Really Need a Victorian Human Rights Charter?', *The Age*, 14 August. Available at: http://www.theage.com.au/victoria/do-we-really-need-a-victorian-human-rights-charter-20110813-1is57.html#ixzz2PBRorGAl.

Travis, A. (2013) 'Can Britain Withdraw from the European Human Rights Convention?', *The Guardian*, 24 April. Available at: http://www.guardian.co.uk/world/2013/apr/24/withdrawal-human-rights-convention-price.

Tulkens, F. (2011) 'The Paradoxical Relationship between Criminal Law and Human Rights', *Journal of International Criminal Justice* 9, 577—95. Available at: http://jicj.oxfordjournals.org/content/9/3/577.full.pdf+html.

US Department of State (2004) 'Introduction', *Trafficking in Persons Report*, US Department of State. Available at: http://www.state.gov/j/tip/rls/tiprpt/2004/34021.htm.

US Department of State (2012) *Trafficking in Persons Report*, US Department of State. Available at: http://www.state.gov/j/tip/rls/tiprpt/2012/index.htm.

Van Dijk, J. (2011) 'Transnational Organized Crime, Civil Society and Victim Empowerment: The New Faces of Victimhood', *Studies in Global Justice*, 8: 99—126.

Woodiwiss, A. (2005) *Human Rights*, Basingstoke: Routledge.

Zedner, L. (2007) 'Preventive Justice or Pre-punishment? The Case of Control Orders', *Current Legal Problems*, 60(1): 174—203.

CHAPTER 7

Crime Prevention

Key concepts

Crime prevention — situational, social, developmental — Primary, secondary, tertiary education and prevention — Post- and pre-crime societies — Surveillance — Pre-emption — Violence against women — Justice reinvestment — War on drugs

7.1 Introduction

From the 1980s onwards, crime prevention, community safety and combating the 'fear of crime' not only became key topics for discussion in criminology, but also developed into important policy priorities for governments (Crawford 2007; Hughes 2007). As we have seen elsewhere in this book, risk and security concerns have also driven recent developments in criminal justice policy and practice, both internationally and domestically. While crime prevention strategies can have important benefits for populations, it has been argued that there are inherent threats to human rights when prevention is driven by fear, risk and security, since it 'permits a dangerously wide range of state interventions and sanctions based on uncertain criteria' (ICHRP 2010: v). Redefining social problems as crime control issues can lead to a situation where people come to be perceived as potentially deviant or risky as a result of their social circumstances or backgrounds, and the consequences of social, economic and health inequalities become criminalized while the socio-economic foundations of crime remain unaddressed.

This chapter begins with a brief overview of what is meant by crime prevention, and then moves on to examine examples of crime prevention strategies and their relationship to human rights principles, with a view to raising awareness of some of their positive outcomes as well as their contradictions and problems.

7.2 Understanding crime prevention

In the 1980s, Left Realist concerns with developing a grounded and communitarian approach to tackling crime (see Newburn 2007: ch. 13) and those criminological approaches that focused on 'crimes of everyday life', 'routine activity' and 'opportunity reduction' theories (see ibid.: ch. 14) brought crime prevention and community safety to the forefront within criminology.

Crime prevention and education for prevention are seen to operate on three levels: *primary*, which entails work directed at general populations before the onset of a problem; *secondary*, involving work with populations defined to be specifically 'at risk'; and *tertiary*, directed towards preventing the recurrence of events by targeting known offenders, victims or locations.

Situational crime prevention, which also encompasses crime prevention through environmental design, focuses on reducing opportunities for crime to occur. To some extent situational crime prevention rejects the idea that crime is linked to social and economic factors, and instead criminal actions are considered to be the result of a rational choice by an offender in weighing up the benefits and disadvantages when a crime opportunity is presented. The routine activity approach considers that there are three immediate preconditions for crime: a likely offender, a suitable target and the absence of a capable guardian (Crawford 2007; Hughes 2007; Newburn 2007). In this view, crime prevention becomes focused on controlling the behaviour of risky individuals in risky situations (Zedner 2009: 76). Situational crime prevention strategies include increased surveillance and the redesign of public and private spaces by the use of closed-circuit television (CCTV), street cameras, better lighting, architectural changes to increase sight lines, and an increased police and security presence. It aims to control access to public and private spaces through monitoring and controlling movement with the introduction of exclusion zones, curfews, control of anti-social behaviour, electronic key pad access and security gates. Through this process populations are sorted and segregated. And, as will be discussed below, the expansion of surveillance and risk technologies in response to security fears can lead to human rights violations.

In contrast, social crime prevention is concerned with the economic, social and cultural conditions associated with crime and criminalization. The work of Elliot Currie in the USA resulting in *Social Crime Prevention Strategies in Market Societies* (2007), and his earlier research on marginalized and excluded communities (Currie 1998), provides a good frame of reference for understanding a social crime perspective. Currie argues that crime needs to be addressed on a number of levels. The first is the macro level, where he advocates an active labour market policy supported by public resources; a reduction in the extremes of social and economic disadvantage, including addressing the gender disparity in incomes; and a reduction in the conflict between work and home demands by increasing the availability of affordable childcare (Currie 2007). At the micro level, Currie suggests that child and family support programmes that deal with care and protection issues in a non-punitive way, youth intervention strategies to increase opportunities in all fields, and user-friendly drug intervention programmes based on health and harm-minimization strategies are examples of good prevention approaches (ibid.). Other social crime prevention strategies might focus on community development – for example, by empowering local communities to design and develop local programmes and services (Ife 2010), providing resources for specific targeted projects, and developing policies and practices that not only protect vulnerable populations but also enhance their capacity to engage in social life by building social capital through deliberative democratic processes. As Hughes points out, these kinds of projects generally operate on the concept of 'partnership', whereby communities, government, non-governmental and criminal justice agencies work together to develop crime prevention and community safety strategies (Hughes 2007).

Amartya Sen (2005, 2010) and Martha Nussbaum (1995, 2000), among others, see that developmental rights and the prevention of human rights abuses are interdependent. Sen points out that, unless second- and third-generation rights are addressed by governments, individuals and groups will not only have little capacity to exercise their first-generation rights, but their right to the full enjoyment of life will also be compromised (Sen 2005). Crime prevention strategies that adopt this broader human rights understanding are holistic and focused on the future. The United Nations Development Programme Associate Administrator, Rebeca Grynspan, for example, argues that hate crime harms individuals in both the short and the long term. As she has stated:

> Homophobia curbs the capacity of individuals to realize their aspirations and potential. Discrimination and harassment in families, schools, workplaces and the military on the basis of sexual orientation and gender identity lead people to drop out of school, prevent them from getting jobs and inhibit [sic] millions across the globe from seeking crucial health services. (*United Nations Daily News*, May 2011)

Appropriate and inclusive development policies increase the autonomy and capacity of groups and individuals to realize their human rights (Nussbaum 1995, 2000; Andreassen 2006; Ife 2010). Tackling poverty, addressing debt, improving education and health, enhancing social and physical environments, and addressing collective rights are all means of reducing crime and harm, and guarding against further human rights violations.

Crime prevention policies can also be seen to incorporate strategies to prevent environmental harm committed by states and corporations (see Chapter 5) (Anton and Shelton 2011; Cantley-Smith 2013; Friends of the Earth International http://www.foei.org/en). In this regard, the developmental concerns of crime prevention outlined above and environmental protection are closely intertwined. Key concerns in this framework revolve around environmental pollution, illegal logging, deforestation, the destruction of ecosystems, access to adequate health care and housing, water security, and indigenous people's rights. The basic survival rights of humans and nature are outlined in the Stockholm Declaration (1972) and the UN Declaration on the Rights of Indigenous Peoples, 2007). This area of criminology remains underdeveloped (see White 2008).

7.3 Crime prevention by the UN and Europe

The United Nations has developed a range of crime prevention initiatives. Within the UN, the Office on Drugs and Crime (UNODC) carries the main responsibility for crime prevention (the key aims and objectives can be found on their website http://www.unodc.org/).

In 2002, the UN developed Guidelines for Crime Prevention, which envisage a broad interpretation of prevention, stating in the Introduction that:

> There is clear evidence that well-planned crime prevention strategies not only prevent crime and victimization, but also promote community safety and contribute to the sustainable development of countries. Effective, responsible crime prevention enhances the quality of life of all citizens. It has long-term benefits in terms of reducing the costs associated with the formal criminal justice system, as well as other social costs that result from crime. Crime prevention offers opportunities for a humane and more cost-effective approach to the problems of crime. (Annex 1)

Yet, as the International Council on Human Rights Policy (ICHRP) report highlights, the approach of the UNODC is also focused on managing risks, reducing the fear of crime and tackling the problems of the 'uncivil society' (ICHRP, 2010: 15).

The UN has also established a Commission on Crime Prevention and Criminal Justice under the auspices of the UN Economic and Social Council, and there is also the UN Congress on Crime Prevention and Criminal Justice which was established in 1955. The Congress covers a wide range of topics from transnational crime to national and local crime prevention and education strategies, and the eradication of poverty and disadvantage.

The UNODC has developed a Compendium of Standards and Norms in Crime Prevention and Criminal Justice, which lists all the relevant crime prevention and related human rights instruments (see http://www.unodc. org/unodc/en/justice-and-prison-reform/compendium.html). There is also a broader social, economic and culturally based programme geared towards improving the lives of vulnerable populations; this can be found at UN-Habitat (http://www.unhabitat.org/categories.asp?catid=9). The UN-Habitat programme includes city development projects, environmental projects and strategies for social inclusion targeted at young people, women and ethnic minorities. It also encompasses a Safer Cities programme, which combines social, situational and developmental strategies.

There is a range of regional human rights crime prevention initiatives. For example, the European Crime Prevention Network, first established in 2001 and re-established in 2009, provides a forum for the exchange of ideas and best practice principles on crime prevention.

The European Union Charter of Fundamental Rights and Justice aims to prevent and combat violence against children, young people and women, and to provide support for victims. It adopts a broad approach to crime prevention and community safety, and integrates criminal justice, health, education and social justice strategies. In Europe, the Daphne programme has compiled an extensive resource of relevant research and policy information, and educational materials, named the Daphne Toolkit (see http://ec. europa.eu/justice_home/daphnetoolkit/html/welcome/dpt_welcome_en.html). In 2013, the European Commission adopted a Recommendation entitled 'Investing in Children: Breaking the Cycle of Disadvantage', which establishes a social investment initiative based on the principle that early investment in families and children prevents the later occurrence of problems, including social exclusion, violence and crime.

7.4 From prevention to pre-emption: surveillance, security and risk

Criminal justice systems have always been concerned with crime prevention through policing, crime deterrence and covert evidence gathering (Zedner 2007; Coleman and McCahill 2011). However, as Zedner argues, an increasing emphasis on crime control, and the management of risk and security, has led to a major social transformation from 'post-crime' to 'pre-crime' societies (Zedner 2007). By this she means that, conventionally, crime is regarded as harm or a wrong that is dealt with post hoc; however, in the emerging pre-crime society, crime is conceived essentially as future risk or potential loss, so that risk assessment becomes the principal tool of crime prevention (Zedner 2009: 78). Zedner has also observed that risk and security assessment and management are increasingly being commodified and contracted out to private concerns (Zedner 2007). Security is no longer the sole concern of states, and the state's involvement becomes one of licensing and regulating the plurality of security services (ibid.). In this context, as in the privatization of policing and prisons, responsibility for the protection and promotion of human rights becomes dispersed (see Chapters 8 and 10 for further discussion).

The extension of policing to private and commercial companies signifies what Zedner denotes as a new set of 'social ordering practices which engages communities, volunteers and individuals in strategies of governance' (2007). She argues that, since the events of 9/11, states have ramped up their risk management and security measures with the stated aim of combating terrorism. This has led to increasingly early interventions aimed at reducing opportunities for crime through the use of target hardening and increasing surveillance even before the 'commission of crime is a distant prospect' (Zedner 2007: 265, 2009). In this context, prevention becomes pre-emption, and information gathering is geared towards calculating risks and potential threats (Zedner 2009).

Other criminologists have written on these phenomena, exploring the move towards what has been termed 'a surveillance society' characterized by a dispersal of discipline across populations (Cohen 1985; Lyon 2001, 2007; Coleman and McCahill 2011). This new surveillance society is characterized by the expansion and use of technologies, as well as different face-to-face policing techniques including increased identity and stop-and-search checks, paramilitary policing, and the use of private security firms (see Chapter 8). Surveillance technologies include the use of drones in domestic settings; CCTV and street cameras; identity and credit checks; biometric testing, racial and offender profiling and DNA registers; telecommunications interceptions and tracking; monitoring and holding of social media and web use data; data mining; and electronic monitoring and implant technology (ICHRP 2010; Coleman and McCahill 2011; Hucklesby 2013; Nellis 2013). There has also been an expansion in policies and technologies to control movements into and out of defensible spaces, and in privatized retail areas and streetscapes with targeted exclusions of such undesirables as young people, the racialized other, the poor and the homeless. Security access control pads in buildings, gated communities, and privately owned and secured leisure, recreation and consumption spaces all facilitate this process (Coleman and McCahill 2011).

Coleman and McCahill also highlight how military tactics of intelligence gathering and security techniques are being transposed into the surveillance of the broader civilian population in ways that are not open to public scrutiny (2011: 91–110). According to Krasmann, the surveillance of private spaces is happening in ways that would have been unimaginable just decades ago (2012: 382). Security government becomes concerned with anticipating abstract risks and diffuse threats, and automated technology facilitates this pre-emptive action (ibid.: 381). In this process, fears and suspicions are created and intensified, not allayed. Threats that are essentially unknowable become articulated in prevention and pre-emption discourse, and implemented through disciplinary techniques. As data obtained via surveillance is aggregated, and processed in relation to risk factors, information is distanced from concrete, identifiable individuals (ibid.: 386). This presents a challenge to human rights discourse, since the targets of the surveillance become disembodied and fragmented, people become sets of profiles and traits – and the citizen, the individual who is the carrier of human rights, no longer exists. It is the enemy, 'the risky other', who is the object of pre-emption (see Coleman and McCahill 2011: ch. 2).

Through the process of information gathering and surveillance, populations, without their knowledge or agreement, are coded, catalogued, managed and controlled according to their data information and risk categorizations. The actions of Edward Snowden in 2013 that exposed the extent of the surveillance and data mining conducted by the National Security Agency in the USA are clear evidence of this. But, as Zedner points out, 'even where surveillance and policies are universalist in conception, they tend to be highly discriminatory in their application, particularly at the hard end of the anti-terrorist measures' (2009: 136).

The sacrifice of individual freedom and invasion of privacy that are the products of intense surveillance are often defended and justified on the basis of a public good such as reduction in crime, or an increase in public safety or national security (Zedner 2009; Coleman and McCahill 2011; Krasmann 2012). However, these public goods are often called upon to justify actions that, in the words of Loader and Walker (2007: 7), 'trample over basic liberties of citizens; that forge security for some groups while imposing illegitimate burdens of insecurity on others or that extend the coercive reach of the state – and security discourse – over social and political life'. As Zedner argues, 'fundamental rights that ought to be considered non-derogable and to be protected are placed in peril by the consequentialist claims of security' (2009: 137).

7.5 Preventing violence against women

Our understanding of human rights is constantly evolving. For many years, and in the face of a great deal of resistance, campaigners fought for the recognition of violence against women as a mainstream human rights issue (Charlesworth and Chinkin 2000). Resistance came from a number of sources. Human rights instruments until the 1990s were generally concerned with state violations of human rights, and State Parties considered the 'private' sphere, including the family, to be a foundational and sanctified unit and not an arena for States Parties intervention (ibid.: 231). Charlesworth and Chinkin observe that it was also believed that linking violence against women to human rights might devalue the 'traditional' notion of human rights as an abuse of publicly based civil and political rights (Charlesworth and Chinkin 2000). Opposition also came from States Parties who claimed the right to retain cultural and religious practices that might be deemed to constitute violence against women when seen in a universal human rights framework (ibid. 2000). As mentioned in Chapter 4, it was not until March 2013 and the meeting of the UN Commission on the Status of Women that the more conservative religious and political states felt able to condemn violence against women and girls outright (including homophobic violence) without invoking cultural or religious defences as excuses for inaction (Ford 2013; UN Commission on the Status of Women 2013). Human rights activists have also highlighted that the discourse of human rights and violence has been resolutely heterosexist. In 2011, the UN Commissioner for Human Rights, Navi Pillay, pointed out that, despite decades of work on tackling race and sex discrimination, homophobia and transphobia are too often overlooked (*UN Daily News*, 17 May 2011).

In 1993, two key actions undertaken by the UN recognized formally that violence against women was a universal human rights issue. The UN Vienna Conference on Human Rights acknowledged that sexual violence was not simply a private problem but a public human rights issue, and in the same year the Declaration on the Elimination of Violence against Women was adopted by the General Assembly. However, as Charlesworth and Chinkin (2000) point out, international human rights discourse and practice continued to marginalize violence against women by designating it as a 'woman's issue' rather than as a core human rights concern.

Today, international definitions of violence against women are encapsulated in human rights law and humanitarian law, and encompass physical, sexual, emotional and economic violence or exploitation, rape, sexual slavery, enforced prostitution, forced pregnancy, enforced sterilization, indecent assault, intimate partner violence, maternal deaths, dowry deaths, honour killings, female infanticide, genital mutilation, inappropriate strip searches, and trafficking, among other actions (True 2012). The UN now recognizes sexual violence as a war crime, a crime against humanity, and an act of torture, or a constituent factor in genocide (True 2012: 115). Such acts can now be prosecuted in the International Criminal Court. Since 2008, the UN Security Council has also passed five resolutions condemning violence perpetrated against women and girls in armed conflict and post-conflict situations, and designated specific measures to be taken to reduce violence and implement gender action plans in relation to peace and security (True 2012: 115).

Despite this plethora of initiatives at international, national and community levels, violence against women continues to be a significant global problem affecting up to 70 per cent of women in some countries (True 2012). Recent media reports have raised awareness of the global nature of violence against women, including the rape of women in India (Shackle 2013), the gang rape of a young woman in Steubenville, Texas (Penny 2013), and in May 2013 the discovery of the abduction, rape, torture and detention of three young women in a suburban house in Cleveland, Ohio. International comparative research evidence does show us that particular groups of women are more vulnerable to violence, and to the short- and long-term effects of violence, and these include indigenous women, women in poverty, women with disabilities, migrants, refugees, and human rights advocates (True 2012: 3). Violence has been found to be more common in societies where there are wide gender disparities in social, economic and political status (True 2012). Research also reveals the continuities of violence in times of peace, conflict and across history (ibid.) (see Box 7.1).

The failure to make a major impact on the elimination of violence against women is a result, it has been argued, of the failure of the UN and States Parties to tackle the systemic nature of the problem. For example, domestic criminal justice systems, their laws, policies and procedures are dealing with

---

Box 7.1   Continuities in violence: domestic violence and torture

Battered women, like official torture victims, may be explicitly punished for infraction of constantly changing and impossible-to-meet rules. Both may be intimidated by the continual threat of physical violence and verbal abuse, and both may be effectively manipulated by intermittent kindness

Source: Report of the Special Rapporteur on Violence Against Women, Its Causes and Consequences, 5 February 1996, UN Doc. E/CN.4/1996/53, para. 47, cited by Charlesworth and Chinkin 2000: 235).

the consequences of violence rather than the causes, and in these circumstances the police and the courts can offer individual prosecution and protection but not prevention (True 2012: 24). A recent World Health Organization (WHO) report found little evidence of the 'deterrent effects of criminal justice sanctions on various forms of violence against women' (cited in True 2012: 24).

A comprehensive human rights understanding of violence against women would not see it simply as an individual, psychological or familial problem but as one that is embedded in the operation of globalized market economies, articulated in localized gendered relations (Charlesworth and Chinkin 2000; True 2012). A focus on the resolution of violence and crime prevention that engages with the criminal justice system alone, or with changing individual behaviours, leaves the day-to-day life experiences of women, and other forms of social, economic and cultural violence, untouched.

The links between violence and the privately based social and economic exploitation of unpaid labour, home working, caring responsibilities, domestic service or small-scale agriculture are often disregarded in UN or WHO development projects, or in International Labour Organization conventions and treaties (Charlesworth and Chinkin 2000; True 2012). As Noreen Burrows points out:

> For most women, what it is to be human is to work long hours in agriculture or the home, to receive little or no remuneration, and to be faced with political and legal processes which ignore their contribution to society and accord no recognition of their particular needs. (Burrows 1986, cited in Charlesworth and Chinkin 2000: 230)

Securing these kinds of economic, educational and political rights is seen to be fundamental to overcoming violence (True 2012). For example, the US National Network to End Domestic Violence's Economic Justice Project has focused on providing education and skills for women escaping violence so that they gain the 'financial capabilities to better assist survivors of domestic violence to move from short-term safety to long-term security, and to an economically sustainable independent life' (Lanning *et al.* 2011). A human rights approach to combating violence against women needs to move beyond merely pressing for reforms to criminal justice systems.

Eliminating violence against women requires work on a number of levels and has to recognize violence against women as a universal human rights issue in private and public domains, and engage in primary, secondary and tertiary education campaigns to ensure that violence is viewed in this way.

Additionally, a comprehensive prevention campaign needs to address second- and third-generation rights in order to increase individual capacity to act, and for women to be able to realize their civil and political rights. Integrating violence against women as a mainstream human rights issue also ensures that prevention is the responsibility of States Parties, and all citizens both male and female (Flood 2010).

7.6 Justice reinvestment

In those jurisdictions where there have been sustained high numbers of people in custody, the costs of justice, in particular the growing expenditure on prisons and juvenile detention, have prompted a rethink on strategies to combat crime and reduce rates of recidivism (Brown *et al.* 2012). Justice reinvestment has been heralded as a new approach to reducing crime, though to many criminologists it may look like old diversionary wines in new cost-effective bottles. The concept has become popular in the USA and the UK and is said to appeal to both progressives and conservatives as it combines commitment to diversion and reducing prison populations with fiscal conservatism (ibid.). Reinvestment recognizes that there are social and economic correlations between crime and recidivism, and that the experience of imprisonment contributes to continued social exclusion for those offenders released back into the community. The focus of justice reinvestment varies from place to place, but in essence it has been brought about by the realization by governments that prison is not an effective deterrent for crime, has no impact on recidivism rates, and can in fact increase them (see, for example, Lanning *et al.* 2011; Brown *et al.* 2012; US Justice Center, Council of State Governments).

Proposals based on the principles of justice reinvestment offer comparisons between the cost-effectiveness and efficiencies of custody, and community-based rehabilitative programmes in a process that has been termed justice and asset mapping (Brown *et al.* 2012). Proponents argue that the community-based option is more economical and has fewer negative repercussions in both the short and long term for offenders, their families and communities. As Lanning *et al.* explain:

> It is a form of preventative financing, through which policymakers shift funds away from dealing with problems 'downstream' (policing, prisons) and towards tackling them 'upstream' (family breakdown, poverty, mental illness, drug and alcohol dependency). (2011: 4)

Justice reinvestment programmes accumulate data about communities that have high offender populations, and divert programme expenditure into

Box 7.2   Prison costs of adult offenders released into London Borough of Lewisham 2009–10

Sentence length	No. of sentences	Average cost (£)	Total* (£)
Less than 12 months	518	5,386	2.8m
Six months and under	406	4,110	1.7m
Three months and under	231	2,188	0.5m

Note: *These represent costs that could be reinvested back into the community
Source: Adapted from Lanning, Loader and Muir, 2011, *Redesigning Justice: Reducing Crime through Justice Reinvestment*, Institute for Public Policy Research, table 1.1 at p. 12. Used with permission.

those communities instead of into prisons. Programmes are targeted at crime prevention, diversion of less serious offenders from custody, and re-entry support for prisoners leaving custody (Lanning *et al.* 2011).

In the USA, a strong cost imperative underpins the push towards justice reinvestment, whereas in Australia the Campaign for Justice Reinvestment for Aboriginal Young People is committed to both a human rights and a social justice agenda, as well as making a strong case for savings. In Australia, Indigenous justice reinvestment is seen as a social crime prevention and community development strategy that aims to prevent children and young people at risk of offending from becoming enmeshed in the juvenile justice system. It demands that resources currently invested in custodial services be redirected into community programmes such as early childhood education in vulnerable communities, targeting young people at risk of school disengagement, intensive case work support with housing and employment support, and job creation. The proposed programmes would involve local Indigenous communities in decision-making, consultation and programme administration, using a multi-agency approach.

In 2010, the UN Committee on the Elimination of Racial Discrimination (CERD) recommended specifically that Australia 'adopt a justice reinvestment strategy, continuing and increasing the use of Indigenous courts and conciliation mechanisms, diversionary and prevention programmes and restorative justice strategies' (AHRLC 2013). In 2011, an Australian Commonwealth Parliamentary Committee lent its support to justice reinvestment in its report on the over-incarceration of Indigenous young people (Brown *et al.* 2012).

Brown *et al.* (2012) express some caution about the ambiguity of the concept of justice reinvestment, and that it might become 'a catch all buzz word' or a passing fad. It could also be argued that investment in social and public policies is a universal human right and should not be determined by criminal justice priorities. Even though advocates of justice reinvestment may be driven by different aims and objectives, and economic arguments may be more convincing for governments than social justice and human rights imperatives, justice reinvestment has been seen by its proponents to sit comfortably with a human rights framework (AHRLC 2013), and more specifically the diversionary, rehabilitation and reintegration goals of human rights which are at the core of criminal-justice-related conventions and treaties.

7.7 The failure of the War on Drugs

> The global war on drugs has failed, with devastating consequences for individuals and societies around the world. (Global Commission on Drugs Policy 2011, Executive Summary)

The so-called War on Drugs provides a fascinating case study of the development of an inappropriate harm-prevention strategy that ultimately exacerbated the very problem it was trying to solve, and in the process led to widespread violations of human rights.

In 1961, the Single Convention on Narcotic Drugs was adopted by the UN General Assembly and introduced in 1964. In 1971, the UN also introduced the Convention on Psychotropic Drugs, followed in 1988 by the UN Convention Against Illicit Traffic in Narcotic Drugs and Psychotropic Substances. The 1988 Convention consolidated transnational co-operation in the policing of trafficking, calling on nation-states to strengthen and expand their national policing policies on illicit drugs as well as extending criminal sanctions (Fox and Matthews 1992). Distinctions were made in the conventions between drugs that were completely prohibited, and those that were restricted to medical and scientific purposes and controlled by pharmaceutical companies (ibid.).

In 1971, then US President Richard Nixon launched the nation's War on Drugs campaign. Together, the UN and the USA launched a period of harsh domestic and transnational law enforcement strategies targeting illicit drug producers, drug markets, distributors and users. It was believed that a tough strategy based on prohibition would have the effect of diminishing the use of drugs worldwide and, according to the Single Convention on Narcotic Drugs (1961), would promote 'the health and welfare of mankind'. Combined international pressure from the USA and the UN led many jurisdictions to criminalize or strictly control drug use and supply, which had until that point been legal (Fox and Matthews 1992).

The language used to describe drugs and drug users was (and continues to be) moralistic and sensational, frequently linking drugs with evil, in turn producing episodic moral panics where drug users became the folk devils of the times (Mena and Hobbs 2010). And, as Ben Bowling argues, the goal of prohibition – to wipe out drugs altogether – was often justified by policymakers with reference to this moralistic language (Bowling, 2011: 367). For example, in 1971, President Nixon identified drugs as the USA's 'public enemy number 1' (Mena and Hobbs 2010: 64).

From the 1960s and 1970s onwards, international resources were poured into the War on Drugs and the USA in particular became involved in militarized campaigns in drug-producing countries such as Panama, Bolivia, Mexico, Colombia (see Mena and Hobbs 2010), and later Afghanistan. Yet, according to the Global Commission on Drugs Policy, the War on Drugs did not reduce drug use:

> vast expenditures on criminalization and repressive measures directed at producers, traffickers and consumers of illegal drugs have clearly failed to effectively curtail supply or consumption. (Global Commission on Drugs Policy 2011, Executive Summary)

The Global Commission on Drugs Policy compiled statistics on drug consumption from United Nations data and found that policies aimed at eradicating drug use have not worked at all; in fact, drug use has risen dramatically. The Global Commission on Drugs Policy found that, according to UN estimates from 1998 to 2008, the consumption of opiates had risen by 34.5% worldwide, the use of cocaine by 27% and the use of cannabis by 8.5% (Global Commission on Drugs Policy 2011: 4).

As Bowling points out, Jock Young's 1971 book *The Drug Takers* was rather prophetic in predicting that prohibition would more than likely entrench and foster the popularity and use of other drugs by linking cannabis markets with those for barbiturates and opiates, and that this, in turn, would have other undesirable effects (Bowling, 2011: 367). According to Bowling, making drugs illegal through prohibition creates clandestine black markets, as those who want to use drugs have to obtain them through criminal sources (ibid.: 368). Repressive, punitive efforts to control drugs have led to a range of human rights abuses.

In 2008, the UNODC published the *World Drug Report*, in which it identified that there have been many serious 'unintended negative consequences' stemming from the War on Drugs, including the creation of a vast criminal market, the displacement of the illegal drugs trade to new areas, a diversion of funding from health, and the stigmatization of users (UNODC 2008). As Count the Costs (CTC), an international consortium on drug use, observed in its 2012 *Alternative Drug Report*:

> In every region of the world the war on drugs is severely undermining human rights. It has led to a litany of abuse, neglect and political scapegoating through the erosion of civil liberties and fair trial standards; the denial of economic and social rights; the demonising of individuals and groups; and the imposition of abusive and inhuman punishments. (CTC 2012a: 1)

US militarized campaigns in South America have also had devastating consequences politically, socially and environmentally. Emerging democracies were undermined through the US supplying aid to dictatorships and support for military coups, leading to serious human rights abuses (Mena and Hobbs 2010). The eradication of illicit crops in Bolivia (and other countries) led to a series of conflicts between coca farmers and the military, and in Colombia constant violence and military campaigns led to the displacement of populations (Mena and Hobbs 2010). The money to be made out of illegal drug markets has also led to the growth of warring drug cartels, and increased corruption as they become involved in extortion, buying co-operation from politicians and policing organizations. The criminal drugs trade in countries such as Mexico, for example, has caused widespread harm, including targeted murders, extrajudicial killings, and associated violence and coercion including the sexual assault and murder of women (Sheptycki 1996; CTC 2012b; Slater 2013). The spraying of illegal crops with aggressive herbicides also poisons domestic agriculture in the country of production, polluting watercourses and poisoning local people, thus denying them the right to life and security. Drug cartels force local farmers into growing illegal crops rather than food, not only through coercion but also through the lure of economic gains (Mena and Hobbs 2010; CTC 2012b). The drugs trade also draws people into smuggling, working as drugs mules or trafficking (Bowling 2011).

The *Alternative Drug Report* also provides evidence of the human costs and human rights abuses that are the product of harsh, punitive, drugs-related policies in domestic criminal justice systems. For example:

- Up to 1,000 people are executed around the world each year for drug offences, in direct violation of international law.
- Between February and April 2003, there were 2,819 extrajudicial killings under the banner of the Thailand Government's War on Drugs crackdown.
- Over 500,000 people are arbitrarily detained in drug detention centres in China, and frequently subjected to forced labour and other cruel, inhuman and degrading treatment. (CTC 2012a)

Drug enforcement in the USA has led to increases in drug-related violence, mandatory detention policies, mass incarceration, and the consequent social, health and economic costs of imprisonment on individuals and their families; but, as seen above, it has not reduced illicit drug use (Global Commission on Drugs Policy 2011; Slater 2013).

Slater argues that women are severely affected by harsh drug prohibition policies (ibid.). Globally, women are imprisoned for drug offences more than for any other crime. One in four women in prison in Europe and Central Asia are incarcerated for drug offences, with levels as high as 70 per cent in some countries. Between 1986 and 1996, the number of American women incarcerated in state facilities for drug offences increased by 888 per cent, surpassing the rate of growth in the number of men imprisoned for similar crimes (Slater 2013).

The War on Drugs has also presented significant human rights challenges for transnational policing agencies in relation to accountability and governance (Bowling 2011; Bowling and Sheptycki 2012). Bowling and Sheptycki (2012) highlight the prevalence of corruption between policing agencies and drug cartels in the transnational policing of drug markets, also pointing out that the secretive nature of transnational policing organizations, management and practices, including intelligence gathering, has pushed the boundaries of the legality of policing practices in relation to civil and political rights.

There has been a global reappraisal of the War on Drugs, and some critics argue that it should be recast as a war on vulnerable people (see Mena and Hobbs 2010). International and domestic campaigns have been initiated to introduce health-based, harm minimization approaches. Some jurisdictions, such as Portugal, have gone even further and decriminalized the purchase, possession and consumption for personal use of all drugs (Mena and Hobbs 2010). These strategies are seen to be more conducive to the prevention and management of drug dependence. The UN is also beginning to change its approach to illicit drug use management. For example, the UN High Commissioner for Human Rights has called for harm reduction to be the basis of policy development (OHCHR 2009 cited in Global Commission on Drugs Policy 2011 n.5 at p.5), and, as the following comments of UN Special Rapporteur Anand Grover reveal:

The current international system of drug control has focused on creating a drug free world, almost exclusively through use of law enforcement policies and criminal sanctions. Mounting evidence, however, suggests this approach has failed … While drugs may have a pernicious effect on individual lives and society, this excessively punitive regime has not achieved its stated public health goals, and has resulted in countless human rights violations. (Anand Grover, UN Special Rapporteur on the right of everyone to the enjoyment of the highest attainable standard of physical and mental health, 2010, cited in the *Alternative Drug Report* 2012)

7.8 Human rights education and prevention

Education is often used as a tool of crime prevention, especially in the areas of sexual assault, domestic violence and drug use, and as with broader crime prevention strategies education for prevention is undertaken at primary, secondary and tertiary levels. Education about human rights is also seen to be an essential tool for fostering a community-wide understanding of, and respect for, human rights, and is seen to be part of the obligations placed on states to fulfill human rights obligations (McCrudden 2005). Human rights have been incorporated into citizenship education in schools, in youth work training and practice, and workplace training courses and accreditation procedures, including for professionals working in the criminal justice field. In sexual assault and anti-racism training and education, a human rights framework can ensure that the message that the issue is a shared one is communicated to both males and females and has underpinned the philosophy of bystander education (Bauman 2003) and community-driven strategies such as the international White Ribbon Campaign (Flood 2010). The UN provides training for criminal justice personnel in human rights as part of its worldwide crime prevention strategies under the auspices of the UN Interregional Crime and Justice Research Institute (http://www.unicri.it/institute/).

Politicians and bureaucrats also need education and awareness training in human rights to ensure that human rights become part of their everyday thinking and practice in the development of human-rights-compliant crime prevention and criminal justice policies.

7.9 Conclusion

As can be seen from the discussion above, the links between human rights and crime prevention are complex. Instead of preventing crime and harm, policies implemented in the name of prevention can lead to violations of human rights. And if they do not get to the heart of the causes of crime they can ultimately be ineffectual. However, as the ICHRP report (2010) says, if key standards and principles such as equality, non-discrimination, dignity, indivisibility, universality, proportionality, accountability and detention as an option of last resort are used as the basis for evaluating the appropriateness of crime prevention strategies, then the far-reaching negative effects of broad social control strategies can be mitigated.

Additional readings and materials

Centre for Human Rights Education at Curtin University
   Available at: http://info.humanrights.curtin.edu.au/.

Justice Reinvestment Campaign for Aboriginal Young People
  Available at: http://justicereinvestmentnow.net.au/.
UN Bangkok Declaration (2005) *Synergies and Responses: Strategic Alliances in Crime Prevention and Justice*. Available at: http://www.un.org/events/11thcongress/declaration.htm.
United Nations Commission on the Status of Women, 57th Session, 4—15 March 2013, New York. Available at: http://www.un.org/womenwatch/daw/csw/57sess.htm.
UN-Habitat Source for social, developmental and environmental approaches to crime prevention. Available at http://www.unhabitat.org/categories.asp?catid=9.
UNODC (2010) *Handbook on the Crime Prevention Guidelines Making them Work*, Criminal Justice Handbook Series, Vienna: United Nations Office on Drugs and Crime. Available at: http://www.unodc.org/documents/justice-and-prison-reform/crimeprevention/10-52410_Guidelines_eBook.pdf.

References

AHRLC (Human Rights Law Centre) (2013) *The Value of a Justice Reinvestment Approach to Criminal Justice*, 10 April. Available at: http://www.hrlc.org.au/submission-the-value-of-a-justice-reinvestment-approach-to-criminal-justice-in-australia; accessed 15 April 2013.
Andreassen, B.A. (2006) 'Development and the Human Rights Responsibilities of Non-state Actors', in B. A. Andreassen and S. P. Marks (eds), *Development as a Human Right: Legal, Political, and Economic Dimensions — A Nobel Book*, Cambridge, MA: Harvard University Press, pp. 119—39.
Anton, D.K. and Shelton, D.L. (2011) *Environmental Protection and Human Rights*, Cambridge: Cambridge University Press.
Bauman, Z. (2003) 'From Bystander to Actor', *Journal of Human Rights*, 2(2) June: 137—51.
Bowling, B. (2011) 'Transnational Criminology and the Globalization of Harm Production', in M. Bosworth and C. Hoyle (eds), *What Is Criminology?*, Oxford: Oxford University Press, pp. 362—79.
Bowling, B. and Sheptycki, J. (2012) *Global Policing*, London: Sage.
Brown, D., Schwartz, M. and Boseley, L. (2012) *The Promise of Justice Reinvestment*. Available at: http://ssrn.com/abstract=2078715; accessed 28 September 2012.
Cantley-Smith, R. (2013) 'A Human Right to a Healthy Environment', in P. Gerber and M. Castan (eds), *Contemporary Perspectives on Human Rights Law in Australia*, Sydney: Thomson Reuters, pp. 448—74.
Charlesworth, H. and Chinkin, C. (2000) *The Boundaries of International Law: A Feminist Analysis*, Melland Schill Studies in Law, Manchester: Juris Publishing, Manchester University Press.
Cohen, S. (1985) *Visions of Social Control*, Cambridge: Polity Press.

Coleman, R. and McCahill, M. (2011) *Surveillance and Crime: Key Approaches to Criminology*, London: Sage.

Count the Costs (2012a) *The Alternative Drug Report*. Available at: http://www.countthecosts.org/alternative-world-drug-report; accessed 31 March 2013.

Count the Costs (2012b) *The War on Drugs: Undermining Human Rights Briefing Paper, Count the Costs: 50 years of the War on Drugs*. Available at: http://www.countthecosts.org/sites/default/files/Human_rights_briefing.pdf; accessed 31 March 2013.

Crawford, A. (2007) 'Crime Prevention and Community Safety', in M. Maguire, R. Morgan and R. Reiner (eds), *The Oxford Handbook of Criminology*, Oxford: Oxford University Press, pp. 866–909.

Currie, E. (1998) *Crime and Punishment in America*, Markham, ON: Fitzhenry & Whiteside.

Currie, E. (2007) 'Social Crime Prevention Strategies in a Market Society', in E. McLaughlin, J. Muncie and G. Hughes (eds), *Criminological Perspectives: Essential Readings*, 2nd edn, The Open University, London: Sage, pp. 369–80.

European Commission (2012) Daphne III Programme. Available at: http://ec.europa.eu/justice/fundamental-rights/programme/daphne-programme/index_en.htm.

Flood, M. (2010) *Where Men Stand: Men's Role in Ending Violence against Women*, White Ribbon Prevention Research Series No. 2, Sydney: White Ribbon.

Ford, L. (2013) 'Activists Welcome Hard Fought Agreement on YN Women's Rights', *The Guardian Online*, 16 March. Available at: http://www.guardian.co.uk/global-development/2013/mar/16/activists-welcome-un-agreeement-womens-rights; accessed 17 March 2013.

Fox, R. and Mathews, I. (1992) *Drugs Policy: Fact, Fiction and the Future*, Sydney: Federation Press.

Global Commission on Drugs Policy (2011) 'Executive Summary', *The War on Drugs Report of the Commission on Global Drugs Policy*, June. Available at: http://www.globalcommissionondrugs.org/wp-content/themes/gcdp_v1/pdf/Global_Commission_Report_English.pdf; accessed 31/3/2013.

Hucklesby, A. (2013) 'Compliance with Electronically Monitored Curfew Orders', in A. Hucklesby and A. Crawford (eds), *Legitimacy and Compliance in Criminal Justice*, New York/London: Routledge, pp. 138–58.

Hughes, G. (2007) *Politics of Crime and Community*, Basingstoke: Palgrave Macmillan.

ICHRP (International Council on Human Rights Policy) (2010) *Modes and Patterns of Social Control: Implications for Human Rights Policy*, Geneva: ICHRP.

Ife, J. (2010) *Human Rights from Below: Achieving Human Rights Through Community Development*, Cambridge: Cambridge University Press.

Krasmann, S. (2012) 'Law's Knowledge: On the Susceptibility and Resistance of Legal Practices to Security Matters', *Theoretical Criminology* 16(4): 379–94.

Lanning, T., Loader, I. and Muir, R. (2011) *Redesigning Justice: Reducing Crime through Justice Reinvestment*, London: Institute for Public Policy Research.

Loader, I. and Walker, N. (2007) *Civilizing Security*, Cambridge: Cambridge University Press.

Lyon, D. (2001) *Surveillance Society: Monitoring Everyday Life*, Buckingham: Open University Press.

Lyon, D. (2007) *Surveillance Studies: An Overview*, Cambridge: Polity Press.

McCrudden, C. (2005) 'Mainstreaming Human Rights', in C. Harvey (ed.), *Human Rights in the Community: Rights as Agents for Change*, Human Rights Law in Perspective, The British Institute of Human Rights, Oxford: Hart Publishing, pp. 9—28.

Mena, F. and Hobbs, D. (2010) 'Narcophobia: Drugs Prohibition and the Generation of Human Rights Abuses', *Trends in Organised Crime*, 13: 60—74.

Nellis, M. (2013) 'Implant Technology and the Electronic Monitoring of Offenders: Old and New Questions about Compliance, Control and Legitimacy, in A. Hucklesby and A. Crawford (eds), *Legitimacy and Compliance in Criminal Justice*, New York/London: Routledge, pp. 159—80.

Newburn, T. (2007) *Criminology*, Uffculme, Devon: Willan Publishing.

Nussbaum, M. (1995) 'Human Capabilities, Female Human Beings', in M. Nussbaum and J. Glover, *Women, Culture and Development: A Study of Human Capabilities*, Oxford: Oxford University Press, pp. 61—104.

Nussbaum, M. (2000) *Women and Human Development*: *The Capabilities Approach*, Cambridge: Cambridge University Press.

Penny, L. (2013) 'Steubenville: This Is Rape Culture's Abu Ghraib Moment', *New Statesman*, 19 March.

Sen, A. (2005) 'Human Rights and Capabilities', *Journal of Human Development*, 6(2): 151—66.

Sen, A. (2010) *The Idea of Justice*, Harmondsworth: Penguin.

Shackle, S. (2013) Will the Delhi Gang Rape Case Actually Change Women's Lives in India?, *New Statesman*, 11 January.

Sheptycki, J. (1996) 'Law Enforcement, Justice and Democracy in the Transnational Arena: Reflections on the War on Drugs', *The International Journal of the Sociology of Law*, 24: 61—75.

Slater, J. (2013) 'The War on Drugs: Time to Count The Costs to Women', 8 March. Available at: http://www.countthecosts.org/blog/war-drugs-time-count-costs-women; accessed 31 March 2013.

Stockholm Declaration 1972 *Declaration on the United Nations Conference on Human Development* United Nations Environment Programme. Available at http://www.unep.org/Documents.Multilingual/Default.asp?documentid=97&articleid=1503 accessed 31 March 2013.

True, J. (2012) *The Political Economy of Violence against Women*, Oxford: Oxford University Press.

United Nations Daily News (2011) 'Homophobic Crimes on the Rise, UN Human Rights Chief Warns', 17 May. Available at: http://www.un.org/news/dh/pdf/english/2011/17052011.pdf; accessed 3 April 2013.

United Nations Declaration on the Rights of Indigenous People (2007) United Nations. Available at http://www.un.org/esa/socdev/unpfii/documents/DRIPS_en.pdf.

OHCHR (Office of the United Nations High Commissioner for Human Rights) (2009) 'High Commissioner Calls for Focus on Human Rights and Harm Reduction in International Drug Policy', Geneva: United Nations. Available at: http://www.ohchr.org/documents/Press/HC_human_rights_and_harm_reduction_drug_policy.pdf.

UNODC (United Nations Office on Drugs and Crime) (2006) *UN Compendium of Standards and Norms in Crime Prevention and Criminal Justice*. Available at: http://www.unodc.org/pdf/compendium/compendium_2006.pdf.

UNODC (2008) *UN World Drug Report*. Available at: http://www.unodc.org/documents/wdr/WDR_2008/WDR_2008_eng_web.pdf.

US Justice Center, The Council of State Governments, *Justice Reinvestment*. Available at: http://justicereinvestment.org/about; accessed 31 March 2013.

White, R. (2008) *Crimes against Nature: Environmental Criminology and Ecological Justice*, Uffculme, Devon/Portland, OR, Willan Publishing.

Zedner, L. (2007) 'Pre-crime and Post-criminology', *Theoretical Criminology*, 11(2): 261–81.

Zedner, L. (2009) *Security*, Key Ideas in Criminology Series, London/New York: Routledge.

CHAPTER 8

Policing

Key concepts
Accountability — Procedural justice — Use of force — Proportionality —
Privacy

8.1 Introduction

The police are a unique institution intimately associated with the nation-state. They are invested by governments with special powers, notably the capacity to use force and invade privacy in ways that would be considered unacceptable if engaged in by other citizens. In this chapter, we consider how police can use their powers and training to both protect and violate human rights, analyse the human rights implications of various ways of approaching the policing task, and consider how human rights policing can be promoted.

8.2 Police as protectors and abusers of human rights

As members of an institution granted wide coercive powers by government and often armed with lethal weaponry, police occupy a special position in the modern state. Because of their crucial social role, police have the potential to act either as protectors or abusers of human rights. On the one hand, police powers and skills are meant to be used to keep the peace and enforce the law. Crawshaw *et al.* (2007) argue that police are pivotal in determining whether states meet their human rights obligations towards their populations, particularly with respect to the rights contained in the International Covenant on Civil and Political Rights (ICCPR), such as the right to life (Article 6). The importance of the police in delivering on these aspects of the social contract has led British police theorists Loader and Walker (2001) to call for 'democratic' policing to be recognized and reinstated as a 'public good'. On the other hand, police may also become abusers of human rights by directly misusing their powers, or by providing inadequate protection for those who need their help. The websites of respected human rights organizations such as Amnesty International and Human Rights Watch are replete with reports alleging serious human rights abuses perpetrated by police: from torture, disappearances and extrajudicial killings, to unwarranted invasions of privacy and discriminatory treatment of minorities (see also Chapter 4). Both rights-respecting and rights-abusing practices may be supported by the unwritten rules that constitute police occupational culture, or through external influences such as the expectations of governments and the wider public, and the relationship between police and government.

Within a *civil police model*, police (unlike the military) are not controlled directly by the government, but are expected to operate within democratic limits (Wright 2002). In so far as this separation is achieved in practice, it protects against police becoming the perpetrators of systematic human rights abuses at the direct behest of government. Wright proposes Britain and the Netherlands as exemplars of this form of police governance, while France and Germany are said to employ a *state police model*. Under such a model, police are still constrained by the rule of law, but have close links with the military, and the concerns of the state predominate. The risk of systematic human rights abuses at the direction of government is arguably highest under what Wright calls *quasi-military* and *martial law* models of policing. In societies adopting these models, the police are directly responsible for state security and operate outside the rule of law under the direct command of government, which is itself under military control in the case of the martial law model. Wright finds examples of these non-democratic modes of policing primarily outside Europe, though they are also characteristic of European colonial rule, in which the rights of subjected populations were routinely breached or unrecognized. Critical criminologists have argued that elements of quasi-military policing styles have become increasingly apparent within liberal democracies in counter-terrorist policing and the policing of political protest (see, for example, McCulloch 2004).

Even within ostensibly democratic modes of policing, the wider social and political context can reduce the capacity of the police to uphold universal human rights standards. In the USA, it has been argued that the histories of vigilantism and slavery in the southern and western states have converged to justify the excessive use of force against African-Americans (Skolnik and Fyfe 1993). In Australia, the historical role of police as enforcers of racist colonial legislation, coupled with pressure from settlers to control Aboriginal populations, has left a lasting legacy of discriminatory policing (Cunneen 2001). More recently, fear of Islamic extremism in many liberal democracies has galvanized public support for counter-terrorism laws and policing that potentially exclude minority Muslim communities from human rights protection (Zedner 2006). In fact, all but the most conservative of policing theorists see differential protection as being inherent within the policing role. For example, Waddington (1999: 42) claims that a key role of the modern police has been to provide 'protection to citizens from the internal threat posed by those on the margins of citizenship'. This raises significant questions about the capacity of police to uphold equally the rights of all sections of the population.

Police occupational culture is also a powerful influence on police practice. It may be harnessed to promote human rights, but more often is seen as antagonistic to human rights norms. Widely observed features of 'cop culture' (Reiner 2000), such as a heightened capacity for suspicion, which encourages stereotyping; a tendency to divide the population into 'respectable citizens' and 'police property'; racial and gender prejudice and an isolationism which, in the extreme, portrays the police as a 'thin blue line' keeping anarchy at bay can create a disdain for due process requirements, most notably rights that provide protection to criminal suspects (see ICCPR, Article 9). The rights of victims may also be undermined where police perceptions about what is and is not police business, and who is and is not a valued member of society, disqualify some victims of crime from receiving adequate protection and redress (see Chapter 12).

8.3 Human rights standards on the use of force by police

Police perform a wide range of tasks in contemporary societies. But it is their mandate to use force that raises the most pressing human rights concerns. Police are authorized to use force where necessary to apprehend a criminal suspect, prevent harm to others, or to restore order. In liberal democracies it is not the role of the police to punish offenders, and guilt and punishment are to be determined by the courts relatively independently of the police. However, studies of police occupational culture often identify scepticism among police officers about the efficacy of the criminal justice process. These perceived shortcomings may be used to justify what Chan (2000) refers to as 'backstage punishment' through the punitive use of force. Even when the police use force for legitimate purposes, human rights norms specify that the type and degree of such force must be proportionate to the risk posed to the police, the public and the targeted person. The United Nations Code of Conduct for Law Enforcement Officers stipulates that force may be used by police 'only when strictly necessary and to the extent required for the performance of their duty' (Article 3), places a duty of care on them in relation to persons in their custody (Article 6), and expressly prohibits torture (Article 5). Paragraph 9 of the UN Basic Principles on the Use of Force and

Firearms by Law Enforcement Officials clarifies the requirement of proportionality as follows:

> Law enforcement officials shall not use firearms against persons except in self-defence or defence of others against the imminent threat of death or serious injury, to prevent the perpetration of a particularly serious crime involving grave threat to life, to arrest a person presenting such a danger and resisting their authority, or to prevent his or her escape, and only when less extreme means are insufficient to achieve these objectives. In any event, intentional lethal use of firearms may only be made when strictly unavoidable in order to protect life.

Overall, there is a standing presumption against the use of force. Kleinig (1996) argues that police training should emphasize the skills of mediation and de-escalation, which are often both more effective and more ethical approaches to handling potentially violent situations. In fact, William Kerr Muir proposed that a 'good policeman' [sic] could be measured, in part, by his/her skill in avoiding the use of force, while being able to resolve successfully the moral contradiction of 'achieving just ends with coercive means' (Muir 1977: 4).

While the legitimate and restrained use of force by police to protect lives is not often celebrated, examples abound of the use of force that does not conform to the well-established human rights principles outlined above. The brutal beating in the USA in 1991 of African-American police suspect Rodney King after a high-speed car chase in Los Angeles (LA) came to public attention worldwide because it was captured on video. The video showed Mr King being beaten and repeatedly shocked with electro-convulsive weapons by LA police long after he had ceased resisting arrest. Moreover, since he was unarmed and massively outnumbered by the police presence, it is implausible to argue that he presented a significant danger at any time in the encounter. Though clearly in breach of human rights standards on the use of force (see American Civil Liberties Union and Human Rights Watch 1993), the police officers who were brought to trial were acquitted of assault, resulting in widespread rioting among African-American communities. American criminologists Skolnick and Fyfe (1993) described the events as a 'symbolic lynching' with deep-seated roots in America's history of publicly supported violence against rebellious slaves. This example demonstrates the practical barriers to achieving human rights compliance within established state institutions in socially divisive and politically charged contexts. However, two of the officers were later convicted in a federal court of violating Rodney King's constitutional civil rights (Human Rights Watch 1998).

The use by police of electro-convulsive weapons has come under intense scrutiny in many countries. Amnesty International claimed in 2012 that these supposedly non-lethal weapons had been involved in at least 500 deaths since 2001 in the USA alone (Amnesty International 2012). A case in point is the death in March 2012 of Brazilian student Roberto Laudisio Curti in Sydney, Australia, who was forcibly restrained and repeatedly stunned with a taser by state police after displaying bizarre but non-violent drug-induced behaviour. Again, much of the action was captured on CCTV cameras and widely viewed by the public. The New South Wales (NSW) State Coroner (2012: 22) described the police involved as having acted with an 'ungoverned pack mentality, like the schoolboys in "Lord of the Flies", with no idea what the problem was, or what threat or crime was supposedly to be averted, or concern for the value of life' (see Box 8.1). However, while recommending internal disciplinary action, the Coroner did not call for criminal charges against the officers because of the medical uncertainty over the exact cause of death, indicating once again the difficulty of using the criminal law to enforce human rights standards.

Electro-convulsive weapons are also widely implicated in torture, precisely because they are usually non-lethal and leave little lasting trace of being used (Kleinig 1996). Since torture is absolutely prohibited by Article 7 of the ICCPR and the Convention Against Torture and Other Cruel, Inhuman or Degrading Treatment or Punishment, it might be tempting to

---

Box 8.1 Human rights limits on police use of force

Statement by the NSW State Coroner regarding the death of Roberto Laudisio Curti on 18 March 2012

[Police] are entitled when necessary to use reasonable force, including weapons, to pursue suspects in vehicles at high speed, to arrest citizens and to place them in custody. As well as tasers, they carry batons, firearms, OC spray and handcuffs. They are trained to use their bodies and appointments to control those who threaten others. These are not entitlements available to almost any other members of our society, and with them come huge responsibilities. Individual officers do not have a licence to act recklessly, carelessly or dangerously or with excessive force. In the pursuit, tasering (particularly in drive stun mode), tackling, spraying and restraining of Roberto Laudisio Curti, those responsibilities were cast aside, and the actions of a number of the officers were just that: reckless, careless, dangerous, and excessively forceful.

Source: NSW State Coroner (2012: 21).

think that it is only practised in overtly repressive states. However, there has been a resurgence of torture in liberal democracies, particularly following the terror attacks of 11 September 2001 (9/11 in New York). The systematic study of torture by criminologists has revealed that it can be deeply embedded within the criminal justice system, may be directed against political opponents, and is often justified by reference to everyday crime-fighting goals. Stanley notes that torture is widely used by state officials to obtain 'confessions', demonstrate the power of the state and damage collective affiliations to cultural or political groups, but may be disguised by political rhetoric:

> It is perhaps not surprising, given such rationalisations, that torture often goes misrecognised since torture engaged in by states is also denied and neutralised by states. As such, torture is euphemistically renamed as 'crime fighting', 'intensive questioning', 'challenging conditions' or 'counterterrorism'. In effect, torture becomes recognised as something else. (Stanley 2004: 3)

8.4 Human rights implications of particular policing strategies and contexts

Particular styles of policing may either support or discourage the observance of human rights principles. So-called *zero tolerance policing*, in which police respond aggressively to even minor infringements and breaches of the peace, has been encouraged in many locations in recent decades, notably in crime-ridden New York City. Many criminologists dispute that the 'New York miracle', in which reported crime rates dropped sharply over the first half of the 1990s, was a result of zero tolerance strategies (see Bowling 1999; Cunneen 1998–9). On the other hand, complaints against police did increase significantly during this period, along with a 35 per cent increase in police shootings, 53 per cent increase in deaths in custody, and many well-documented human rights abuses. One example was the torture of Haitian immigrant Abner Louima in 1997, which the New York City Public Advocate identified as part of a 'pattern of police abuse, brutality and misconduct' (Cunneen 1998–9).

The advent of *intelligence-led* approaches, in which police resources are targeted towards risky people and places, seems at first to promise a shift towards less aggressive policing. However, the use of aggregate-level risk estimates to target particular groups equates in practice to systemic discrimination (see Chapter 4). Equally, the identification of 'hot spots' for intensive policing efforts often impacts disproportionately on particular groups frequenting those areas, either inadvertently or by design. The Equality and

Human Rights Commission (2012) concluded that police stops authorized under section 60 of the Criminal Justice and Public Order Act 1994 in particular locations in Britain were sometimes focused on certain minority groups, and that the use of undisclosed police intelligence to justify these practices meant they lacked the level of transparency expected within democratic systems. Parmar (2011) also noted that Muslim populations were effectively being recast as providers of intelligence regarding terrorist activity and subjected to unwarranted police stops, with damaging implications for community relations. Even intelligence-led targeting based on individual, rather than aggregate, risk assessments – on the basis of criminal record, for example – is potentially contrary to the rehabilitation ideals set out in Article 10 of the ICCPR.

Public order policing presents a particular human rights challenge for police as they attempt to reconcile protestors' rights of peaceful assembly and freedom of association (Articles 21 and 22 of the ICCPR) with the police mandate to maintain the peace and protect life and property. Violent suppression of dissent is often associated with authoritarian regimes that deploy military-style tactics against their own citizens. The fatal shooting by police of more than 30 striking miners from the Marikana platinum mines in South Africa on 16 August 2012 was particularly shocking because it was reminiscent of the brutal tactics of the former Apartheid regime (see Box 8.2). The events raise many questions about the operations of multinational mining companies in the region, as well as the actions of the police on the day. Within liberal democracies, complaints about public order policing may concern the disproportionate use of force (see the debates between Jefferson (1990) and Waddington (1993)), or may focus on tactics that ostensibly breach protestors' freedom of movement, such as the cordoning off of large security zones, or using heavy-handed tactics such as 'kettling' (Fenwick 2009).

In the post–9/11 world, enhanced powers of search and surveillance have been granted to police and security agencies in liberal democracies for the purposes of *security policing*. Most human rights criticisms are aimed at the permissive nature of the laws themselves (see Chapter 6), which often contravene long-established legal rules (Zedner 2007). Some critics have argued that counter-terrorist policing more closely resembles the martial law model described earlier than the civil policing model that applies to general policing. In Australia, Pickering *et al.* (2008: 22) have noted that '[s]acrificing human rights, and in particular sacrificing the human rights of segments of the population which are stereotyped as terrorist, undermines efforts to counter or minimise terrorism'. In the USA, revelations that the Bush administration had granted exceptional powers to security officials to eavesdrop on telephone conversations without court-issued warrants created a public furore

Box 8.2   Three views of the Marikana Mine shootings

SAHRC condemns the violence in Marikana, calls for an investigation

Statement issued by South African Human Rights Commission,
17 August 2012

While it's still not clear what happened prior to the police opening fire and fatally wounding several miners, we believe there were no grounds for excessive force to be used. We are of the view that the police should have used other means at their disposal to disperse the crowd and to arrest the situation. Ironically, this sad and shocking incident happened on the day when the National Council of Provinces unanimously passed the Criminal Procedures Act Amendment Bill, curtailing the use of force by the police in situations like the one in Marikana. The Bill, which intends to bring section 49 of the Act in line with the Constitution, provides guidelines on why and how force, and deadly force, may be used to carry out an arrest or deal with a violent crowd.

Government respects the constitutional rights of Marikana residents but has to promote peace and order

Statement issued by President Jacob Zuma, 16 September 2012

The Presidency wishes to point out that the law enforcement measures undertaken in Marikana are not in any way aimed at undermining the civil liberties of strikers and residents of the area. The people of Marikana, including the strikers, are entitled to the rights of freedom of association, expression, assembly and association like all South Africans, as enshrined in the Constitution of the land. Clause 17 of the Constitution states that everyone has the right, 'peacefully and unarmed', to assemble, to demonstrate, to picket and to present petitions. All South Africans, including those in Marikana, also have the right to fair labour practices as enshrined in Clause 23 (1) of the Constitution ... Government has not and will never take away the constitutional rights of our people that they worked so hard for during the struggle for liberation. Government action in Marikana is directed at ensuring that citizens exercise their rights peacefully and within the ambit of the law, as would be required in any democratic country in the world.

A view from the mountain

Eyewitness reports published in Los Angeles Review of Books *(Lichtenstein, 4 January 2013)*

People were not killed because they were fighting ... 'We were shot while running. We went through the hole [in the fence], and that is why we were shot.' In this encounter, 12 more miners met their deaths. In the third and final phase, police literally hunted down escaped workers at a distance from the initial encounter on what Alexander calls the 'Killing Koppie.' There, without any provocation, they simply murdered at least 13 more unarmed and terrified men, Alexander charges. 'Whatever view one takes of the initial killings, it is clear that the men who died on the Killing Koppie were fleeing from the battlefield,' he observes. 'This was not public order policing,' Alexander concludes. 'This was warfare.'

about breaches of privacy (Risen and Lichtblau 2005). Still, surveillance techniques widely associated with counter-terrorism and the policing of serious crime appear set to become a regular feature of everyday policing (House of Lords Select Committee on the Constitution 2009).

Another powerful trend in contemporary policing is the re-emergence of *networked* and *privatized* forms of policing (Loader 2000). While governments generally retain legal responsibility for regulating private policing, privatization can complicate the task of tracing lines of accountability where human rights abuses occur. In the Australian state of NSW, minimally trained transit officers employed by public transport providers to maintain security on trains were the subject of 400 complaints over a six-month period (Smith and Marinner 2005). The security and law enforcement functions performed by these transit officers have since been transferred back to specialist state police. Lines of responsibility may become even more blurred if not only the providers of policing services but also the body authorizing policing is no longer the state (Wood and Shearing 2007). While state police have fallen well short of achieving equal protection for all (see Chapter 4), private policing based on a 'user pays' system presents an even greater challenge with respect to the universalist principles of human rights.

Community policing aimed at maximizing non-conflictual contacts with the public and forming police–community partnerships seems to be the form of policing most likely to promote respect for human rights. Its companion policing model, *problem-oriented policing*, which directs police to analyse recurring patterns of local crime and disorder and to take steps to implement long-term solutions, also seems to favour reflective and open policing rather than the more aggressive and secretive approaches discussed above. However, both of these models also potentially raise human rights concerns. Community policing begs the question of who is to be included in 'the community', and who represents it. Approaches to community policing that elevate a homogeneous conception of 'community values' over more abstract systems such as the rule of law or respect for human rights have given rise to *quality of life* policing, which often shares some characteristics with zero tolerance. Equally, problem-oriented policing is not prescriptive about the type of solutions to local crime problems that might be proposed, which could be either rights-respecting or rights-abusing. The model also envisages that police retain control over crime-related data, which could foster a lack of transparency that is characteristic of some forms of intelligence-led policing.

New thinking about *procedural justice* within policing highlights the central importance of police demeanour, towards both suspects and other members of the public, in building or eroding trust in police and perceptions of legitimacy (Tyler 1997; Sunshine and Tyler 2003; Bradford and Jackson 2010; Jackson *et al.* 2013). Research has shown that respectful treatment and reasoned explanations may ameliorate resentment about unwarranted intrusions during street stops, while genuine concern and provision of information can increase the satisfaction levels of victims of crime, even where no resolution of the criminal matter follows (Hough 2013). Disrespectful treatment by police can erode trust and perceptions of legitimacy, not only among the individuals who have direct contact with the police, but also throughout their wider community networks (Brunson and Miller 2006; Sharp and Atherton 2007; Bradford *et al.* 2008; Bridenball and Jesilow 2008). The 'asymmetry hypothesis' (Skogan 2006, 2009) contains even worse news for police who do not respect human rights, since it suggests that negative interactions cannot simply be 'cancelled out' by a similar number of positive ones. These findings have serious implications for the police, since all forms of policing ultimately depend on co-operation from the public. Furthermore, if labelling theorists such as Becker (1963) are correct, consistently treating certain young people as if they were criminals might indeed have 'self-fulfilling prophecy' effects, which would be counterproductive to police crime reduction objectives.

8.5 Promoting human rights in policing

Article 2 of the UN Code of Conduct for Law Enforcement Officers stipulates that 'in the performance of their duty, law enforcement officials shall respect and protect human dignity and maintain and uphold the human rights of all persons'. This goal of human-rights-based policing requires that police are aware of what human rights standards apply to their occupation, and are trained and motivated to uphold them. In the USA, several police agencies are trialling 'procedural justice policing' approaches developed by academic criminologists on the basis of the empirical evidence outlined above (Dai *et al.* 2011; Schulhofer *et al.* 2011). In Britain, former senior police officers have been influential in promoting human rights training for police (Neyroud and Beckley 2001; Crawshaw *et al.* 2007). The passage of the Human Rights Act (HRA) in 1998 forced the British police to assess their level of human rights compliance. Neyroud and Beckley (2001) concluded that key areas for police training and practice were the proportionate and non-discriminatory use of police powers, the 'absolute necessity' criterion in relation to the use of force, reasonable and lawful decision-making, duty of care towards people in custody, and openness and accountability. Despite these good intentions, criminological research has indicated that the HRA has failed to embed a human rights culture within policing organizations in England and Wales:

> We argue that there is little evidence to suggest that [the HRA] has promoted a greater awareness of, and respect for, human rights amongst police officers. Rather, the HRA has become institutionalized by the police service into a series of bureaucratic processes that, although requiring conformity by officers, do not encourage active consideration of human rights issues. Instead of shaping police work to make it more responsive to human rights, bureaucratic processes are used by officers to legitimize and justify their existing practices. (Bullock and Johnson 2012: 630)

Evidence such as this supports the view that police occupational culture is antithetical to human rights, monolithic and resistant to change. Moreover, despite several decades of anti-racism initiatives and training within the London Metropolitan Police following the McPherson Inquiry, the association representing minority officers claims that institutional racism persists (Muir 2013). However, Chan's conceptualization of police culture as dynamic and knowledge-based provides some basis to hope that change may be possible in the longer term (Chan 1997). Drawing on Bordieu's concepts of *field* and *habitus*, Chan argues that the habitus of police culture (that is, the internal systems of occupational norms, knowledge and informal rules that arise from police practice) can be reformed from the outside if they are also supported by appropriate changes in the field (that is, the socio-political context of laws, policies, institutions and public opinion that also influence police practice). In this view, legislation such as bills of rights, effective institutions that implement human rights standards, and a population that is socially inclusive and accepting of universal claims to human rights protection, accompanied by appropriate police leadership, could potentially support the development of a human rights culture within police institutions in the longer term.

While voluntary compliance with human rights norms is always preferable, human-rights-compliant policing can also be promoted through the enforcement of treaties to which governments have formally assented. In one of its regular treaty monitoring reports, the UN Human Rights Committee concluded that the use of force by Australian police in relation to 'indigenous people, racial minorities, persons with disabilities, as well as young people' at times breached

Articles 6 (right to life) and 7 (prohibition against torture) of the ICCPR (Human Rights Committee 2009, para. 21). Particular criticism was directed towards the overuse of tasers. The committee recommended that this weapon should only be used in cases where lethal force (such as the use of a firearm) would be justified. In the years leading up to the death of Roberto Laudisio Curti (discussed earlier), the NSW Ombudsman had also warned repeatedly that better police training was needed, and had called for a moratorium on the roll-out of these weapons until the benefits and dangers were better understood (NSW Ombudsman 2008). Since this fatality, the Ombudsman has publicly criticized the police handling of the inquiry into the death and called for further restrictions on the use of the weapon (NSW Ombudsman 2012, 2013). While this example seems to confirm the ineffectiveness of human rights enforcement in the face of entrenched police practice, it also highlights practical steps that could be taken if supported by sufficient political will and leadership.

In jurisdictions with long-standing traditions of seeking remedies for human rights breaches in local courts (see Chapter 6), human rights defenders can point to case law as a powerful argument against policing practices that violate human rights. In the USA, civil liberties groups have launched many successful challenges against zero-tolerance-style policing that have been underpinned by local ordinances banning otherwise non-criminal behaviour such as 'panhandling' (known outside the USA as begging). Box 8.3 includes extracts from a letter written by the American Civil Liberties Union to the political administration of the city of Madison, Wisconsin, which summarize some of the important legal precedents upholding the right to beg, based on principles of free speech.

Despite their generally negative research findings (outlined above), Bullock and Johnson are not entirely pessimistic about the potential impact of the HRA on British policing. They believe that some improvements in accountability have resulted, but without the development of a true understanding of human rights principles – an outcome they claim is not unique to the police. They conclude that deeper change will require:

> the development of new 'cultural capacities' based on the ideas of respect, equality, toleration, dignity, fairness, transparency and democratic accountability from which police officers can draw inspiration in carrying out their work. It demands an appreciation among police officers of how police work might contribute to greater respect for, and protection of, human rights in society. At the very least, it necessitates an understanding of the fundamental objectives of the HRA and the framework that it provides for achieving a fair balance between the demands of the community and the protection of human rights. (Bullock and Johnson 2012: 647)

Box 8.3 Zero tolerance policing and civil liberties

Some types of aggressive street policing have been held to breach the civil liberties protections within the US Constitution. The following US court decisions striking down local ordinances promoting zero-tolerance-style policing against 'panhandlers' were listed in a letter from the American Civil Liberties Union to the city of Madison, Wisconsin.

The U.S. Supreme Court has consistently held that 'mere public intolerance or animosity cannot be the basis for abridgment of ... constitutional freedoms,' *Coates v City of Cincinnati*, 402 US 611, 615 (1971), and speech cannot be punished on account of its 'profound unsettling effects,' 'public inconvenience, annoyance, or unrest.' *Terminiello v City of Chicago*, 337 US 1, 4 (1949); see also *Forsyth County v Nationalist Movement*, 505 US 123, 134 (1992).

Lower courts have concluded that begging is a form of political speech. *Gresham v Peterson*, 225 F.3d 899, 904 (7th Cir. 2000); *Loper v NY City Police Dep't*, 999 F.2d 699, 704 (2d Cir. 1993); *Speet v Schuette*, ___ F. Supp. 2d ___, 2012 WL 3865394, *3-*4 (W.D. Mich. Aug. 24, 2012); *Blair v Shanahan*, 775 F. Supp. 1315, 1322-3 (N.D. Cal. 1991); *Benefit v City of Cambridge*, 679 N.E.2d 184, 188 (Mass. 1997).

In addition, content-based restrictions on speech are 'presumptively invalid.' *R.A.V. v St. Paul*, 505 US 377, 382 (1992); see also *Police Dep't of City of Chicago v Mosley*, 408 US 92, 95 (1972). Thus, the City cannot single out the speech of panhandlers for punishment, while permitting the speech of others who solicit funds.

The desire to protect people from the discomfort caused by panhandlers (or other charitable solicitations) or exposure to poor people does not justify suppressing speech. See *Coates*, 402 US at 615; *Terminiello* 337 US at 4. Even words and conduct that are 'deeply offensive to many,' including 'virulent ethnic and religious epithets, vulgar repudiations of the draft, and scurrilous caricatures' are protected from prosecution. *United States v Eichman*, 496 US 310, 318–19 (1990) (citations omitted); see also *Cohen v California*, 403 US 15, 18–22 (1971). Certainly, the much more commonplace urban inconvenience of being asked peacefully for a donation cannot be banned in a traditional public forum.

Source: http://aclu-wi.org/sites/default/files/stories/press-releases/20121004PanhandlingBanMadisonLetter.pdf.

This conclusion highlights the dynamic relationship between the internal police culture and the external context of policing, and suggests that the reconstitution of policing as a 'public good' depends to a large extent on the development of a broader human rights culture.

8.6 Conclusion

Arguably, the fundamental requirement for rights-respecting policing is the recognition that *all* individuals, whether persistent offenders or pillars of the community, are possessors of inalienable human rights, and policing that upholds the rights of all people is not only possible, but has practical advantages. Police do infringe certain individual rights when seeking to protect the rights of the majority, but they must do so for lawful reasons and within acceptable limits. Moreover, criminological research is beginning to establish that *how* police perform their law enforcement and order maintenance activities – particularly the level of respect they demonstrate for human rights – may be just as important as *what* they actually achieve.

Additional reading and resources

Basic Principles on the Use of Force and Firearms by Law Enforcement Officials, UN Doc. A/CONF.144/28/Rev.1 at 112 (1990).
  Available at: http://www1.umn.edu/humanrts/instree/i2bpuff.htm.
Code of Conduct for Law Enforcement Officials, adopted by UN General Assembly resolution 34/169 of 17 December 1979.
  Available at: http://www.ohchr.org/EN/ProfessionalInterest/Pages/Law EnforcementOfficials.aspx.
Crawshaw, R. and Holmström, L. (eds) (2008) *Essential Texts on Human Rights for Police: A Compilation of International Instruments*, Leiden: Martinus Nijhoff.
Office of the UN High Commissioner for Human Rights (2004) *Human Rights Standards and Practice for the Police: Expanded Pocket Book on Human Rights for the Police*, Professional Training Series No. 5/Add. 3, New York/Geneva, United Nations.
  Available at: http://www.ohchr.org/Documents/Publications/training5Add3en. pdf.

Court cases cited

Benefit v City of Cambridge, 679 N.E.2d 184, 188 (Mass. 1997) (US).
Blair v Shanahan, 775 F. Supp. 1315, 1322–3 (N.D. Cal. 1991) (US).
Coates v City of Cincinnati, 402 US 611, 615 (1971) (US).
Cohen v California, 403 US 15, 18–22 (1971) (US).

Forsyth County v Nationalist Movement, 505 US 123, 134 (1992) (US).

Gresham v Peterson, 225 F.3d 899, 904 (7th Cir. 2000) (US).

Loper v NY City Police Dep't, 999 F.2d 699, 704 (2d Cir. 1993) (US).

Police Dep't of City of Chicago v Mosley, 408 US 92, 95 (1972) (US).

R.A.V. v St. Paul, 505 US 377, 382 (1992) (US).

Speet v Schuette, __ F. Supp. 2d __, 2012 WL 3865394, *3–*4 (W.D. Mich. Aug. 24, 2012) (US).

Terminiello v City of Chicago, 337 US 1, 4 (1949) (US).

United States v Eichman, 496 US 310, 318–19 (1990) (US).

References

American Civil Liberties Union and Human Rights Watch (1993) *Human Rights Violations in the United States: A Report on US Compliance with the International Covenant on Civil and Political Rights*, American Civil Liberties Union and Human Rights Watch. Available at: http://www.hrw.org/sites/default/files/reports/US941.pdf.

Amnesty International (2012) 'Statistical Analysis of Deaths Following Police Taser Use (AMR 51/013/2012)', Amnesty International, London. Available at: http://www.amnesty.org/en/library/asset/AMR51/013/2012/en/6ac90938-73f2-41d3-aa08-bd971f2dffa0/amr510132012en.pdf.

Becker, H. (1963) *Outsiders: Studies in the Sociology of Deviance*, New York: The Free Press.

Bowling, B. (1999) 'The Rise and Fall of New York Murder: Zero Tolerance or Crack's Decline?' *British Journal of Criminology*, 39: 531–54.

Bradford, B. and Jackson, J. (2010) 'Trust and Confidence in the Police: A Conceptual Review', 29 September Available at: http://papers.ssrn.com/sol3/papers.cfm?abstract_id=1684508.

Bradford, B., Jackson, J. and Stanko, E. (2008) 'Contact and Confidence: Revisiting the Impact of Public Encounters with the Police', *Policing and Society*, 19(1): 20–46.

Bridenball, B. and Jesilow, P. (2008) 'What Matters: The Formation of Attitudes Toward the Police', *Police Quarterly*, 11(2).

Brunson, R. and Miller, J. (2006) 'Young Black Men and Urban Policing in the United States', *British Journal of Criminology*, 46(4): 613–40.

Bullock, K. and Johnson, P. (2012) 'The Impact of the Human Rights Act 1998 on Policing in England and Wales', *British Journal of Criminology*, 52(3): 630–50.

Chan, J. (1997) *Changing Police Culture: Policing in a Multi-cultural Society*, Cambridge: Cambridge University Press.

Chan, J. (2000) 'Backstage Punishment: Police Violence, Occupational Culture and Criminal Justice', in T. Coady, S. James, S. Miller and M. O'Keefe (eds), *Violence and Police Culture*, Melbourne: Melbourne University Press, pp. 85–108.

Crawshaw, R., Cullen, S. and Williamson, T. (2007) *Human Rights and Policing*, Leiden: Martinus Nijhoff.

Cunneen, C. (1998–9) 'Zero Tolerance Policing and the Experience of New York City', *Current Issues in Criminal Justice*, 10(3): 299–313.

Cunneen, C. (2001) *Conflict, Politics and Crime: Aboriginal Communities and the Police*, Sydney: Allen & Unwin.

Dai, M., Frank, J. and Sun, I. (2011) 'Procedural Justice During Police–Citizen Encounters: The Effects of Process-Based Policing on Citizen Compliance and Demeanor', *Journal of Criminal Justice*, 39(2): 159–68.

Equality and Human Rights Commission (2012) *Briefing Paper 5: Race Disproportionality in Stops and Searches under Section 60 of the Criminal Justice and Public Order Act 1994*, London: Equality and Human Rights Commission.

Fenwick, H. (2009) 'Marginalising Human Rights: Breach of the Peace, "Kettling", the Human Rights Act and Public Protest', *Public Law* 4: 737–65.

Hough, M. (2013) 'Procedural Justice and Professional Policing in Times of Austerity', *Criminology and Criminal Justice*, 13: 181–97.

House of Lords Select Committee on the Constitution (2009) *Surveillance, Citizens and the State*, 6 February. Available at: http://www.publications.parliament.uk/pa/ld200809/ldselect/ldconst/18/18.pdf.

Human Rights Committee (2009) *Consideration of Reports Submitted by States Parties under Article 40 of the Covenant: Concluding Observations of the Human Rights Committee*, CCPR/AUS/CO/5 7, Geneva: United Nations.

Human Rights Watch (1998) *Shielded from Justice: Police Brutality and Accountability in the United States*, New York: Human Rights Watch. Available at http://www.hrw.org/legacy/reports/reports98/police/uspo72.htm.

Jackson, J., Bradford, B., Stanko, B. and Hohl, K. (2013) *Just Authority? Trust in the Police in England and Wales*, London: Routledge.

Jefferson, T. (1990) *The Case against Paramilitary Policing*, Milton Keynes: Open University Press.

Kleinig, J. (1996) *The Ethics of Policing*, Cambridge: Cambridge University Press.

Lichtenstein, A. (2013) 'Marikana, Part II: Looking for Answers to a South African Massacre', in *Los Angeles Review of Books*, Los Angeles, 4 January. Available at: http://lareviewofbooks.org/review/marikana-part-ii-looking-for-answers-to-a-south-african-massacre/

Loader, I. (2000) 'Plural Policing and Democratic Governance', *Social and Legal Studies*, 9(3): 323–45.

Loader, I. and Walker, N. (2001) 'Policing as a Public Good: Reconstituting the Connections between Policing and the State', *Theoretical Criminology*, 5(1): 9–35.

McCulloch, J. (2004) 'Blue Armies, Khaki Police and the Cavalry on the New American Frontier: Critical Criminology for the 21st Century', *Critical Criminology*, 12(3): 309–26.

Muir, H. (2013) 'Metropolitan Police Still Institutionally Racist, Say Black and Asian Officers', *The Guardian*, 21 April 2013. Available at: http://www.theguardian.com/uk/2013/apr/21/metropolitan-police-institutionally-racist-black.

Muir, W.K. (1977) *Police: Streetcorner Politicians*, Chicago: University of Chicago Press.

New South Wales Ombudsman (2008) *The Use of Taser Weapons by the NSW Police Force: A Special Report to Parliament under Section 31 of the Ombudsman Act 1974*, Sydney: New South Wales Ombudsman.

New South Wales Ombudsman (2012) *How Are Taser Weapons Used by the NSW Police Force? A Special Report to Parliament under s. 31 of the Ombudsman Act 1974*, Sydney: New South Wales Ombudsman.

New South Wales Ombudsman (2013) *Ombudsman Monitoring of the Police Investigation into the Death of Roberto Laudisio-Curti: A Special Report to Parliament under s.161 of the Police Act 1990*, Sydney: New South Wales Ombudsman.

New South Wales (NSW) State Coroner (2012) 'Inquest into the Death of Roberto Laudisio Curti (File number 2012 / 00086603)', Sydney: New South Wales State Coroner. Available at: http://www.coroners.lawlink.nsw.gov.au/agdbasev7wr/_assets/coroners/m40160114/curti%20decision%2014%20nov%202012.pdf.

Neyroud, P. and Beckley, A. (2001) *Policing, Ethics and Human Rights*, Uffculme, Devon: Willan Publishing.

Parmar, A. (2011) 'Stop and Search in London: Counter-Terrorist or Counter-Productive?', *Policing and Society*, 21(4): 369—82.

Pickering, S., McCulloch, J. and Wright-Neville, D. (2008) *Counter-terrorism Policing: Community, Cohesion and Security*, New York: Springer.

Reiner, R. (2000) *The Politics of the Police*, 3rd edn, Oxford: Oxford University Press.

Risen, J. and Lichtblau, E. (2005) 'Bush Lets US Spy on Callers without Warrant', *The New York Times*, 16 December.

Schulhofer, S., Tyler, T. and Huq, A. (2011) 'American Policing at a Crossroads: Unsustainable Policies and the Procedural Justice Alternative', *The Journal of Criminal Law & Criminology*, 101(2): 335—74.

Sharp, D. and Atherton, S. (2007) 'To Serve and Protect? The Experience of Policing in the Community of Young People from Black and Other Ethnic Minority Groups', *British Journal of Criminology*, 47(5): 746—63.

Skogan, W. (2006) 'Asymmetry in the Impact of Encounters with Police', *Policing and Society*, 16(2): 99—126.

Skogan, W. (2009) 'Concern about Crime and Confidence in the Police: Reassurance or Accountability?', *Police Quarterly*, 12(3): 301—18.

Skolnik, J. and Fyfe, J. (1993) *Above the Law: Police and the Excessive Use of Force*, New York: Free Press.

Smith, A. and Marinner, C. (2005) 'Complaints Prompt Rail Staff Inquiry', *Sydney Morning Herald*, 19 March. Available at: http://www.smh.com.au/news/National/Complaints-prompt-rail-staff-inquiry/2005/03/18/1111086017193.html.

Stanley, E. (2004) 'Silencing torture', in Victoria University online *Human Rights Research Journal*. Available at: http://www.victoria.ac.nz/law/centres/nzcpl/publications/human-rights-research-journal/publications/vol-2/Stanley.pdf.

Sunshine, J. and Tyler, T. (2003) 'The Role of Procedural Justice and Legitimacy in Shaping Public Support for Policing', *Law and Society Review*, 37(3): 513—47.

Tyler, T. (1997) 'The Psychology of Legitimacy: A Relational Perspective on Voluntary Deference to Authorities', *Personality and Social Psychology Review*, 1(4): 323–45.

Waddington, P.A.J. (1993) 'The Case against Paramilitary Policing Considered', *British Journal of Criminology*, 33(3): 353–73.

Waddington, P.A.J. (1999) *Policing Citizens: Authority and Rights*, Abingdon: Routledge.

Wood, J. and Shearing, C. (2007) *Imagining Security*, Uffculme, Devon: Willan Publishing.

Wright, A. (2002) *Policing: An Introduction to Concepts and Practice*, Uffculme, Devon: Willan Publishing.

Zedner, L. (2006) 'Neither Safe nor Sound: The Perils and Possibilities of Risk', *Canadian Journal of Criminology and Criminal Justice*, 48(3): 423–34.

Zedner, L. (2007) 'Pre-crime and Post-criminology?', *Theoretical Criminology*, 11(2): 261–81.

CHAPTER 9

Criminal Courts

> **Key concepts**
> Fair trial right — Proportionality principle — Miscarriage of justice —
> Mandatory sentencing — Therapeutic jurisprudence — Restorative justice

9.1 Introduction

In the aftermath of the 15 April 2013 bombing at the Boston Marathon in the USA, with one suspect gunned down by police a few days later and another confined to a hospital bed, badly injured, the ongoing discussion was focused on the fact that what are known as the Miranda rights in the USA had not been read to the surviving suspect. This issue of the Miranda warning (the right to remain silent and have a lawyer present) had the USA holding its breath for a few days, debating whether the interest of public security should prevail over the individual rights of Dzhokhar Tsarnaev, a 19-year-old naturalized American citizen. Is the handling of a terrorist case by the domestic criminal justice system a reason not to apply a right guaranteed by the US Constitution and protected at the international level? Are immediate threats to public safety valid reasons to infringe human rights? The solution came to the US authorities in the form of a delayed reading of the Miranda rights, using the exception clause in relation to the collection of information on possible immediate threats to public safety.

The need for the Miranda warning was first established in the 1966 US Supreme Court case *Miranda v Arizona*. Incriminating evidence rendered by the suspect to police can be used by the prosecution in court only if the prosecutor can prove that the defendant, prior to interrogation in police custody, had been informed and showed understanding of the rights related to self-incrimination (that is, the right to silence) and of the right to consult with a defence lawyer. This right is closely linked to the International Covenant on Civil and Political Rights (ICCPR), Article 14(3:g); and the European Court of

Human Rights has since held that the rights against self-incrimination are 'generally recognised international standards which lie at the heart of the notion of a fair procedure under Article 6 [of the European Convention for the Protection of Human Rights]' (*Murray v UK* [1996] para 45).

The first exception to the Miranda principle occurred in 1984 (*New York v Quarles*), and was used to allow the prosecution to make use of the statements provided by a defendant when questioned by police on a matter related to the protection of public safety. In this case, a man accused of rape was believed to have on his person a loaded gun and this fact took priority over reading him his Miranda rights. The public safety exception was later also used in two US terrorist cases: the underwear bomber, Umar Farouk Abdulmutallab, in 2009; and the Times Square bomber, Faisal Shahzad, in 2010.

Emerging from the cases above is the important role invested in criminal courts in seeking to balance powers between the state and individuals or groups of people. Achieving an equitable balance between public expectations and recognition of human rights is a challenging task. The protection of individuals and collective groups from interference by the state during the criminal justice process is a foundational principle in Western legal systems. The right to life, liberty and security, the right to be free from arbitrary arrest and detention, the right to a fair trial, the right to be presumed innocent, and the right to freedom from torture and degrading treatment or punishment are embedded in many rules and statutes. And yet, other developments, such as victims' rights movements, popular punitivism and processes of securitization constantly challenge the capacity, reach and limits of the legal system. The issue of internal and external influences on the criminal justice process reflects how any form of decision-making is generally a product of competition between several diverging interests. How to prioritize these interests entails a process of compromise informed by the assimilation of higher values and principles as priorities over other competing interests. When the government declares it is pursuing certain objectives in the name of the public interest, we should question what portion of the public is represented. This direct way of expressing political opinion is filtered by the fact that the relationship between the electorate and the government's final decisions is rarely direct: political parties, pressure groups and, increasingly, transnational corporations, moderate this link (Hill in Alcock *et al.* 1998). This approach is also undermined by inequalities: we do not compete equally – some interests and groups are stronger than others. One need only think of the 2013 gun control debate in the USA led by President Barak Obama to appreciate how lobbies and transnational corporations can influence policy decisions.

This brings us back to the cases involving Miranda rights, mentioned earlier: is there ever a legitimate case to claim exception to a fundamental set of human rights? The shared legal values found in several Western criminal justice systems are informed by the principle of the right to life. Once we are bound, as we are, to this principle, the social order and productive functioning within these societies are shaped by this value. Shared sentiment, or collective conscience (Durkheim 1960 [1893]), is the glue that holds together a reality composed of many different elements (such as institutions, individuals, roles and values). The right to life is a shared value that can bring together different groups in the face of adversity. Principles such as the right to life create positive obligations to protect individuals. In the eyes of several international lawyers (Cassese 1990; Bassiouni 1993; Delmas-Marty and Summers 1995), the collective conscience is synchronized to fight injustice using the tool of human rights frameworks (however, see Lazarus (2012) on coercive duties and the right to security). And courts at the national and supranational levels are at the forefront of these progressive changes. While this chapter focuses on human rights protection as applied by criminal courts, civil remedies are also a fruitful arena that can be explored further (Friedmann and Barak-Erez 2001). Furthermore, alternative settings, such as Royal Commissions, are primary examples of the prioritization of human rights positive obligations over other socio-political factors in venues other than criminal courts.

9.2 The court's role

Whether a national or an international court, an inquisitorial or adversarial framework, in the criminal justice system the accused has to respond to allegations of criminal conduct by the state, represented by the judge. A case before a criminal court symbolically represents the state investigating and deciding on behalf of the people. The evidence is offered to build a narrative, a story intended to be the closest version to the truth. Examination and counter-examination of identified victims, witnesses and defendants are a representation of justice, to produce a prevailing narrative that should be shaped by the defendant's right to the presumption of innocence until proven otherwise. The resolution of the case is not the resolution of a dispute; often the court resolution can be a further exacerbation of underlying issues. Still, the courts are required to assert a normative order of events (Cotterrell 1984). Inevitably, this is a compromise between reality and what has been possible to establish in court, given its many constraints. These constraints may be internal or external to the court proceedings, and profoundly affect the outcome for the defendant. Such constraints limit the defendant's rights in both a covert and overt manner. Often identifying a link between these constraints and the breach of human rights is problematic, since such constraints are systemic. In recent years, however, we have seen a more critical reflection on the importance of human rights, such as the right to life, the right to liberty, the presumption of innocence and the right to a fair hearing. This has allowed us to highlight, and in part address, the ways in which the legal system produces denial or miscarriage of justice. This section explores this further by looking first at internal constraints, as those constraints on the full application of the law as a result of inevitable internal competitive demands; and then at the infringement on or obstacles to the application of the law in court as a result of external factors (external constraints), focusing on the proportionality principle.

9.2.1 Internal constraints

The right to a fair, public and impartial hearing within a reasonable time by an independent and impartial tribunal established by law is a basic principle proclaimed in Article 10 of the Universal Declaration of Human Rights (UDHR), Article 6 of the European Convention on Human Rights (ECHR), Article 8 of the American Convention on Human Rights, and Article 7 of the African Charter on Human and Peoples' Rights. Yet internal constraints, including those related to time and the management of backlogs, financial pressures, lack of personnel and organizational relationships, often limit the application of such a right.

Trial delays are common in many jurisdictions. For example, in Australia, research has shown that more than half of all criminal trials do not start on the listed day, and are often adjourned and relisted (Payne 2007). According to the Council of Europe (2010), 26.37 per cent of all European Court of Human Rights (ECtHR) cases between 1959 and 2009 involved an infringement of Article 6 of the ECHR concerning the length of proceedings – the highest proportion compared to other violations. Even if the average working day for judges is around 10 hours, and 9 hours for magistrates, with a quarter of magistrates' working days being longer than 11 hours (Mack *et al.* 2012), there seems to be insufficient time and resources to give adequate attention to each case.

Further, the judgement in cases is routinized and constrained by a number of other competing tasks and requirements of various court players (such as judges, prosecutors, defence lawyers and police), impacting on the impartial conduct of the court. Organizational relationships involve a complex combination of personal and professional interconnections among the key court players, which are often prioritized over establishing the events within a case or a link between facts, evidence and outcome. Prosecutorial decision-making powers have the capacity to influence the course and outcomes of a trial

(O'Brien 2009). However, such powers often receive little scrutiny (Zedner 2004), especially compared to police discretionary powers. Yet prosecutors' discretionary powers allow for the investigation of a case or interrogation of a suspect without many restrictions, and a prosecutor can also use such powers to refuse to co-operate with the defence and to delay a trial – all of which can have an enormous impact on the defendant and outcome of the case. This increases the inequalities generated by the criminal justice system, and the creation of alliances between powerful parties in the courts. The 1999 Standards of Professional Responsibility of the International Association of Prosecutors, linked directly to the UDHR and related instruments, advocate the proper ethical conduct of prosecutors, and that they should reflect on their role in shaping the adoption of human rights in the criminal justice system. These standards contain guiding principles for prosecutors related to professional conduct, independence, impartiality, and their role within criminal proceedings (for example, 'prosecutors shall perform their duties fairly, consistently and expeditiously', and co-operate with other parties). Yet, prosecutors' actions are frequently driven by a conviction of the defendant's guilt, and a belief that they are operating in the public interest, as well as by opportunistic determinations of whether a case will 'stand' in court (with rape and sexual assault cases providing evidence of this). Further, the close link between prosecutors and the police, the fact that evidence is collected by the police, and the lack of time and internal resources, can all limit the ability of the prosecutor to move forward independently. In such a complex scenario, the rights of suspects must be weighed against the many other expectations, compromises and demands that are intrinsic, normalized aspects of court life. The need for a speedy trial, even if guaranteed by international human rights (Bassiouni 1993), may be against the defendant's interests, in a scenario in which efficiency and crime control aims may be built around the concept of guilt (Packer 1968). This, in turn, compromises other important human rights, such as the right to a fair trial and the right to be presumed innocent until proven otherwise according to law and by a tribunal established by law.

The dynamics in court should also be shaped by fundamental rights such as the right to examination and counter-examination, and the right to evidence, rather than being dictated by the jurisdiction in which a case is heard and its domestic criminal laws. A universal understanding of human rights should mean that the difference in approaches to justice adopted across various geographic locations is tempered by a widely agreed need for consistent treatment of the defendant. During the hearing, the trial should be conducted in a way that respects the defendant's right to a public hearing, the right to an independent and impartial tribunal and juries, the right to adequate defence and free legal assistance, and the right to examine witnesses. The combination of these rights should inform the criminal proceedings within countries that are signatories to the UN conventions and other regional and national protocols. However, very often internal constraints, such as financial and other resource limitations, restrain the opportunity to make good use of such rights. For example, in Victoria, Australia, Supreme Court Chief Justice Marilyn Warren has recently complained that cuts to the legal aid budget have led to the rising occurrence of self-representation in cases of domestic violence in a context in which the Victorian Government has prioritized a crackdown on family violence. The over-policing and consequent increased rates of prosecution in this area have generated a demand for legal aid assistance among an unanticipated number of defendants – a demand that cannot be met by legal aid staff because of budgetary cuts (Lee 2012).

Further, the right to a fair trial is often obscured by the formalities of the court. The language used in court and the requirements on defendants regarding their behaviour in court may limit their capacity to explain their position. Courtroom interaction is traditionally based on formal rules combined with an informal but internalized code of professional conduct known to more experienced legal practitioners. The way defendants, witnesses and experts interact in court influences how they are perceived by other parties, which is particularly significant if a jury is present. Issues of power, social status and privilege can affect the defendant's experience of the courtroom process, and can lead to misunderstandings or the silencing of already powerless parties. The impact of such issues on young defendants, or defendants from lower socio-economic, indigenous or foreign-speaking language backgrounds can be enormous. How can a defendant be given a fair trial when he or she does not understand the proceedings, or have limited control over them? The 1999 Bulger case is exemplary here. In this case, two-year-old James Bulger was abducted, tortured and murdered by two 10-year-old boys. Here, the ECtHR highlighted how obscure adult court dynamics can impair young defendants' access to a fair trial and therefore access to an adequate defence (*V v UK* and *T v UK*).

Further, the male-dominated internal culture of the legal profession contributes to the construction of the victim as 'deserving', often via a judge's commentary or a defence lawyer's strategies of cross-examination. This is seen in particular in cases of sexual assault; the case of *R v Middendorp* before the Victorian Supreme Court (Australia), as discussed by Tyson (2011), is an example of a male judge trivializing the tragic event of the female victim's death at the hands of a male perpetrator after years of domestic violence:

When sentencing the defendant, His Honour described the defendant's act in killing his ex-partner a 'foolish act' committed against a 'troubled young woman' (*R v Middendorp* [2010] VSC 202 per Byrne J:[17]). Comments such as these only serve to minimise the significance of the death threats and a prior history of domestic violence perpetrated against the woman victim. (Tyson 2011: 218)

The isolation and silencing of indigenous defendants and witnesses in court are further examples of how the right to a fair trial may be compromised. Despite widespread awareness of Aboriginal over-representation in the criminal justice system – for example, in Canada (Rudin 2007) and Australia (Eades 2008) – hegemonic court practices persist.

The power differentials and formalities of court proceedings represent legal impediments to the creation of a court narrative that resembles the true sequence of events. The masculinity and racial bias of the legal system are transcendental elements that influence the outcome of court cases and are intrinsic to a way of thinking that appears to be 'against human rights', but which are difficult to discuss in precise terms in order to bring about change. Rather, these issues engender ongoing debates, which require the input of internal participants to the criminal justice process as well as scholars: the human rights lens can offer an anchor with which to focus on values and principles that have already been embraced, albeit informally, in the criminal justice process.

9.2.2 External constraints: proactive judiciary and securitization processes

External constraints also exert a significant influence on court proceedings and can contribute to the infringement of human rights. The Bulger case mentioned above received an enormous amount of media attention and generated a public outcry. The desire to be seen to be 'taking a stand' was felt strongly at all levels of the criminal justice system, from the police to prosecutors and judges. This example reveals how the public, media and political response can generate concerns that have the capacity to override the human rights linked to criminal proceedings that are usually applicable to the defendant. This point has become more evident in recent years as external processes of securitization have influenced the sentencing process increasingly, or have strengthened the platform from which to criticize the proactive role of the judiciary in sentencing in favour of defendants' human rights rather than prioritizing the safety of the public. This section begins with a discussion of the proactive role of the judiciary in a networked society, and then considers the influence of external agencies on the sentencing process and the proportionality test.

A judge bound to the rule of law and to performing his/her duties in line with human rights (as per the 2002 UN Bangalore Principles of Judicial Conduct) comes to a conclusion based on a case-by-case approach (for example, guilty or not guilty) in the exercise of discretionary power, as is the case for judicial decisions on possible penalties if a guilty verdict follows. Judges from both national and international courts have been criticized for making use of sovereign powers in sentencing beyond statutory agreements (Malleson and Russell 2006). This process of judicialization (Tate and Vallinder 1995) has been informed and empowered directly by international human rights. In the emergent New World Order, which has contributed to the construction of a global legal system (Slaughter 2004), international and domestic judges are increasingly sharing experiences of legal practice, even in an area – criminal law and proceedings – that is still dominated by a rigid interpretation of the Westphalia concept of the nation-state and territorially bound sovereignty. Senior domestic judges are contributing to the development of a 'global community of Human Rights Law' (Slaughter 2004: 79), via a process of cross-fertilization. The extent of these developments has meant that judicial decision-making has been informed by a desire to bring uniformity in opposition to the arbitrariness of territoriality – representing an ongoing attempt to reduce justice by geography through a more uniform interpretation of human rights within criminal proceedings and criminal law. Successful examples of this search for a homogenous approach to human rights can be found in Western Europe, where the courts of the European Union and Council of Europe have been working towards this aim for over 40 years. In Europe, we see more examples of domestic judges bypassing their own governments to look at case law developed by supranational courts with a view to incorporating those principles into their rulings.

In other regional areas, the situation is more complex as a result of cultural-political circumstances. In the USA, for example, we have seen the Supreme Court divided between taking a proactive role in embracing international laws, and following the nation's traditional domestic-focused interpretation of the law. Sometimes this contrast is evident in the same court case, such as in the 2006 *Hamdan v Rumsfeld*. This case concerned the military commission established by the administration of George W. Bush, which had jurisdiction over Guantanamo Bay detainees, among whom was included the defendant, Salim Ahmed Hamdan, charged with terrorist conspiracy. In this case, Justice Stevens made an open and positive reference to the international principles of due process, in particular that judgment ought to be pronounced by a regularly constituted court. In contrast, Justice Scalia returned the focus to an original interpretation of the law as domestic development. With much historical significance, the case symbolizes this country's greater willingness to adopt a broader commitment to international legislation, in particular the 1949 Geneva Conventions on the wartime rights of prisoners.

Other judges in senior domestic courts around the world have also had opportunities to reflect on their role in a globalized society that supports human rights. The positioning of the former Chief Justice of Israel, Aharon Barak (a Holocaust survivor from Lithuania), has been rather powerful in those cases where suspects were subjected to moderate physical pressure to obtain information that can save lives (famously known as the 'ticking bomb scenario'). In the 1999 court case *Public Committee Against Torture v The State of Israel*, Judge Barak embraced a categorical defence of individual rights. This approach was framed by former South African judge, Richard Goldstone – renowned for undermining apartheid within the South African legal system and for being the first chief prosecutor of the UN International Criminal Tribunal for the former Yugoslavia (ICTY) and for Rwanda – as 'uncompromising' (2006; see also critique in Mann and Shatz 2010).

Criminal sentencing is an area that is being investigated increasingly via a human rights lens. Penalties are decided against the test of proportionality: a compromise among the right of freedom and the right to privacy, the certainty of penalty, and other rights. However, the aims of sentencing (deterrence, retribution and rehabilitation) are influenced heavily by external agents. For example, external agencies, such as executives, can limit the range of punishment, decisions on which historically have been left to judicial discretionary powers (with some statutory limits), breaching in many cases the proportionality principle. This explains why stealing three golf clubs (worth US$399 apiece in this case) under California's Three Strikes Law can translate into a 25-years-to-life sentence (*Ewing v California* 2003). It also explains why, under US federal law on mandatory minimum sentences, a judge is forced to impose a minimum 10-year sentence for the possession of a kilogram of heroin, whereas in the UK a similar offender would receive a maximum sentence of six months, according to De la Vega *et al.* (2012). How this can be reconciled with human rights is a matter no longer left to the judiciary, since the desire of government to be seen to be taking a stand on street crime is increasingly prevailing over other values and principles.

Such external constraints and interference in the sentencing process do not reflect a geographically isolated trend. In civil law countries, such as many European countries with continental legal systems, and increasingly in common law countries, using statutory enforcement, the state has attempted to limit progressively judicial discretionary powers (see Box 9.1).

Examples of this approach, however, reveal an impoverishment of judicial discretionary powers in many countries. The mandatory sentencing in

---

Box 9.1   Mandatory sentencing in the Northern Territory (Australia): an extract from Hansard

Anyone with a working knowledge of teenage culture knows that shoplifting is not an uncommon behavioural pattern. Indeed, I have known over the years of school students from very well-connected families who needed naught by way of material possessions but were caught shoplifting for the thrill of it. Under Northern Territory laws, such offenders would not be subject to mandatory detention, nor should they. Nor will tourists, kids from well-off family circumstances or perhaps the good burgher's wife in the Territory face mandatory detention for stealing a can of coke or a bottle of spring water, even if it is their second or third offence. Ways will be found to circumvent penalties for such transgressions.

But that was not the case for an Aboriginal youth from Bagot community at Ludmilla in the Northern Territory who was sent to jail for 28 days as a 17-year-old adult, by Territory definition, for receiving a bottle of spring water to the value of [Australian]$1 which had been received by means of a crime, namely stealing, knowing it to have been so obtained. Indisputably these laws are biased, unstated but very clear, if you scratch the skin, against the indigenous population. Why, even if it is the fourth, fifth, 10th or 20th offence, are we jailing for 28 days or even one day the young woman on this charge sheet from Argulluck Camp, Oenpelli, Northern Territory for receiving two litres of unleaded petrol worth [Australian]$2, knowing it to be stolen? Why are we jailing any person whose need of petrol is a sniffing dependency? We are simply locking away the problem.

Source: House of Representatives Hansard of 10 April 2000. Used with permission.

Australia, as in the USA, has produced absurd situations that have been criticized by the UN. A UN legal opinion argued that Australia's mandatory sentencing laws violate both the ICCPR and the Convention on the Rights of the Child.

In the UK, the anti-social behavioural package introduced with the Crime and Disorder Act 1998 brought a new level of limitation on the proportionality principle, in effect diminishing the fundamental rights of the defendant to a fair trial. The Act implemented a number of initiatives, including:

- curfew orders (dusk-to-dawn curfews on all children aged under 10);
- anti-social behaviour orders (ASBOs) (on children aged 10 and over, for behaviour that 'causes alarm, distress or harassment to one or more people not in the same household');

- parenting orders (on parents responsible if curfews or ASBOs are breached, involving training or counselling for parents); and
- child safety orders (on children under the age of 10 deemed to be 'at risk' of criminal or anti-social behaviour, involving supervision by the 'responsible officer').

ASBOs have been applied to a number of young people whose behaviour has ranged from 'being rude to members of the public', littering and 'urban exploration', to vandalism. An ASBO is an order of the court in civil proceedings regarding 'how to behave', and its breach is an automatic criminal offence, to be tried in a criminal court: this is clearly an infringement of the proportionality test. Home Office data suggests that 57.3 per cent of ASBOs were breached between 2000 and 2011 (Ministry of Justice 2012). Even though ASBOs have recently been replaced with 'community-based' social control policies, the essence of an executive limitation on judicial discretionary power remains. These types of orders breach a number of human rights, from the right to a fair trial to the right to privacy; and because they may remain in force 'until further notice', these orders also breach the legal certainty principle.

Further, these limits to judicial discretionary powers exacerbate an issue that has already been considered problematic in a normal court setting: the intersection of multiple demographic or socio-cultural factors, which has always had an impact on the sentencing process. For example, if we consider race and ethnicity: in 2010, for each white person in a US prison, there were 2.5 Hispanic/Latino people and 5.8 black people (NCJ 2011). In England and Wales, 'black prisoners make up 15 per cent of the prisoner population and this compares with 2.2 per cent of the general population' (Equality and Human Rights Commission 2010, no page number). Sentencing guidelines

---

Box 9.2   A few examples of ASBOs

Take a few recent examples [of ASBOs]. A 23-year-old woman who repeatedly threw herself into the [river] Avon was served with an ASBO banning her from jumping into rivers or canals. A man with mental health problems was banned from sniffing petrol anywhere in Teesside. A woman living on an estate in East Kilbride was given an ASBO ordering her not to be seen wearing her underwear at her window or in her garden. The local ASBO unit handed out diaries to her neighbours to record when she was seen in her underwear, giving a new meaning to neighbourhood watch. (Foot 2005)

for judges were introduced with a view to limiting discretionary powers and discriminatory outcomes in response to such issues.

Yet policies aimed at incapacitating offenders and populist policy that have inspired approaches aimed at limiting judicial discretionary powers have aggravated this problem further. And this issue is becoming more evident with the targeting of subjects classified as problematic. The pre-emptiveness of such labelling of criminals before trial serves to justify the usefulness of (pre-emptive) action in the public interest, rather than the protection of individual civil liberties.

Inevitably, the running of the court and the sentencing process are influenced in either a direct or indirect manner by external socio-political agendas. In the twenty-first century, the politics surrounding courts have largely been dominated by crime control policies, which have in turn been influenced by penal populism (Pratt 2007). These policies are aimed at people who can be categorized as 'others' rather than ordinary citizens (Pratt 2007: 96), and at bringing unity to the constituency against what is constructed as different socio-politically.

In recent years, we have witnessed an increased drive by the executive to normalize the exclusion and punishment of those people framed as outsiders. Processes of securitization include international state immunity, which Mann and Shatz (2010) call 'un-prosecution': revealing the emerging gap between the law and executive power that is capitalized on by the immediacy of 'national interests'. This is a grey area where the rule of law cannot find application because it does not appear under the radar of a public prosecutor or a court established by law. Relevant to this is the 'promise not to talk' extracted from individuals who have been subjected to (unlawful) detention at Guantanamo Bay. Two such cases, that of British citizen Binyam Mohamed (2009) and Australian David Hicks (2007), with two different outcomes, reveal examples of un-prosecution. As part of their plea bargain, both individuals were asked to confess to terrorism crimes, to deny having been tortured by the state and to promise not to talk about any aspects of their imprisonment. Binyam Mohamed did not agree to the plea bargain, did not plead guilty and returned to Britain in 2009 with no charges filed against him. David Hicks entered into a plea bargain (an Alford plea) based on charges of providing material support for terrorism and served the final part of his prison time in Australia; and a condition of his plea included a suspension of the right to approach the media for a given period of time (see Box 9.3).

Similarly, targeted killing is furthering un-prosecution by eliminating undesirable subjects without allowing them access to justice or individual civil liberties, effectively rendering the court system redundant and undermining the

Box 9.3   Charge sheet for David Hicks issued in 2007 while imprisoned by the US Guantanamo military commission from 2001 to 2007

CHARGE SHEET		
I. PERSONAL DATA		

1. NAME OF ACCUSED:
DAVID MATTHEW HICKS

2. ALIASES OF ACCUSED:
a/k/a "David Michael Hicks," a/k/a "Abu Muslim Australia," a/k/a "Abu Muslim Austraili," a/k/a "Abu Muslim Philippine," a/k/a "Muhammad Dawood"

3. ISN NUMBER OF ACCUSED (LAST FOUR):
0002

II. CHARGES AND SPECIFICATIONS

4. CHARGE: VIOLATION OF SECTION AND TITLE OF CRIME IN PART IV OF M.M.C.

SPECIFICATION:

See Attached Charges and Specifications.

III. SWEARING OF CHARGES

5a. NAME OF ACCUSER (*LAST, FIRST, MI*)	5b. GRADE	5c. ORGANIZATION OF ACCUSER
Tubbs, II, Marvin, W.	O-4	Office of the Chief Prosecutor, OMC

5d. SIGNATURE OF ACCUSER	5e. DATE (*YYYYMMDD*)
	20070202

AFFIDAVIT: Before me, the undersigned, authorized by law to administer oath in cases of this character, personally appeared the above named accuser the __2nd__ day of __February__, __2007__, and signed the foregoing charges and specifications under oath that he/she is a person subject to the Uniform Code of Military Justice and that he/she has personal knowledge of or has investigated the matters set forth therein and that the same are true to the best of his/her knowledge and belief.

Kevin M. Chenail	Office of the Chief Prosecutor, OMC
Typed Name of Officer	*Organization of Officer*

O-5	Commissioned Officer, U.S. Marine Corps
Grade	*Official Capacity to Administer Oath* (See R.M.C. 307(b) must be commissioned officer)
Signature	

MC FORM 458 JAN 2007

Blocks I through IV of this MC Form 458, including the continuation sheets for Block II, are duplicate originals, replacing misplaced originals.

basic right to life. Targeted killing is the premeditated elimination of an individual, often executed extra-territorially by a state, outside a battlefield, and therefore in contravention of the Geneva Convention. The elimination of targets is justified by immediate threats that the person poses to the state and its people. The killing of Osama bin Laden in 2011, much celebrated in the USA, engendered an infantilized reaction on the part of media celebrities (Younge 2011).

Unfortunately, this event also signalled an escalation of further initiatives (such as the Obama administration Tuesday 'kill-list' meetings – see Becker and Shane 2012) assisted by new forms of technology, such as combat drones. This process is one of many that have entailed a narrative around the need to protect the public through the enforcement of regulations that require no, or minimal, interventions by the courts. If an authority decides to enforce a rule by which the suspect's rights are below UN standards on human rights, the court can – and should – intervene. Any other solution constitutes a mere tactic of political survival, which can be minimized with the development of a more coherent foreign policy.

9.3 Therapeutic jurisprudence (TJ), restorative justice and 'problem-solving' courts

Reflection on the barriers formal court settings can pose for the fairness of proceedings and their outcome has informed considerations about the effects of the law on the parties involved. The law can produce harmful effects for people directly or indirectly involved in a court case (anti-therapeutic effects). Since the 1990s legal practitioners and scholars have reflected on how the law can be used in a therapeutic manner to produce better results for the defendants and other parties, such as victims. Originally, therapeutic jurisprudence (TJ) was considered in relation to cases involving individuals with a form of mental impairment, as a way of recognizing the needs generated by what are deemed to be exceptional circumstances. Within this context, the UN Convention on the Rights of Persons with Disabilities, adopted in December 2006, encapsulates the spirit of the right to life and to dignity for those groups who so often become the forgotten parties of the UDHR, with the UN underlining that 10 per cent of the world's population have some form of disability. An integral part of the 2006 Convention are rights related to access to a fair trial. Article 12 on equal recognition before the law, and Article 13 on access to justice are the key points that have direct application by police, courts and prisons. Perlin (2011) has discussed the ratification and application of this Convention to explore anti-discrimination law and to confront a shared history of mistreatment and marginalization.

Mental health, however, has raised wider questions, primarily regarding social attitudes towards normality in the criminal justice system, which have found broader application in problem-solving courts (Winick 2002). Problem-solving courts are specialized courts that aim to offer innovative responses to criminal activity by addressing the behaviour and socio-cultural conditions underlying a problem. Based on the positive results of drug treatment courts, other treatment courts have emerged, from youth courts, family (or domestic violence) courts, mental health courts, veterans' courts, and homelessness courts, to child abuse and neglect courts. Daicoff (2000) claims that TJ and problem-solving courts represent just some of the various possible ways to address holistically the law's impact on individuals. TJ has therefore evolved as an umbrella concept closely linked to restorative justice (Braithwaite 2002), and aimed at highlighting the impact of the law and legal and court proceedings on the social and psychological well-being of participating actors. While 'TJ remains normatively neutral in principle' (Schopp 1998: 666), restorative justice offers a further opportunity to involve all the parties in a reconciliatory process aimed at re-establishing some level of harmony. All of these mechanisms of justice reflect the underlying principles and values of human rights, because these approaches prioritize the restoration of human dignity, the inalienable rights of all individuals, access to justice, and freedom from external constraints, as per the 1993 Vienna Declaration and Programme of Action (VDPA) and the UDHR. Further, in 2002, the UN Economic and Social Council (ECOSOC) adopted the Basic Principles on the Use of Restorative Justice as a way to assist UN Member States to adopt and standardize restorative initiatives in their justice systems.

Closely linked to these principles is the importance of redistributing power among the participating parties in a court case, specifically to return power to the main agents (the defendants and victims) to tell their stories, to facilitate reparation. The aim is also to offer judges the flexibility to explore solutions together with the participants to prevent recurring court involvement (known as the revolving door effect).

Within a problem-solving framework, through a process of empowerment the defendant is 'coached' by the judge during the trial to take responsibility for the underlying problem (for example, mental health, family and domestic violence, or drug addiction) and its possible resolution. Judges are involved in motivating individuals to accept the help of services and make commitments (to apologise, for example). Judges reward each step made by the defendant towards success via progress monitoring visits. The role of the judge is thus demanding, both professionally and emotionally (Duffy 2011), and is being changed by these innovative approaches to justice. This has raised questions around whether the principles underpinning problem-solving courts conflict with the core values of the legal system – and of human rights principles – of due process and the rights of the defendant (Berman and Fox 2010). Consistency of treatment and equal access to opportunities – basic human rights principles – have also offered a platform for raising doubts about such approaches (Raine 2011).

The application of the law as a healing process and restorative justice ought to be influenced by human rights principles. The values of ensuring fairness in a trial, respect for difference, and the right to be treated with dignity are fundamental human rights principles that underpin this approach to the court system. Yet, rarely can a direct reference to human rights values be found (with a recent exception seen in Perlin 2011), unless it is framed within the context of restorative justice. TJ and restorative justice are innovative mechanisms that embrace the practicability of human rights values, entailing the easy translation of these abstract principles into the everyday practice of the court environment, with the aim of minimizing the negative impact of the law on subjects and reducing the prevalence of imprisonment, making it 'a last resort'. A closer look at the 2006 Compendium of UN Standards and Norms in Crime Prevention and Criminal Justice would suggest that any form of innovative justice has deep roots in UN human rights principles. This is especially evident in the importance given to self-determination in promoting positive behavioural change free from external constraints, for both victims and offenders.

Restorative processes should be used only where there is sufficient evidence to charge the offender, and with the free and voluntary consent of both victim and offender. Both parties should be able to withdraw such consent at any time during the process. Agreements should be arrived at voluntarily and should contain only reasonable and proportionate obligations (UN Compendium, Part 1, ch. 3, para. 7).

Self-determination underpins the UN Declaration on the Rights of Indigenous Peoples and the UN International Covenant on Economic, Social and Cultural Rights. Yet the collective need and anxiety that emerges in response to certain situations that attract media and political attention are prioritized, and the explorative mode surrounding TJ and restorative justice reverts quickly to professional justice or even stricter intervention. An example of this was seen in the Northern Territory Emergency Response, a militarized, executive-led response to numerous reported cases of child sexual abuse in Aboriginal communities in this regional area of Australia. As noted by King and Guthrie (2008), the 2007 Little Children Are Sacred report recommended an intervention inspired by therapeutic approaches; yet the report generated a media hysteria that led to coercive rather than consultative action on the part of the federal government – a reaction criticized by many, including the

UN Special Rapporteur, James Anaya (2010), for infringing individual auton-omy. King and Guthrie (2008) have reflected on the mismatch between the intention of the government and the militarized response, which resulted in an anti-therapeutic approach and a denial of rights with a negative legacy that will scar the people of this region.

9.4 Conclusion

This chapter has explored the role of the courts by using human rights as a lens to reflect on selected court dynamics. The adoption of human rights within the criminal justice process can help legal practitioners and scholars to identify values and principles that should find application at all times. The chapter also considered the internal and external constraints that limit the reach and capacity of human rights in the criminal justice system. Such constraints have been investigated by criminologists, but without explicit reference to human rights frameworks. Therapeutic jurisprudence and restorative justice are examples of this point: even if they clearly advance the human rights agenda, little reference to such positive obligations is made within these systems. Human rights can offer a common language and joint values across jurisdictions, and it is a legacy already shared by many judges, prosecutors and other legal practitioners of different tradi-tions, whether adversarial or inquisitorial, or from common law or civil law traditions.

Additional readings and materials

Christoffersen, J. and Rask Madsen, M. (2011) *The European Court of Human Rights: Between Law and Politics*, Oxford: Oxford University Press.

Conforti, B. and Francioni, F. (1997) *Enforcing International Human Rights in Domestic Courts*, The Hague: Martinus Nijhoff.

Fair Trials International website. This website contains up-to-date information on the infringement of fair trial right across the world, and interactive maps. Available at: http://www.fairtrials.net.

UN Bangalore Principles of Judicial Conduct 2002. Available at: http://www.unodc. org/pdf/crime/corruption/judicial_group/Bangalore_principles.pdf.

UN Basic Principles on the Use of Restorative Justice Programmes in Criminal Matters 2002. Available at: http://www.un.org/en/ecosoc/docs/2002/ resolution%202002-12.pdf.

UN Compendium of United Nations Standards and Norms in Crime Prevention and Criminal Justice 2006 (esp. Part 1, ch. 3). Available at: http://www. unodc.org/pdf/criminal_justice/Compendium_UN_Standards_and_Norms_ CP_and_CJ_English.pdf.

Court cases cited

Campbell and Fell v UK (1984) 4 E.H.R.R. 293 (UK).

Ewing v California, 538 US 11 (2003) (US).

Hamdan v Rumsfeld, 548 US 557 (2006) (US).

Miranda v Arizona, 384 US 436 (1966) (US).

Murray v UK, (1996) 22 EHRR 29, at para. [45] (ECtHR 1973) (UK).

New York v Quarles, 467 US 649 (1984) (US).

Public Committee Against Torture v Israel, CHAI 5100/94 [1999]) (Israel).

R v Middendorp [2010] VSC 202 per Byrne J:[17] (Australia).

V v United Kingdom Application no. 24888/94, and *T v United Kingdom* Application 24724/94, 16.12.99, European Court of Human Rights (Europe).

References

Alcock, P., Erskine, A. and May, M. (eds) (1998) *The Student's Companion to Social Policy*, Oxford: Blackwell.

Anaya, J. (2010) 'Observations on the Northern Territory Emergency Response in Australia', United Nations Special Rapporteur on the Situation of Human Rights and Fundamental Freedoms of Indigenous People, UN General Assembly

Bassiouni, C. (1993) 'Human Rights in the Context of Criminal Justice: Identifying International Procedural Protections and Equivalent Protections in National Constitutions', *Duke Journal of Comparative and International Law*, 3: 235—97.

Becker, J. and Shane, S. (2012) 'Secret "kill list" Proves a Test of Obama's Principles and Will', *New York Times*, 29 May. Available at: http://www.nytimes.com/2012/05/29/world/obamas-leadership-in-war-on-al-qaeda.html?pagewanted=all&_r=0.

Berman, G. and Fox, A. (2010) 'The Future of Problem-Solving Justice: An International Perspective', *University of Maryland Law Journal of Race, Religion, Gender and Class*, 10(1): 1—24.

Braithwaite, J. (2002) 'Restorative Justice and Therapeutic Jurisprudence', *Criminal Law Bulletin*, 38(2): 244—62.

Cassese, A. (1990) *Human Rights in a Changing World*, Philadelphia, PA: Temple University Press.

Cotterrell, R. (1984) *The Sociology of Law: An Introduction*, London: Butterworths.

Council of Europe (2010) *The European Court of Human Rights: 50 Years of Activity — Some Facts and Figures*, Strasbourg: Public Relations Unit. Available at: http://www.echr.coe.int/Documents/Facts_Figures_1959_2009_ENG.pdf.

Daicoff, S. (2000) 'The Role of Therapeutic Jurisprudence within the Comprehensive Law Movement', in D. P. Stolle, D. B. Wexler and B. J. Winick (eds), *Practicing Therapeutic Jurisprudence*, Durham, NC: Carolina Academic Press.

de la Vega C., Solter, A., Kwon, S. and Isaac, D. (2012) *Cruel and Unusual US Sentencing Practices in a Global Context*, San Francisco: University of San Francisco School of Law.

Delmas-Marty, M. and Summers, M. A. (eds) (1995) *The Criminal Process and Human Rights: Toward a European Consciousness*, Dordrecht: Martinus Nijhoff.

Duffy, J. (2011) 'Problem-solving Courts, Therapeutic Jurisprudence and the Constitution: If Two Is Company, Is Three a Crowd?', *Melbourne University Law Review*, 35(2): 394–425.

Durkheim, E. (1960 [1893]) *The Division of Labor in Society*, trans. G. Simpson, New York: The Free Press.

Eades, D. (2008) 'Telling and Retelling Your Story in Court: Questions, Assumptions, and Intercultural Implications', *Current Issues in Criminal Justice*, 20(2): 209–30.

Equality and Human Rights Commission (2010) *How Fair Is Britain?* Available at: http://www.equalityhumanrights.com/key-projects/how-fair-is-britain/.

Foot, M. (2005) 'A Triumph of Hearsay and Hysteria', *The Guardian*, 5 April.

Friedmann, D. and Barak-Erez, D. (Eds) (2001) *Human Rights in Private Law*, Oxford: Hart Publishing.

Goldstone, R. (2006) 'Combating Terrorism: Zero Tolerance for Torture', *Case Western Reserve Journal of International Law*, 37(2/3): 343–8.

King, M. and Guthrie, R. (2008) 'Therapeutic Jurisprudence, Human Rights and the Northern Territory Emergency Intervention', *Precedent*, 89: 39–41.

Lazarus, L. (2012) 'Positive Obligations and Criminal Justice: Duties to Protect or Coerce', in J. Roberts and L. Zedner (eds), *Principled Approaches to Criminal Law and Criminal Justice: Essays in Honour of Professor Andrew Ashworth*, Oxford: Oxford University Press.

Lee, J. (2012) 'Right to Fair Trial at Risk: Judge', *The Age*, 5 December. Available at: http://www.theage.com.au/victoria/right-to-fair-trial-at-risk-judge-20121204-2atcv.html.

Mack, K., Wallace, A. and Roach Anleu, S. L. (2012) *Judicial Workload: Time, Tasks and Work Organisation*, Melbourne: Australian Institute of Judicial Administration.

Malleson, K. and Russell, P. (eds) (2006) *Appointing Judges in an Age of Judicial Power: Critical Perspectives from Around the World*, Toronto, ON: University of Toronto Press.

Mann, I. and Shatz, O. (2010) 'The Necessity Procedure: Laws of Torture in Israel and Beyond, 1987–2009', *Unbound: Harvard Journal of the Legal Left*, 6: 59–110.

Ministry of Justice (2012) *Statistical Notice: Anti-Social Behaviour Order (ASBO) Statistics England and Wales 2011*. Available at: https://www.gov.uk/government/uploads/system/uploads/attachment_data/file/116702/asbo11snr.pdf.

NCJ (National Criminal Justice) (2011) *Correctional Population in the United States at June 30, 2010*, US Department of Justice NCJ, Bulletin no 236319.

O'Brien, B. (2009) 'Recipe for Bias: An Empirical Look at the Interplay between Institutional Incentives and Bounded Rationality in Prosecutorial Decision Making', *Missouri Law Review*, 1016–50.

Packer, H. (1968) *The Limits of the Criminal Sanction*, Stanford, CA: Stanford University Press.

Payne, J. (2007) 'Criminal Trial Delays in Australia: Trial Listing Outcomes', Research and Public Policy Series, No. 74, Canberra: Australian Institute of Criminology.

Perlin, M. (2011) *International Human Rights and Mental Disability Law: When the Silenced Are Heard*, New York: Oxford University Press.

Pratt, J. (2007) *Penal Populism*, Abingdon: Routledge.

Raine, J. (2011) 'Community Justice and the Courts: A Step Forwards, Backwards or Sideways?', in K. Doolin, J. Child, J. Raine and A. Beech (eds), *Whose Criminal Justice?: State or Community?*, Hook, Hants: Waterside Press, pp. 173—86.

Rudin, J. (2007) *Aboriginal Peoples and the Criminal Justice System*. Available at: http://www.attorneygeneral.jus.gov.on.ca/inquiries/ipperwash/policy_part/research/pdf/Rudin.pdf.

Schopp, R. (1998) 'Integrating Restorative Justice and Therapeutic Jurisprudence', *Revista Juridica Universidad de Puerto Rico*, 67: 665—9.

Slaughter, A. (2004) *A New World Order*, Princeton, NJ: Princeton University Press.

Tate, N. and Vallinder, T. (eds) (1995) *The Global Expansion of Judicial Power*, New York: New York University.

Tyson, D. (2011) 'Victoria's New Homicide Laws: Provocative Reforms or More Women "Asking for It"?', *Current Issues in Criminal Justice*, 23(2): 203—35.

Winick, B. (1999) 'Therapeutic Jurisprudence and the Civil Commitment Hearing', *Journal of Contemporary Legal Issues*, 10: 37—60.

Winick, B. (2002) 'Therapeutic Jurisprudence and Problem Solving Courts', *Fordham Urban Law Journal*, 30(3): 1055—90.

Younge, G (2011) Osama bin Laden's Death: The US Patriot Reflex', *The Guardian*, 3 May Available at: http://www.guardian.co.uk/commentisfree/2011/may/03/bin-laden-death-us-patriot-reflex.

Zedner, L. (2004) *Criminal Justice*, Oxford: Oxford University Press.

CHAPTER 10

Detention

Key concepts

Deprivation of liberty — Torture — Cruel, unusual and inhumane punishment — Degrading treatment — Unlawful detention — Prisoners as citizens — The right to vote — Privatization — Women in prison — Scandinavian exceptionalism

10.1 Introduction

The deprivation of liberty; the inherent human right of detainees to be treated with dignity, humanity and respect; protections against torture, cruel and other degrading treatment and punishment; and prohibitions against the arbitrary taking of life, are all foundational human rights concerns. The haunting images and testimony of the survivors of concentration camps, the more recent revelations of torture in Abu Ghraib, the reports of conditions in labour camps in North Korea, and the accounts of those imprisoned at Guantanamo Bay detention camp remind us of the shocking inhumanity that results from abuses in the exercise of state power against those deprived of liberty.

Yet, on a day-to-day level, in prisons and immigration detention centres in countries all over the world, routine administrative practices and poor conditions mean that the violation of human rights of those individuals in detention has become routinized. Commentators such as Christie (1994), Parenti (1999), Carlton (2006), Scraton and McCulloch (2006) and Easton (2011), among many others, have highlighted the systematic abuse and degradation of those incarcerated in prison regimes.

In some liberal democracies, the punitive politics of the 1980s has led to a rapid rise in prison numbers in countries such as the USA, the UK, Australia and New Zealand (Lacey 2008; Easton 2011). Lacey notes that, at the peak of this mass detention, the incarceration rate across the developed world ranged, per 100,000 population, from 36 in Iceland to 737 in the USA (2008: 27). The USA has led the charge in expanding crime control (Currie 1998; Garland 2001a, 2001b) and in governing through crime (Simon 2007). By 2009, the US prison population was eight times higher than it had been in 1970, and by December 2008 it exceeded 2.3 million, compared to 1.2 million in 1990 (Easton 2011: 1). The USA also has large numbers of individuals on parole and on probation (Easton 2011: 1), and racialized moral panics about drugs and street crime have seen an exponential rise in the numbers of Afro-American and Hispanic youth in detention. In Australia, Indigenous Australians are overrepresented in prisons and youth detention centres (see Chapter 4). In many countries, prisons are overcrowded – for example, in Haiti, the occupancy rate is 335 per cent over capacity; in Italy the rate is 140.4 per cent; in the UK 107.7 per cent; but, in contrast, in Sweden the rate is just 92 per cent (ICPS 2013). And in other countries, migrant communities and communities deemed to be living on society's fringes are the targets of punitive law-and-order campaigns, heavy policing and mass imprisonment (Currie 1998; Young 1999; Lacey 2008). Those in detention are characterized as dangerous, risky and deserving of harsh punishment, and prisons have become warehouses – places to incapacitate, contain and manage inmates rather than to reform or even to deter them from crime (Lacey 2008). In some societies, the fear of others has also led to a willingness to accept increasing violations of human rights in the name of public safety (Lacey 2008).

In addition to this punitive shift, global crises, poverty, political repression, and the devastation in countries such as Afghanistan, Iraq and Sri Lanka have led to growing numbers of displaced persons seeking refuge in other countries, and being placed in immigration detention. The demonization of 'the other', Lacey argues, has led in effect to a penal apartheid and a need for ever more incapacitating penal policies (2008).

This chapter explores selected issues relating to human rights and detention. It focuses mainly on criminal justice detention but also considers examples from administrative detention. It provides information on relevant human rights instruments, and questions why we continue to permit the violation of the rights of people incarcerated in our institutions. The chapter examines how the state's duty of care towards prisoners and other persons under its authority is often undermined in the pursuit of other ideological goals, such as the need to exact punishment, bolster securitization or increase electoral popularity, and asks why detainees are seen to be less deserving of rights and protection than the rest of the population.

10.2 Rights of individuals deprived of their liberty

The people who are classed as being deprived of their liberty by the state comprise the following: those convicted of criminal offences and incarcerated; individuals charged with offences and not convicted but are placed in custody; political prisoners and prisoners of conscience or religion; undocumented migrants and asylum seekers placed in administrative detention; victims of crime who are placed in detention; individuals considered to be in need of care and protection; scheduled psychiatric patients; and persons with intellectual or physical disabilities who are placed in institutions. The United Nations Human Rights Council (UNHRC) has argued that human rights protection should also extend to prevent corporal punishment in schools, and teaching and medical institutions (UNHRC GC No. 20 1992, para. 5), and to situations in which medical experimentation is conducted without consent (ibid., para. 7).

Despite what some governments might wish, all persons deprived of their liberty continue to be protected by foundational human rights instruments that are universal and indivisible. Moreover, the UNHRC has made it clear that prisoners are to enjoy all the rights set out in the International Covenant on Civil and Political Rights (ICCPR), and that those deprived of liberty should enjoy the same rights as those of a free person, and only be subject to 'restrictions that are unavoidable in a closed environment' (UNHRC GC No. 21, para. 3).

Alongside the universal protections offered by human rights conventions there are also specific provisions, guidelines and standards in international treaties that relate to persons deprived of their liberty. The two key UN Articles are seen to be Article 7 and Article 10 of the ICCPR, which are generally read together. Article 7 refers to the right not to be subjected to torture or to cruel, inhuman or degrading treatment or punishment, and Article 10 states that it is the 'right of all persons deprived of liberty to be treated with humanity and with respect for the inherent dignity of the human person'. The UNHRC General Comment No. 20 and UNHRC General Comment No. 21 provide further guidance on the interpretation of Articles 7 and 10 of the ICCPR. Article 1 of the UN Convention against Torture and Other Cruel, Inhuman or Degrading Treatment or Punishment (CAT) defines torture and incorporates the prohibition of extradition of individuals to states where they might be tortured. The UN Committee against Torture was set up in 1988 to audit State Party actions and ensure compliance. The Optional Protocol attached to CAT was adopted in 2002 and introduced in 2006, with the intention of enabling the inspection and monitoring of detention facilities. In 2007, a Subcommittee to the Optional Protocol was established, with the remit of working with States Parties to develop initiatives, advice and guidance on the prevention of torture. In this regard, the Universal Declaration of Human Rights (UDHR) Article 5 states that 'No one shall be subjected to torture or to cruel, inhuman or degrading treatment or punishment.' General Comment 21 also states that the material resources available to the state should not impact on the treatment of those deprived of their liberty (UNHRC GC No. 21, para. 4).

The Standard Minimum Rules for the Treatment of Prisoners were adopted in 1957 and Principle 6 states that torture is not permissible in any circumstances. Article 10.3 of the ICCPR states that the principal aim of the penitentiary system should be the reformation and social rehabilitation of prisoners, and, by implication, not further punishment. Articles 10 and 7 have been seen by the UNHRC to impose positive obligations on states not to inflict any hardship or constraint on those deprived of their liberty other than that resulting from the deprivation of liberty itself. UNHRC General Comment No. 21 at para. 11 states that no penitentiary should be based purely on retribution, and 'should seek the reformation and social rehabilitation of the prisoner'. This Comment emphasizes how important it is for States Parties to indicate in their reports to the Committee what measures are being taken to 'provide teaching, re-education, vocal guidance and training and work programmes for prisoners inside and outside the penitentiary'. Article 10.2(a) of the ICCPR calls for the segregation and separate treatment of convicted and unconvicted offenders, except in exceptional circumstances.

Other key Articles of the ICCPR that relate to prisons and detention include the procedural rights of Articles 14, 15 and 16; Article 8 on the right not to be held in slavery or servitude or to perform forced or compulsory labour; Article 9 on the right to liberty and security of the person; Article 17 on the right not to be subject to arbitrary interference with privacy, family, home or correspondence; Article 19 on the right to hold opinions without interference, and freedom of expression; Article 25 on the right to take part in the conduct of public affairs and the right to vote; and Article 26 on the right to equality and to non-discrimination, among many others.

Article 3 of the European Convention on Human Rights reflects the ICCPR, and also states that no one should be subjected to torture or to inhuman or degrading treatment and punishment. The European Court of Human Rights (ECtHR) has been active in reinforcing the rights of prisoners in many of its judgments, and minimum standards are set for the treatment of prisoners within the European Prison Rules. The European Convention for the Prevention of Torture and Inhuman or Degrading Treatment or Punishment is overseen and administered by the European Committee for the Prevention of Torture and Inhuman or Degrading Treatment or Punishment (CPT). For a full discussion of European human rights relating to prisons and detention, see Easton (2011), ch. 3.

10.3 Violations of the human rights of detainees

The General Comments of the UNHRC, a wide range of international case law, and reports from non-governmental organizations (NGOs) provide us with many examples of violations of Articles 7 and 10 of the ICCPR and Article 1 of the CAT, as well as other relevant Articles. There are too many examples of violations to discuss them all in detail here, but the following provides a brief overview. For further information, organizations such as Amnesty International, Human Rights Watch, Open Society, nationally based prisoner advocacy organizations, and refugee advocacy groups, among others, provide details on their websites. The case law of international and national courts and State Party reports are also rich sources of information.

The harsh, and often brutal, conditions of maximum security units such as Supermax, involving extended periods of confinement, are not only considered to breach human rights but also have a devastating impact on the individuals exposed to them (Carlton 2006; Scraton and McCulloch 2006; Shalev 2007). A study of 100 randomly selected inmates from California's Pelican Bay Supermax prison noted that after months or years of complete isolation, many prisoners:

> begin to lose the ability to initiate behavior of any kind – to organize their own lives around activity and purpose ... Chronic apathy, lethargy, depression, and despair often result. In extreme cases, prisoners may literally stop behaving, becoming essentially catatonic. (Craig Haney, a psychology professor at the University of California at Santa Cruz, cited in Cure International 2010: 1)

The justification for such units lies with the identification of inmates as threats to national security and public safety, and as being unpredictable, dangerous, violent and unmanageable (Carlton 2006). Prisoners are thus reconstructed as sub-human or as perpetual threats. This image of danger is projected on to the entire prison population and thus justifies the maintenance of harsh prison regimes. This is despite the fact that the majority of prisoners are on the whole people who are not dangerous; they are repeat offenders; are dealing with cognitive impairment issues such as mental illness, intellectual disability and brain damage; have had difficult or traumatic childhoods; or are long-term older inmates with chronic illnesses.

Holding prisoners on death row for an extended period of time has also been found to cause high levels of stress and anxiety, and has been deemed to constitute cruel and unusual punishment. Other violations that can be seen as inhuman, cruel, degrading or constituting torture include random and disruptive inspections of cells involving deliberate disruptions of sleep; daily shackling, and the use of restraints; and the use of boot camps and chain gangs as punishment. Violations may also include lack of contact with family, and withholding contact as punishment, or treating it as a privilege to be earned rather than a right; lack of appropriate services for detainees with cognitive impairment; poor treatment of mentally ill prisoners and the use of drugs to subdue prisoners in the main prison and hospital units; and failure to provide adequate healthcare. In *Estelle v Gamble*, 429 US 97 (1976), it was found that deliberate indifference to the serious medical needs of prisoners constitutes 'unnecessary and wanton infliction of pain', whether the indifference is displayed by prison doctors in their response to prisoners' need or by prison guards who deny or delay access to, or interfere with, treatment (Cure International 2010, no p. no.). Violations can also include lack of recreational facilities, and failure to provide rehabilitative services. In the USA, the judgment in the case of *Brown v Plata* (2011) No. 09-1233 United States Supreme Court, May 23, provides a clear illustration of the horrendous conditions that existed in overcrowded Californian prisons at the time. Together, the conditions were judged to amount to torture and cruel and unusual punishment, and seen to be the result of poor political policy choices, and inadequate funding, management and administration (see Simon 2011).

The kinds of harsh conditions experienced by prisoners can also be found in administrative detention. In January 2011, the Grand Chamber of the ECtHR found that the conditions in a Greek migration detention centre were so poor that returning an asylum seeker who had escaped would violate Article 3 of the ECtHR (*MSS v Belgium and Greece*, Application no. 30696/09). In 2013 the UN Human Rights Committee found that the Australian Government had breached the ICCPR by holding 46 refugees in indefinite detention for over four years. The refusal of the government to provide the detainees with reasons for their detention or to provide them with visas because of alleged security risks was found to be procedurally unfair and amounted to 'cruel, inhuman and degrading treatment'. The Committee called for Australia to release the detainees immediately (UN News Centre, 22 August 2013).

10.4 Transnational detention, extraordinary rendition

Violations of detainee rights have risen since the terror attack on the USA on 11 September 2001 (hereafter, 9/11). A number of jurisdictions have introduced exceptional emergency legislation that has had a major impact on the conditions of those who are detained in the name of anti-terrorist measures. This is despite the fact that the rights of those deprived of their liberty are said to be inalienable, and the UNHRC's General Comment No. 20 reaffirmed that Article 7 is absolute, has no limitations and even in situations of emergency no derogation from its provisions are allowed (UNHRC GC No. 20, para. 3).

To guard against torture and guarantee the further protection of detained persons, General Comment No. 20 warns against holding individuals incommunicado (para 11), and places a duty on states to provide clear records of interrogation. It also requires that the place where a detainee is held must be a designated place of detention, that States Parties should ensure that any places of detention are free from any equipment liable to be used for inflicting torture or ill treatment, and that detainees should receive prompt and regular access to doctors, lawyers and family members. The General Comment also states that States Parties should not expose those who have been returned by way of extradition, expulsion or refoulement to degrading treatment or punishment (GC No. 20, para. 9).

The actions of the George W. Bush administration, and other States Parties complicit in extraordinary renditions, have seen the arbitrary detention, transfer, illegal detention and torture of those accused of terrorist activities, or of associating with alleged terrorists. Prisoners continue to be held at Guantanamo Bay and other secure units under conditions of torture with very little access to review. In the USA, the Senate Intelligence Committee's long-awaited report on the secret detention and interrogation programme of the Central Intelligence Agency (CIA) after 9/11 was tabled on 13 December 2012. The Senate Select Committee on Intelligence approved the report, which contains important information on the use and ineffectiveness of torture. However, the Senate has refused to release the report to the public.

Box 10.1   Unlawful rendition and detention

The ECtHR found that a German citizen, Khaled el Masri, who was subjected to a forced disappearance, unlawful detention and extended solitary confinement outside any legal process, was the subject of extraordinary rendition.

El Masri was sodomized, shackled, hooded and beaten by CIA agents in the presence of Macedonian state police, and thus was found to have been tortured. He had been seized by a CIA rendition team in 2004 in Macedonia and then secretly rendered to Afghanistan. The Court found that Macedonia had contravened Article 3 of the European Human Rights Convention by allowing the CIA to inflict harm and suffering intentionally in order to obtain information (Singh 2012).

10.5 Violence and deaths in custody

The failure of the state to fulfil its duty of care is evident in the level of violence and deaths in custody to be found in some places of detention, especially police custody and prisons. Violence in many prisons is endemic, both between inmates, and between guards and inmates. Violence towards prisoners includes beatings, homicides and the sexual assault of both males and females. Women prisoners, for example, have been found to be particularly vulnerable to sexual assault from prison staff, and young men to rape and violence from other inmates. The despair engendered by the prison environment can also be measured by the high levels of self-harm and suicide seen in prisons and in administrative detention.

Deaths in custody can occur as a result of a lack of appropriate medical treatment for prisoners with physical as well as mental illnesses; the failure to check regularly on suicidal prisoners or those in isolation; and overcrowding, which can place prisoners in dangerous and risky situations (see Scraton and McCulloch 2006).

For some groups of prisoners, such as Indigenous prisoners, there are even higher rates of deaths and harm experienced in custody. In Australia, the Report of the Royal Commission into Aboriginal Deaths in Custody produced damning evidence of the massive overrepresentation of Indigenous prisoners in detention, and while the report proposed many recommendations for reform, relatively few have been introduced, and high rates of violence continue to be experienced in both adult and juvenile custodial settings (Cunneen 2006).

Violence and abuse in prison tend to be hidden from view. If prisoners try to take action, or if such violence is the subject of condemnation by human rights bodies or prison inspectorates, more often than not the result is inaction (Scraton and McCulloch 2006).

10.6 Deprivation of life, and life without parole

The USA remains the last Western democratic country to retain the death penalty (Garland 2010). While UN treaties do not prohibit the use of the death penalty, there are very stringent rules relating to the circumstances in which capital punishment can take place, and the conditions under which individuals can be executed. Article 6(2) of the ICCPR states that:

> In countries which have not abolished the death penalty, sentence of death may be imposed only for the most serious crimes ... and not contrary to the provisions of the present covenant.

The Rome Statute of the International Criminal Court, adopted by the UN in July 1998, declares that, for all life sentences, a review is mandated after 25 years and, if warranted, a lesser sentence may then be imposed (Article 110 No. 3). By October 2009, 110 states had become party to the treaty, with 38 states signed but not yet ratified. The UNHRC states that, if the death penalty is to be applied it must be undertaken 'in a way that causes the least possible physical and mental suffering' (GC No. 20, para. 6). Article 6.1 of the ICCPR states that 'Every human being has the inherent right to life. This right shall be protected by law. No one shall be arbitrarily deprived of his life.' The aim of this Article is to stop the indiscriminate execution of persons by states as a form of punishment or a means of containing, controlling or eliminating undesirable persons, including political and religious dissidents, or ethnic and religious groups. It places an obligation on States Parties to establish due process, and accountable and reviewable decision-making procedures.

It could be argued that some states in the USA are arbitrarily depriving people of their right to life because of the lack of due process in capital cases and leading to a number of wrongful convictions and executions (see the work of the Innocence Project, available at: http://www.innocenceproject.org/). It is argued that the high rate of exonerations of people on death row awaiting execution is evidence of the state condoning the 'arbitrary deprivation of life', by consistently failing to establish adequate proof and procedural safeguards in capital cases (Cure International 2010).

Box 10.2   Life sentences and life-without-parole sentences in the USA

- In five states — Alabama, California, Massachusetts, Nevada and New York — at least one in six people in prison are serving a life sentence.
- The highest proportion of life sentences relative to the prison population is in California, where 20 per cent of the prison population are serving life sentences, up from 18.1 per cent in 2003. Among these 34,164 life sentences there are
  - 6,807 juveniles serving life sentences; and
  - 4,694 women and girls serving life sentences.
- Two-thirds of people with life sentences (66.4 per cent) are non-white, reaching as high as 83.7 per cent of the life-sentenced population in the state of New York.
- Seventy-seven per cent of juveniles sentenced to life are youth of colour.

Source: Cure International 2010.

The rapid increase in the USA of life-without-parole sentences is also considered to amount to an arbitrary 'slow death' deprivation of life, which is predominantly the result of politically motivated changes in state policy rather than increases in violent crime or a greater need for public safety (Cure International 2010).

In summary, the prioritization of punishment, retribution and incapacitation in many countries continues to override the ICCPR's declaration that rehabilitation should be the sole purpose of incarceration in prison.

10.7 'Social death' of the prisoner

Raising issues about prisoners' human rights has never been easy, but in a post–9/11 world, and in the context of 'punitive political environments', there are a number of distinct challenges (Lacey 2008; Naylor 2013). One key challenge relates to how to convince politicians and the public that detainees should have any rights at all. At common law, it used to be the case that those who were convicted of crimes were deemed to be 'civilly dead' – that is, they lost all rights and recognition as a person (Naylor 2013; Ridley-Smith and Redman 2002). Though this doctrine has not been applied for a long time, some societies operate with the view that anyone convicted of a crime is a lesser person, and that their actions, in breaching society's codes, mean that they are 'less eligible' for the protection of the law, including human rights (Naylor 2013).

Recent political controversies in the UK and Australia over the rights of prisoners to vote have provided these governments with the opportunity to make a public symbolic stance on the issue of 'less eligibility' (Naylor 2013). Article 21 of the UDHR confirms the rights of prisoners to vote, and Article 25 of the ICCPR states that prisoners should have 'the right and opportunity to take part in the conduct of public affairs, to vote and be elected and have equal access to public service'. The UN Human Rights Committee, in its General Comment No. 25, considers that depriving people who have been convicted of a felony of the right to vote does not fulfil the obligations set out in Article 25 of the ICCPR, nor does it serve the rehabilitation goals of Article 10(3) of the Covenant, since denying citizenship rights to prisoners inhibits their reintegration into civil society (18 December 2006, cited in Ridley-Smith and Redman 2002: 293). Despite this interpretation, the Committee has stated that the right to vote is not absolute (Ridley-Smith and Redman 2002).

In Australia, convicted persons who are sentenced to more than three years in prison forfeit their right to vote in federal elections while they are serving their sentence, though the law at the state level varies (Naylor 2013). In 2006, a proposal by the Australian Government to remove the right of prisoners to vote was challenged in the High Court (*Roach v AEC and the Commonwealth of Australia* 2007 233 CLR 167). The High Court found that the Australian Constitution enshrined the right to vote of all citizens including prisoners, but accepted that the right could be subject to 'proportionate' restrictions for a 'substantial reason', and upheld the previous limitation on the right to vote (Naylor 2013).

In the UK, a blanket ban (with few exceptions) on convicted prisoners voting in elections was introduced in Section 3 of the Representation of the People Act 1979 (amended in 1983 and 2000) (Easton 2011: 211). The law was challenged by a prisoner, John Hirst, who took the case to the High Court in England. When the case was dismissed he appealed to the ECtHR (*Hirst v UK* (No. 2) Application 74025/01, 6 October 2005). The UK was found by the Court to have breached the European Convention Protocol 1, Article 3. As Easton (2011) states, a central element of the UK's voting ban was that allowing prisoners to vote would cause offence to the public – a decision not informed by principled policy or evidence but by political pragmatism. Hirst argued that the ban was disproportionate as it did not relate to the seriousness of the offence, and that it was also arbitrary, since it depended on the timing of the period of punishment and the calling of elections (Easton 2011). It was also claimed that there was no link between disenfranchisement and the prevention of crime or deterrence, and that the ban alienated prisoners and denied them a voice (Easton 2011: 212). The ECtHR agreed that, while States Parties had some flexibility in the administration and interpretation of provisions, the UK law was clearly outside the margin of appreciation, since it constituted a blanket ban and did not relate to the seriousness of the offence or the individual circumstances of the prisoner. The case was referred to the Grand Chamber of the court at the request of the UK Government. The Grand Chamber also found that there was no link between the ban and principles of punishment, and that voting was a right and not a privilege (Easton 2011). Despite this ruling, the UK has continued to resist lifting the ban and was admonished by the Council of Europe in December 2012 for its refusal to comply with the ECtHR ruling. In 2013, the Scottish Parliament has taken the interpretation of the phrase 'election' narrowly and is proposing that Scottish citizens in prison will be disenfranchised in the 'referendum' on Scottish independence in 2013, with no explanation provided (*The Scotsman* 2013). This is despite the fact that European Prison Rule 24:11 states that the right to vote should include referenda. In contrast, most European countries allow prisoners to vote, as does South Africa (Easton 2011).

In the USA, 48 states have banned voting for prisoners (only Vermont and Maine retain the vote), which means that because of the high levels of incarceration in the USA, half of all prisoners in the world who are denied the right to vote reside in the United States (Easton 2011: 231) and that, nationally, an estimated 5.3 million Americans are denied the right to vote (Cure International 2010; Easton 2011). Two states permanently ban voting by anyone with a felony record of any sort (Cure International 2010). In effect, this leads to discrimination against African Americans, of whom 13 per cent have lost their vote – seven times the national average (Easton 2011: 231). In Virginia, for example, African Americans make up 20 per cent of the population but over half of the disenfranchised population (Easton 2011: 231). This constitutes a clear breach of the anti-discrimination provisions of human rights. Moreover, the rules relating to the right to vote are confusing and complex, and voters and election officials are not necessarily aware of felon enfranchisement rights (Easton 2011).

Denial of the right to vote flies in the face of the principles of rehabilitation and reintegration that underpin human rights treaties. Disenfranchisement might appeal to the punitive politics of governments but it reinforces the idea of prisoners as non-citizens and continues to segregate offenders and ex-offenders from the rest of the population.

10.8 Privatization

The increasing privatization of prisons, security services and administrative detention raises a number of human rights concerns. Privatization ranges from the use of voluntary workers in some settings, to the outsourcing of specific services such as policy development, prisoner transfer, transport and building services; and the design, building, management and delivery of an entire facility (see Naylor 2001). It is questionable whether such a central and significant site of state power, which has profound implications for fundamental human rights and is exercised in the public's interest, should be tendered on a for-profit basis (Naylor 2001; Culp 2005; ICHRP 2010; Mason 2013). In the words of the Open Society Institute:

> For profit private prisons, jails and detention centers have no place in a democratic society and profiteering from the imprisonment of human beings compromises public safety and corrupts justice. (Open Society Institute 2004, cited in Culp 2005: 434)

In Israel, the High Court found that transferring the management of prisons to private corporations whose main aim is to make money in effect undermines human rights and, further, that 'the act of depriving someone of their liberty loses much of its legitimacy' (case cited in ICHRP 2010: 68).

Since the early 1980s there has been a global expansion in the use of privatization in a range of custodial services (see Table 10.3 Number of Prisoners Held Privately). The modern trend towards privatization of prisons began in the USA in the 1980s (Mason 2013). From 2002 to 2009, there was a 37 per cent increase in the USA in the number of inmates in privately run facilities, including prisons and administrative detention (Lee 2012). Today, as US prison populations drop, and questions have been raised about the cost-effectiveness of privately run prisons, the numbers of private prison contracts have stabilized (Culp 2005; Lee 2012; Mason 2013). However, other markets have been opening up. A small group of multinational corporations, including the GEO Group, Corrections Corporation of America and its subsidiary the Correctional Corporation of Australia, and British-based companies G4S and Serco, provide a wide range of prison, security and custodial services globally. In the late 1990s, the Australian State of Victoria had the greatest proportion of inmates held in private facilities than any other part of the world (Naylor 2001). Since then, the numbers of Australian prisoners held in privately run facilities have increased dramatically, so that Australia now has the highest proportion of prisoners held in privately run facilities than any other country (see Box 10.3).

For-profit companies have also moved into other forms of detention- and security-related markets. Nearly half of all administrative detainees in the USA are held in private detention (Lee 2012). In the UK, 73 per cent of inmates held in immigration detention are in privately run institutions, and all of Australia's immigration detention centres and alternative places of detention are operated by for-profit companies (Mason 2013: 5). In the UK, companies such as Serco and G4S have expanded their interests into a range of other security, health, welfare and administrative services.

Box 10.3   Number of prisoners held privately

	Privately held prisoners	Publicly held prisoners	Percent held privately
Australia	5,520	23,191	19%
Scotland	1,408	6,770	17%
England & Wales	10,936	74,030	13%
New Zealand	925	7,508	11%
United States	130,941	1,467,839	8%
South Africa	5,952	152,838	3%

Note: Data from Australia and the USA is from 2011; data from Scotland and South Africa from fiscal year 2011; data from NZ, England & Wales is from 2012.
Source: Mason 2013: 9 (reproduced with kind permission of the Sentencing Project).

The move towards privatization in the USA was driven in part by an ideological belief prevalent during the Reagan presidency in the capacity of the competitive market to deliver higher quality services at less cost to the tax payer compared to state-run facilities (Culp 2005). But it was also motivated in the 1990s by the fact that the rapid rise in the numbers of people in prison was leading to overcrowding and increased expenditure; in the USA, governments were not able to build prisons quickly enough to cope with the results of mass incarceration policies and practices (Culp 2005). As stated above, it could be argued that the privatization of detention is antithetical to fundamental human rights. The fact that private companies are run on a for-profit basis should preclude them on human rights grounds from being involved in running prisons or detention centres. For example, it could be argued that treating detainees as for-profit commodities is degrading and in breach of Article 7 of the ICCPR. In privately run prisons, work schemes could also be seen to be in breach of Article 8(1), which states that 'No one shall be held in slavery; slavery and the slave trade in all their forms shall be prohibited.' While public prisons have always run work schemes, ostensibly to offer rehabilitation services, private prisons operate on a per-diem payment system, whereby they are paid per prisoner, per day of incarceration. This could be said to mirror a system of slavery, such that prisoners are used to generate profits as underpaid contract workers for other industries (Naylor 2001; Cure International 2010). A report on the privately run Yarl's Wood Immigration Removal Centre in the UK found that detainees were being paid far less than the minimum wage and in some cases as little as 50p an hour to work on menial tasks for private businesses. Detainees described the work as 'modern-day slavery' and accused the UK Border Agency (UKBA) and Serco, the highly profitable outsourcing company that runs the Bedfordshire centre, of exploiting them. The UKBA's guidance, written in 2008, recommends that detainees are paid £1 per hour for routine work, with 'specified projects' such as painting a room, to be paid at a higher rate of £1.25 an hour. Detainees are exempt from being paid the minimum wage under immigration laws (McVeigh 2011).

Since the objective of private prison companies is to generate profit, it is claimed that companies will put profit first and not prioritize the reform or rehabilitation of prisoners, in contravention of Article 10(3). As Cure International (2010) has argued, 'companies have a duty to their shareholders to make money; they do not have a duty to help prisoners better their lives'.

Naylor (2001) raises important concerns about the capacity of States Parties to regulate private contractors and to monitor human rights compliance in privately run facilities and services. She argues that there is a lack of openness in Australia in particular, about whether compliance with human rights is built into the private providers' contractual obligations. Questions have also been raised about the extent to which private companies might derogate from their human rights responsibilities because of economic pressures. Cutbacks to staffing levels, the withdrawal of more expensive rehabilitation and treatment programmes, the reduction in health care and psychiatric services, and extended lockdowns have been introduced as cost-cutting measures in some custodial settings (Naylor 2001; Culp 2005). In the USA, a series of lawsuits from prisoners complaining about violence in prisons, abusive treatment from guards, poor prison conditions and failure to provide rehabilitation services, coupled with publicly reported stories of serious riots, deaths in custody and escapes, prompted governments to introduce more comprehensive legislation, to monitor private prison standards more closely, and in some cases led to the review and withdrawal of contracts (Culp 2005). The Howard League for Penal Reform in the UK is maintaining a watching brief over the poor quality of conditions in privately run adult and juvenile detention facilities (http://www.howardleague.org/). Private security companies in the UK are also involved in the repatriation of asylum seekers who have been refused residency (see Box 10.4). The UK Inspectorate of Prisons has on a number of occasions raised concerns about the substandard conditions of privately run prisons and administrative detention centres in the UK (Mason 2013: 10).

Studies of the links between private companies and government in the USA have revealed corrupt practices in tendering processes, and undue lobbying influence from private corporations on the individuals responsible for introducing laws and policies relating to the policing and detention of undocumented migrants, including reforms that have benefited the financial interests of the corporations (Lee 2012; Jones 2013). These close links between business interests and government decisions raise important questions about openness and accountability in the governance of privatization. As Mason (2013: 12) argues, the poor standards, practical failures and moral

---

Box 10.4   G4S and the death of Jimmy Mubenga

In the UK, a coroner presiding over the case of the death of Jimmy Mubenga while being deported from Britain raised numerous concerns about the ways in which the UK Government and the security firm G4S conduct deportations. After the jury at the inquest had recorded a verdict of unlawful killing, the coroner's report stated that there was pervasive racism among G4S security guards, inadequate training; evidence that the guards had used dangerous restraint techniques, and that there was a system of rewards for keeping detainees quiet (Taylor 2013).

implications of privatization deserve 'serious attention and scrutiny' by the international community, policy-makers and citizens. There are systemic issues and fundamental human rights principles to be addressed in relation to detention, and it is questionable whether States Parties should be leaving profit-motivated companies to deal with them.

10.9 Women prisoners

Since the early 1980s (see Carlen 1983), there have been sustained campaigns for greater recognition of the needs and rights of women prisoners, and of their children, to address the differential impact of prison on women and their families (Easton 2011; Malloch and McIvor 2013). The role of women as primary carers often results in the children of women prisoners being taken into out-of-home care if mothers receive custodial sentences (Easton 2011).

Corrective services in many jurisdictions have now introduced what have become known as 'gender-responsive' penal policies and programmes as a means of incorporating the specific circumstances surrounding women's offending patterns and pathways into prison, addressing issues related to women's victimization, trauma, relationships with family, mental illness, addiction, and low socio-economic status, among others (Hannah-Moffat 2010). Reformers have campaigned for more community-based options for women prisoners, such as bail hostels, mother and baby units, and a range of gender-specific health, welfare and vocational services. For many women prisoners and their children there have been benefits from the system-wide changes to the administration of prisons and the delivery of targeted programmes (Hannah-Moffat 2010). In the UK, for example, children are allowed to stay with mothers who are classified as low security for up to 18 months after birth, whereas in some other countries, including Germany, children are permitted to stay with their mother until they are much older (Easton 2011: 187). However, Hannah-Moffat argues that within the current risk-dominated culture of many prison regimes there is a need to be cautious where 'relationships, children, past victimisations, mental health, self injury and self esteem all become correctional targets in the pursuit of normative femininity and gender conformity' (Hannah-Moffat 2010: 9). Women come to be seen not as clients in need of support or prisoners with rights, but as risks to be managed, whether they are 'high risk', 'risky' or 'at risk' (Hannah-Moffat 2010: 11). Access to rehabilitative-type programmes and post-release support becomes dependent on such classification. In this context, it is then difficult to incorporate the diversity of women's experiences such as poverty, Aboriginality, mental illness or sexuality as factors to be taken into consideration because the issues are complex and not dealt with easily via risk classificatory systems (Hannah-Moffat 2010). As Hannah-Moffat reminds us, gender-responsive programmes are still delivered in the context of punishment in a closed system that causes harm, and cautions that a human rights approach should not be lost to the lure of gender responsivity. Hannah-Moffat (2010) calls for systemic accountability and monitoring to become essential features of penal strategies that respond to women's needs, and argues that a rights-based approach should also recognize the need to incorporate the views and opinions of women prisoners (see also Malloch and McIvor 2013).

10.10 Accountability

The isolation of prisons and detention centres from public scrutiny presents a number of distinct challenges for the monitoring and reviewing of human rights violations. Unfortunately, even on the occasions where abuse is reported, there may be subsequent inaction on the part of prison authorities or governments (Scraton and McCulloch 2006).

International report and review mechanisms can provide a means for NGOs to present information on violations, and for international bodies to audit human rights. The Optional Protocol attached to the CAT requires that its signatories develop independent inspection mechanisms to ensure that places of detention, including public and private custodial settings, are available for regular visits and review.

Most European jurisdictions have national independent prison inspection authorities, or Ombudsman's Offices or Commissioners. The UK's Inspector of Prisons has been proactive in monitoring and reporting on conditions inside prisons and administrative detention centres in Britain (Easton 2011).

However, in many jurisdictions, prisoners' lack of access to complaints mechanisms and to legal representation further compromises their rights. Complainants in some custodial institutions may be physically and mentally vulnerable to isolation or retribution by other detainees and staff. The machinery of the law can also move very slowly. For example, in the UK, the case of *Campbell and Fell v UK* (1984) EHRR took 16 years to be heard in the ECtHR (see Easton 2011: 10 for a discussion of the case).

Some prisoners are denied access to freedom of speech. For example, in Queensland, Australia, prisoners have to seek permission from prison administrators before they can speak publicly. Lex Wotton, a prisoner who was released on parole, was not allowed to attend meetings about a death in custody that occurred on Palm Island in Queensland, where he lived; was forbidden from attending a subsequent official inquiry; and was not allowed to contact the media. The High Court of Australia ruled that while the Queensland laws did impinge on Wotton's freedom of political communication, they were deemed to be reasonable and served a legitimate end (*Lex Patrick Wotton v The State of Queensland & Anor [2011] HCA 2*). In Queensland, investigative journalist, Anne Delaney, who wanted to speak to a female inmate regarding making a documentary about her case, was prosecuted for attempting to contact the inmate, and was consequently charged and fined.

10.11 Humane systems in a punitive world

It is important to note that not all jurisdictions have emulated the punitive excesses mentioned in this chapter, and that penal regimes vary from country to country and even within countries. International comparative work conducted by Mick Cavadino and Jim Dignan (2006) found strong correlations between the political economy of nation-states and the operation and ethos of their prisons. The corporate welfare systems of Scandinavian countries, for example, were reflected in their humane approach to penality, in contrast to the neo-liberal economies of the USA and to some extent Australia, New Zealand and the UK. The work of Pratt and Eriksson (2012) examined the differences between Anglophone and Scandinavian penal policies and practices, and highlighted the exceptionalism of the welfare-focused approach that, in contrast to most penal regimes, has supported the human rights of prisoners in the criminal justice system. Bastøy prison in Norway is probably the best-known example of an enlightened and humane prison (http://www.bastoyfengsel.no/English/). Many European countries have highly developed systems of prisoner rights, including monitoring and inspection mechanisms, and prison is used as an option of last resort when all other options have been explored (Easton 2011).

Within the USA, some states, such as Minnesota, have maintained more liberal penal systems that encompass progressive rehabilitative programmes for both adults and juveniles (Lacey 2008; Easton 2011). In the Australian context, the legislative and policy framework of the Alexander Maconochie prison in the Australian Capital Territory (see Corrections Management Act 1997 [ACT]) has explicitly incorporated human rights principles (Mackay 2012). The day-to-day operational culture of custodial institutions can either support or undermine the policy and procedural safeguards of human rights (Liebling and Arnold 2005). In some settings, such as open prisons, where there is consultative decision-making, prioritization of rehabilitation, treatment and pre-release programmes, and staff who are committed to a more progressive ethos, there is a greater likelihood of compliance with human rights standards.

10.12 Conclusion

It has not been possible to discuss in detail the human rights of prisoners with complex needs, such as prisoners with cognitive impairments including mental illness, intellectual disability or acquired brain injury, or those detainees dealing with drug dependency. The chapter is also not able to cover the day-to-day injustices in the form of discrimination and harassment facing transgender, transsexual, gay and lesbian prisoners in detention (Easton 2011). However, it is important to note that in many jurisdictions around the world, conditions are slowly improving as the result of sustained advocacy and recognition of relevant human rights issues by governments.

This chapter has revealed how contemporary penal policy in some jurisdictions continues to violate the human rights of prisoners, and how governments, under the veil of security, public safety and popular demand perpetuate the violations that continue away from the public gaze (Lacey 2008). Garland reminds us that:

> The prison is a machine that silences as well as segregates. It deprives inmates of their voices along with their liberty. By hiding prisoners behind the scenes of social life, prison walls serve as a means of political as well as civil exclusion. The lawbreaker is incapacitated but also excommunicated. (Garland, Foreword in Brown and Wilkie 2002: v)

In her book, *The Prisoner's Dilemma* (2008), Nicola Lacey argues that, on the one hand, without advocacy it would be difficult to raise awareness of human rights violations, but on the other, there is a danger that, in drawing attention to prisoners' rights there might be a punitive backlash from both the public and governments.

In the long term, the segregation and poor treatment of prisoners and the denial of their citizenship status can have damaging effects, whereas respect for the human rights of prisoners could be seen to be supporting strategies that reduce reoffending and increase public safety (see Chapter 7 for a discussion of justice reinvestment). According to Easton (2011: 8), 'Respect for rights may limit the negative impact of imprisonment and by treating prisoners as autonomous individuals capable of making choices and as responsible citizens, better prepare them for release.' Rights also offer a means of challenging social exclusion and segregation. Recognition of prisoners as citizens, and not simply harbingers of risk, facilitates their reintegration back into society (Easton 2011).

Additional reading and resources

American Civil Liberties Union (2013) Interactive Infographic on State Prison Rates in the US. Available at: http://www.aclu.org/maps/americas-addiction-incarceration-state-state.

Coyle, A. (2003) *A Human Rights Approach to Prison Management: Handbook for Prison Staff*, Oxford: Blackwell.

Drake, D. (2012) *Prisons, Punishment and the Pursuit of Security*, Basingstoke: Palgrave Macmillan.

Murphy, T. and Whitty, N. (2007) 'Risk and Human Rights in UK Prison Governance', *British Journal of Criminology*, 47: 798—816.

Padfield, N. (2002) *Beyond the Tariff: Human Rights and the Release of Life Sentence Prisoners*, Uffculme, Devon, Willan Publishing.

Theroux, L. (2008) *Behind Bars*, British Broadcasting Corporation (BBC), DVD.

Theroux, L. (2011) *Miami Mega Jail, Part 1 and Part 2*, British Broadcasting Corporation (BBC), DVD.

Van Zyl Smit, D. and Snacken, S. (2009) *Principles of European Prison Law and Policy Penology and Human Rights*, Oxford: Oxford University Press.

Court cases cited

Estelle v Gamble, 429 US 97 (1976) (US).

Brown v Plata (2011) No. 09-1233 United States Supreme Court May 23 (US).

ECtHR (*MSS v Belgium and Greece*, Application no. 30696/09) (Europe).

Roach v AEC and the Commonwealth of Australia 2007 233 CLR 167 (Australia).

ECtHR (*Hirst v UK* (No. 2) Application 74025/01, 6 October 2005) (Europe).

Campbell and Fell v UK (1984) EHRR (Europe).

Lex Patrick Wotton v The State of Queensland & Anor [2011] HCA 2) (Australia).

References

Brown, D. and Wilkie, M. (2002) *Prisoners as Citizens: Human Rights in Australian Prisons*, Annandale, NSW: Federation Press.

Carlen, P. (1983) *Women's Imprisonment: A Study in Social Control*, London: Routledge & Kegan Paul.

Carlton, B. (2006) 'From H Division to Abu Ghraib: Regimes of Justification and the Historical Proliferation of State Inflicted Terror and Violence in Maximum Security', *Social Justice* 33(4): 15—36.

Cavadino, M. and Dignan, J. (2006) *Penal Systems: A Comparative Approach*, London: Sage.

Christie, N. (1994) *Crime Control as Industry*, London: Routledge.

Culp, R. (2005) 'The Rise and Stall of Prison Privatization: An Integration of Policy Analysis Perspectives', *Criminal Justice Policy*, 16: 412—42.

Cunneen, C. (2006) 'Aboriginal Deaths in Custody: A Continuing Systematic Abuse', *Social Justice*, 3(4): 37—51.

Cure International (2010) *United States Human Rights Violations in Correctional Practices: A Contribution to the 2010 UN Universal Periodic Review*. Available at: http://www.internationalcure.org/UPR_USA.htm; accessed December 2012.

Currie, E. (1998) *Crime and Punishment in America*, New York: Henry Holt & Co.

Easton, S. (2011) *Prisoners' Rights: Principles and Practice*, Uffculme, Devon: Willan Publishing.

Garland, D. (2001a) *The Culture of Control*, Oxford: Oxford University Press.

Garland, D. (ed.) (2001b) *Mass Imprisonment in the United States: Social Causes and Consequences*, London: Sage.

Garland, D. (2010) *Peculiar Institution: America's Death Penalty in the Age of Abolition*, Cambridge, MA: Harvard University Press.

Hannah-Moffat, K. (2010) 'Sacrosanct or Flawed: Risk, Accountability and Gender Responsive Penal Politics', *Current Issues in Criminal Justice*, 22(2): 1—25.

International Centre for Prison Studies (ICPS) (2013) Entire World Occupancy Rates. Available at: http://www.prisonstudies.org/info/worldbrief/wpb_stats.php?area=all&category=wb_occupancy.

International Council on Human Rights Policy (ICHRP) (2010) *Modes and Patterns of Social Control: Implications for Human Rights Policy*, Versoix, Switzerland: ICHRP.

Jones, A. (2013) 'The For Profit Immigration Imprisonment Racket', *Rolling Stone*, 25 February.

Lacey, N. (2008) *The Prisoners' Dilemma: Political Economy and Punishment in Contemporary Democracies*, The Hamlyn Lectures, Cambridge: Cambridge University Press.

Lee, S. (2012) 'By the Numbers: The US's Growing For Profit Detention Industry', *ProPublica*, 20 June. Available at: http://www.propublica.org/article/by-the-numbers-the-u.s.s-growing-for-profit-detention-industry; accessed 26 January 2013.

Liebling, A. and Arnold, H. (2005) *Prisons and their Moral Performance: Studies of Values, Quality and Prison Life*, Clarendon Studies in Criminology Series, Oxford: Oxford University Press.

Mackay, A. (2012) 'The Road to the ACT's First Prison (the Alexander Maconochie Centre) Was Paved with Rehabilitative Intentions', *Canberra Law Review*, 11(1): 33—57.

Malloch, M. and McIvor, G. (2013) *Women, Punishment and Social Justice: Human Rights and Penal Practices*, London: Routledge.

Mason, C. (2013) *International Growth Trends in Prison Privatization*, The Sentencing Project, Washington, DC, August. Available at: http://www.sentencingproject.org/doc/publications/inc_International%20Growth%20Trends%20in%20Prison%20Privatization.pdf; accessed 22 August 2013.

McVeigh, K. (2011) 'Yarl's Wood Detainees Paid 50p an Hour', *The Guardian*, 2 January. Available at: http://www.guardian.co.uk/uk/2011/jan/02/yarls-wood-detainees-paid-50p-hour; accessed 10 January 2011.

Naylor, B. (2001) 'Prisons, Privatisation and Human Rights', *Castan Centre for Human Rights Law Conference Proceedings*, Melbourne: Monash University.

Naylor, B. (2013) 'Protecting the Human Rights of Prisoners in Australia', in P. Gerber and M. Castan (eds), *Contemporary Perspectives on Human Rights Law in Australia*, Pybank, NSW: Thomson Reuters, (pp. 395–416).

Parenti, C. (1999) *Lock Down America: Police and Prisons in the Age of Crisis*, New York: Verso.

Pratt, J. and Eriksson, A. (2012) *Contrasts in Punishment: An Exploration of Anglophone Excess and Nordic Exceptionalism*, London: Routledge.

Ridley-Smith, M. and Redman, R. (2002) 'Prisoners and the Right to Vote', in D. Brown and M. Wilkie (eds), *Prisoners as Citizens: Human Rights in Australian Prisons*, Annandale, NSW: Federation Press, pp. 283–307.

Scotsman, The (2013) 'Independence: Prisoners Challenge Voting Ban', 24 March. Available at: http://www.scotsman.com/scotland-on-sunday/independence-prisoners-challenge-voting-right-ban-1-2854664.

Scraton, P. and McCulloch, J. (2006) 'Deaths in Custody and Detention', *Social Justice*, 33(4): 1–14.

Shalev, S. (2007) 'The Power to Classify: Avenues into a Supermax Prison', in Downes *et al.* (eds), *Crime, Social Control and Human Right: From Moral Panics to States of Denial — Essays in Honour of Stanley Cohen*, Uffculme, Devon: Willan Publishing, pp. 107–19.

Simon, J. (2007) *Governing through Crime: How the War on Crime Transformed American Democracy and Created a Culture of Fear*, New York: Oxford University Press.

Simon, J. (2011) 'Editorial: Mass Incarceration on Trial', *Punishment and Society*, 13: 251–5.

Singh, A. (2012) 'European Court of Human Rights Finds against CIA Abuse of Khaled el Masri', *The Guardian* online, 13 December. Available at: http://www.guardian.co.uk/commentisfree/2012/dec/13/european-court-human-rights-cia-abuse-khaled-elmasri; accessed 3 February 2013.

Taylor, M. (2013) 'Jimmy Mubenga Coroner Issues Damning Report On Deportations', *The Guardian* online, 4 August. Available at: http://www.theguardian.com/uk-news/2013/aug/04/jimmy-mubenga-coroner-report-deportations.

UNHRC (United Nations Human Rights Committee) 1992 General Comment No. 20, Article 7

UNHRC (United Nations Committee for Human Rights) 1992 General Comment No. 21

UN News Centre (2013) 'Australia Must Release Refugees Subjected to Cruel Treatment — UN Human Rights Experts', 22 August. Available at: http://www.un.org/apps/news/story.asp?NewsID=45672&Cr=australia&Cr1=#; accessed 23 August 2013.

Young, J. (1999) *The Exclusive Society: Social Exclusion, Crime and Difference in Late Modernity*, London: Sage.

CHAPTER 11

Juvenile Justice

Key concepts

Children as citizens — Children who come into conflict with the law — The best interests of the child — A child's right to be heard — Developing capacity of the child — Age of criminal responsibility — Adultification and responsibilization — Children in adult detention — Child-friendly justice — A children's human rights approach

---

11.1 Introduction

The Convention on the Rights of the Child (CROC) is the key global international instrument on children's rights. It was adopted by the United Nations in 1989, and came into force in 1990. The CROC is the most widely ratified human rights treaty; by January 2013, 193 nations had signed and ratified it. Somalia and the USA are the only countries that have, at the time of writing, failed to do so. The USA did in fact become a signatory in 1995 but did not take the next step to ratification; it stands alone as the only liberal democratic nation not bound by the Convention.

It is generally agreed that, since 1990, there have been substantial improvements in many jurisdictions in children's human rights and in the way that juvenile justice systems operate. According to Kilkelly, there is now 'an impressive body of international law, that collectively describes the position of "children in conflict with the law" and prescribes the rights to which they are entitled' (2008: 188).

However, there remains a significant shortfall between the commitment of many States Parties to the Convention and regional human rights instruments, and what is delivered on the ground. The general punitive turn in criminal justice (discussed elsewhere in this book) has compromised human rights for adults and children alike, and it is argued that there have been shifts towards 'adultification' and 'responsibilization' in the discourses, laws, policies and practices relating to children and young people which have had a particular impact on youth justice (Muncie 2008; Goldson and Muncie 2012).

Sadly, the rights of children and young people continue to be violated widely (CRC 2007; Kilkelly 2008; Muncie 2008; Goldson and Muncie 2012). As the United Nations Committee on the Rights of the Child (CRC) stated in its 2007 General Comment (GC) on Juvenile Justice, 'it is ... clear that many States Parties have a long way to go in achieving full compliance' (CRC 2007 para. 1:3).

This chapter will examine some of the reasons why this has occurred, and the effects it has had on children and young people. It starts with an overview of the CROC and regional human rights instruments relevant to children, and then considers a number of issues specific to juvenile justice.

11.2 The CRC and juvenile justice

Article 1 of the CROC defines the term 'child' as anyone under the age of 18. The CRC, in General Comment No. 10, states that, in relation to criminal proceedings, those children 'who are alleged to have, or accused of or recognized as having, infringed the penal law are termed "children in conflict with the law"', and that every person under the age of 18 years at the time of an alleged offence must be treated in accordance with the rules of juvenile justice (CRC 2007 para. 37).

One of the most innovative (and for some people the most challenging) aspects of the CROC is its recognition of children as active rights-bearers and relatively autonomous individuals. At the same time, the Convention recognizes the specific welfare, care and protection needs and rights of children resulting from their vulnerability and dependency, as well as their developing maturity and emerging capacities. Freeman describes this dual conceptualization of children as both 'being' and 'becoming' (Freeman 2011: 26). The rights contained in the CROC are normative, while also being procedural, thus providing guidelines on how justice is to be achieved (Tobin 2013).

The CROC covers all aspects of children's lives, including family life, out-of-home care, education, health care, protection and employment, among others. Articles 32–39 are concerned specifically with protecting children from illicit drugs (Article 33); economic, sexual and other forms of exploitation (Articles 32, 34 and 36); and abduction and trafficking (Article 35). Articles 37 and 40 relate specifically to juvenile justice. The Articles of the Convention are universal and indivisible. They apply equally to children in the juvenile justice system, including children in detention, as they do to other children.

It is generally considered that there are four key principles that underpin all Articles of the CROC (UN International Children's Emergency Fund

(UNICEF); Hamilton 2011; Tobin 2011, 2013). The first of these (Article 3) states that the 'best interests' of the child shall be the 'primary consideration' in all matters affecting children, including the development of policy and legislation. Hamilton points out that, while the term 'best interests' has not been defined precisely, it prioritizes rehabilitation, reintegration and restorative justice as responses to offending behaviour over repressive or retributive measures (2011: 24). The second is 'non-discrimination' (Article 2); the third is the 'right to life, survival and development' (Article 6); and the fourth and final principle is that the child has 'a right to be heard' (Article 12). Article 12 calls on states to assure children who are capable of forming their own views the right to express them freely in all matters affecting them, and that 'they are given due weight in accordance with their age and maturity'. Tobin argues that there are two other principles that underpin the CROC: one he calls 'due deference', which refers to the requirement that States Parties respect the rights, duties, responsibilities and role of parents, guardians and families towards children (Article 5); and the second is the principle of recognizing the child's evolving capacities, which is threaded throughout the Convention (Tobin 2011: 72).

Articles 37 and 40 of the Convention reiterate foundational civil and political human rights, but also contain specific provisions for children. For example, Article 37(a) states that 'Neither capital punishment nor life imprisonment without the possibility of release shall be imposed for offences committed by persons below the age of eighteen.' Article 40(1) identifies that age should be a key factor to be taken into consideration in the treatment of children, while Article 40(2)i calls for children to have access to a parent, guardian or legal representative in preparing their defence to charges. Article 40(3) calls for States Parties to develop specific criminal justice measures that are appropriate for children, and this is seen to apply 'from the initial contact … until all involvement with the system ends' (Hamilton 2011: 12). The CRC advocates the establishment of a comprehensive, separate juvenile justice system with laws, procedures, authorities, institutions and programmes designed and implemented specifically for children. The Committee also recommends that specialized units and training be introduced into all juvenile-justice-related agencies including the police, judiciary and custodial services (CRC 2007, paras 92, 93, 94). The requirement for the development of specialized services is also seen to include those run by non-governmental organizations (NGOs) (Hamilton 2011: 12–14). Article 40(3)a calls for the establishment of a minimum age of criminal responsibility, 'below which children shall be presumed not to have the capacity to infringe the penal law', and 40(3)b privileges diversion from formal judicial proceedings as the most desirable method of dealing with children's offending.

11.3 Implementation and monitoring

The CRC oversees the implementation and interpretation of the CROC. Until 2012, the only mechanism available for monitoring the compliance of States Parties was the State Party and NGO reporting process. However, in 2012, the CRC adopted an Optional Protocol for Communication, which allows children and others to take complaints directly to the Committee. The Optional Protocol is now open for signature by States Parties, and it will be interesting to see how many – and which – countries become signatories.

The reporting process is considered to be a fairly weak method for ensuring compliance (Goldson and Muncie 2012). It relies on States Parties acting on the recommendations of the Committee without the threat of any sanctions for failure to comply. For example, it has taken Australia over 20 years to appoint an independent National Commissioner for Children, despite repeated requests to do so.

The CROC is supplemented by specific juvenile justice instruments, which, while not binding, provide supporting guidelines and standards for States Parties. These include the 1985 UN Standard Minimum Rules for the Administration of Juvenile Justice (the Beijing Rules); the 1990 UN Guidelines for the Prevention of Juvenile Delinquency (the Riyadh Guidelines); the 1990 UN Rules for the Protection of Juveniles Deprived of their Liberty (the Havana Rules); and, while not specifically developed for children and young people, the 1990 UN Standard Minimum Rules for Non-custodial Measures (the Tokyo Rules). The CRC also publishes General Comments on key issues relating to the Convention, and in 2007 issued General Comment No. 10 on juvenile justice (CRC 2007).

International organizations and NGOs, including UNICEF and Defence for Children International, play a crucial, and active, role in the development and promotion of the CROC. Many jurisdictions have established Independent Children's Rights Institutions, including ombudsmen and commissioners to monitor and audit children's rights. Their role and responsibilities vary across jurisdictions (see Gan 2011).

11.4 Regional children's rights

There are a number of regional human rights instruments that address children's rights. The African Charter of Human and People's Rights 1979 (the Banjul Charter) includes a brief reference to children, and the African Charter on the Rights and Welfare of the Child (the African Children's Charter, or ACC) was adopted in 1990 and came into force in 1999. The ACC incorporates the principles of the CROC and addresses specifically the social, economic and cultural experiences of children's lives in Africa (Njungwe 2009).

In the Americas, there are no specific treaties for children. The main treaty is the American Convention on Human Rights (the American Convention), but the Inter-American Court and Commission on Human Rights have used the CROC to guide their actions and judgments in the defence of children's rights (Alston *et al.* 2005). Exemplary here is the judgment of the Inter-American Committee in relation to the failure of the Guatemalan Government to protect the lives of its street children in *Guatemala Villagran Morales et al. v Guatemala Judgment of Nov. 19 1999 Inter-American Court of Human Rights (Ser. C) no. 63.*

In Europe, the Court of Justice of the European Union (CJEU) and the European Court of Human Rights (ECtHR) have been proactive in their support of children's human rights. The organizations of the European Union and the European Commission, including the Council of Europe, have slowly been working towards integrating children's rights (Stalford and Drywood 2011; Stalford 2012). In 2006, the European Commission published *Towards an EU Strategy on the Rights of the Child*, EU COM 2006 (Stalford and Drywood

---

Box 11.1   Selected European children's rights documents

- European Commission 2006, Towards an EU Strategy for the Rights of the Child. Available at: http://eur-lex.europa.eu/LexUriServ/LexUriServ. do?uri=COM:2006:0367:FIN:EN:PDF.
- Council of Europe 2009, Commentary on the European Rules for Juvenile Offenders Subject to Sanctions or Measures. Available at: http://www.coe.int/t/dghl/standardsetting/prisons/Commentary_Rec_ 2008_11E.pdf.
- Council of Europe 2010, Guidelines of the Committee of Ministers of the Council of Europe on Child Friendly Justice. Available at: http://www.coe.int/t/dghl/standardsetting/childjustice/Guidelines%20 on%20child-friendly%20justice%20and%20their%20explanatory%20 memorandum%20_4_.pdf.
- European Commission 2011, An EU Agenda for the Rights of the Child. Available at: http://ec.europa.eu/justice/fundamental-rights/rights-child/eu-agenda/index_en.htm.
- European Forum on the Rights of the Child, Available at: http://ec.europa.eu/justice/fundamental-rights/rights-child/european-forum/ index_en.htm.
- The Lisbon Treaty, Available at: http://europa.eu/lisbon_treaty/full_ text/.

2011: 199). Since then there has been a raft of further initiatives including the Council of Europe's *Guidelines for Child Friendly Justice* developed in 2010 (see Alston *et al.* 2005; Jensen and Jepsen 2006a; Kilkelly 2008, 2011; Stalford and Drywood 2011; Goldson and Muncie 2012; Stalford 2012).

11.5 Attitudes to children's rights

As stated earlier, there is still a strong antipathy towards the recognition of children's rights, and accepting that children are legitimate human rights subjects. According to Freeman, philosophical hostility to the concept of children's human rights can even be found among general human rights advocates (Freeman 2011: 23). Other resistance stems from the belief that parents' rights in the home are sacred, and that children are the property of their parents. Freeman argues that too often children are seen as objects to be dealt with (Freeman 2011). These attitudes are encapsulated in the following statement of opposition to the USA's proposed ratification of the CROC:

> this Treaty would virtually undermine parents' rights as we know it [*sic*] in the United States. Parents no longer would have the basic right to control what their children watch on TV, whom they associate with and what church they attend. Parents could be prosecuted and children be taken away, simply because they spank their children or fail to honor the various rights that the children are guaranteed. (C.J. Klicka, 2006, cited in Alston, *et al.* 2005;12)

Abramson (2006) points out that it is even harder to gain support for children's rights when the subject of the rights is an older juvenile offender and not the vulnerable, innocent child represented in the bulk of children's rights discourse. This lack of empathy towards young offenders persists, he argues, despite the fact that evidence suggests that many offenders have themselves been victims of physical and sexual abuse or neglect and are in need of the same kinds of rights protections and support (Abramson 2006; see also Goldson and Muncie 2012). Research published in the *Report on Violence against Children* identified children who come into conflict with the law as 'one of the most vulnerable groups to the *worst forms of violence*' (Pinheiro 2005: 17–18, cited in Goldson and Muncie 2012: 56).

The prevalence of negative political, public and media attitudes to children's and young people's behaviour has been well documented in criminological and juvenile justice literature (Muncie 2008). These attitudes have been used to justify the development of laws, policies and practices that would not be tolerated if they were proposed in relation to adults. Children and young people are heavily policed in public and privatized spaces. In the UK, for example, the Anti-Social Behaviour Act 2003 provided the police with powers to create dispersal zones, which allow them to move on or send home any young person under 16 not accompanied by an adult if they are found in the zone between 9pm and 6am (Crawford and Lister 2007). In 2005, lawyers working on behalf of the civil liberties organization Liberty acted for 'W', a 15-year-old boy from Richmond, London, who successfully challenged the legality of curfews for under-16s (Liberty undated). In another example of discrimination against young people, shopkeepers and retail centres in the UK have introduced a high-pitched electronic device called the Mosquito, originally used to deter vermin. The irritating noise can generally only be heard by those aged under 25 year of age and is used to exclude young people, effectively introducing 'no go' areas (Liberty UK, *Curfews* undated). As the Director of Liberty UK has said:

What type of society uses a low-level sonic weapon on its children? Imagine the outcry if a device was introduced that caused blanket discomfort to people of one race or gender, rather than to our kids. The Mosquito has no place in a country that values its children and seeks to instil them with dignity and respect. (Liberty UK, *Buzz Off*, undated, Director Shami Chakrabarti)

Goldson and Muncie argue that there has also been a marked racialization of juvenile justice policies and practices. Systemic discrimination against particular ethnic groups such as Afro-American children, Roma and 'traveller' children, immigrant children, and Indigenous children in Australia, Canada and

---

Box 11.2   Systematic denial of rights: children in military detention in Israel

In February 2013, UNICEF released a briefing paper on the treatment of Palestinian children in Israeli military detention — *Children in Military Detention in Israel* (UNICEF 2013). Each year around 700 Palestinian children aged between 12 and 17, mainly boys, are arrested, interrogated and detained by the Israeli army, police and security agents. The report found that, from arrest to custody and release, the ill-treatment of children, and the abuse of their fundamental rights, including torture, appeared to be widespread, systematic and institutionalized.

For a full copy of the briefing paper, go to: http://www.unicef.org/oPt/UNICEF_oPt_Children_in_Israeli_Military_Detention_Observations_and_Recommendations_-_6_March_2013.pdf.

the USA has meant that these groups are over-represented in all stages of the juvenile justice system (Goldson and Muncie 2012; see also CRC GC No. 11, 2009). Other children who live on the social margins, such as those living on the streets, children with disabilities, children who are repeatedly in conflict with the law, and children from dysfunctional families, are also more likely to be targets of juvenile justice interventions (Hamilton 2011).

Attitudes towards children that show them as being less deserving of human rights are also evident in the cultural acceptance of the use of violence against children. For example, the 2006 *UN World Report on Violence against Children* found that:

> violence exists in every country of the world, cutting across culture, class, education, income and ethnic origin. In every region, in contradiction to human rights obligations and children's developmental needs, violence against children is socially approved, and frequently legal and State-authorised. (Pinheiro 2006 I(1): 5)

The CROC forbids the use of corporal punishment on children in detention (and in other institutions, such as schools). The *UN World Report on Violence against Children* found that, despite 124 countries having fully banned corporal punishment in penal institutions, in at least 78 countries it remained legal as a disciplinary measure (Pinheiro 2006: 175).

The Global Initiative to End All Corporal Punishment of Children (2012) has audited the use of corporal punishment worldwide and found that 33 states (including New Zealand and countries in Europe, Africa and South America) have prohibited corporal punishment against children in all settings, and that the majority of states have banned its use in schools and other institutional settings, or as a court-mandated sentence. The rest of the world, including 50 of the states in the USA, continue to accept the use of physical punishment against children in private, in a way that violence against women is no longer tolerated (Pinheiro 2006).

The CRC advises that physical restraints are only to be used on children in detention in exceptional circumstances where the child might be in imminent danger of harming him/herself or when all other avenues have been tried but have failed; and further, that they should never be used as a means of punishment (CRC GC No. 10, para. 64). In 2008, a case that went to the English Court of Appeal concerned the use of pain-inducing techniques to restrain detainees. The case followed the death in a secure training centre of a boy who killed himself after being pinned down, and another who died while being restrained (*R (on the application of C) v Secretary of State for Justice [2008]*, cited in Hamilton 2011: 102). The Court found that the use of

---

Box 11.3   Corporal punishment as reasonable chastisement?

A case was brought against the UK Government by a boy who had been repeatedly caned by his stepfather, causing significant bruising (*A v United Kingdom Application No. 25599/94 23 Sept 1998*). The stepfather had been charged with causing actual bodily harm, but his case was dismissed by the court as his actions were seen to constitute 'reasonable chastisement' and to be permissible under law. The child took the case to the ECtHR, on the basis that the state had denied him a remedy under domestic law for a violation of his rights, and that the law discriminated against children (Alston *et al.* 2005). The Court found in his favour, stating that children are entitled to effective deterrence against serious breaches of their personal integrity. In response, the UK Government changed the law so that reasonable chastisement became a defence to common assault, but not to the more serious charges of wounding causing grievous bodily harm, assault occasioning actual bodily harm or cruelty to children.

---

restraints in this way constituted humiliating and degrading treatment, thus breaching Articles 3 and 8 of the European Convention on Human Rights (Hamilton 2011).

11.6 From welfare to injustice

From the late nineteenth century onwards, and the establishment of separate children's courts, the age, welfare needs and social background of children and young people in conflict with the law have been taken into consideration in all aspects of criminal proceedings. However, as stated earlier, attitudes towards children in some jurisdictions have shifted from a concern for the child's welfare towards a focus on treating children as being fully responsible, rational actors (Muncie 2008; Goldson and Muncie 2012). In the words of Michael Howard, a former Conservative Party Home Secretary in the UK, children should be seen 'as adults in everything except years' (cited in Goldson 2009: 514). These moves towards responsibilization and adultification can have devastating consequences (Goldson and Muncie 2012).

The minimum age of criminal responsibility is a legal principle which recognizes that under a certain age children are not seen as being sufficiently mature to be fully aware of the criminal nature of their actions (Telford 2012). In some jurisdictions, the age at which children are considered to be criminally responsible is extremely low. For example, it is as young as seven or eight years old in countries such as Yemen and the United Arab Emirates, while in the UK and New South Wales (NSW), Australia, this age is set at 10.

However, NSW retains the principle of doli incapax for children aged between 10 and 14. Doli incapax places an onus on the prosecution to prove that the child does have the mental capacity to form the requisite criminal intent, and is criminally responsible. In comparison, the age of criminal responsibility ranges from 14 to 16 in other jurisdictions, especially in countries where there is still a strong welfare focus in juvenile justice (Jensen 2006; Goldson 2009; Hamilton 2011; Telford 2012). As most commentators note, the age of criminal responsibility often bears no relation to the age at which children are considered to be mature enough to get married, have sex, vote, drink alcohol or drive.

The CRC has endeavoured to provide guidance to States Parties on the interpretation of CROC Article 40(3), and has stated that setting the age of criminal responsibility below the age of 12 is not acceptable, and that a higher age, such as 14 or 16, is much more in line with the foundational principles contained in the Convention (2007: 11, para. 32). The Beijing Rules also stipulate that the age should not be set too low, and that the emotional, mental and intellectual maturity of the child should be taken into account.

The CRC is of the view that younger children are not sufficiently mature to be fully responsible for their actions, and in addition, early contact with the justice system is detrimental to children's welfare (CRC 2007, para. 32). The Committee also considers principles such as doli incapax to be confusing and detrimental to children (2007, para. 34). It argues that those States Parties who use what is in effect two ages of criminal responsibility should instead simply increase the minimum age to 14 (GC No. 10 2007, para. 34). Despite its recommendations, the CRC has had a tough battle in achieving change. It has recommended on at least 65 occasions that States Parties increase the age of criminal responsibility, or at least introduce a minimum age in the case of countries where one did not previously exist (Hamilton 2011: 16).

As discussed earlier, international human rights instruments require that children in conflict with the law be dealt with separately from adults at all times through a child-focused system of justice. Many jurisdictions do maintain separate systems of juvenile justice that include child-friendly procedures that are very different from those in the adult courts (see Hamilton 2011: 67–81). In some jurisdictions, the developing capacity of children and their lack of maturity are recognized in that they are dealt with in separate proceedings until their early twenties (see Jensen and Jepsen 2006b: 3, table 3). However, in other states, children are being subjected increasingly to adult-based proceedings and penal sanctions before they are 18. For example, jurisdictions that have mandatory or three strikes sentencing laws do not take children's individual circumstances or age into consideration. In other situations, children accused of serious crimes may be transferred automatically to adult courts and be subject to the full force of the adversarial system (Goldson 2009). In the UK, since 1993 and the trial of two 10-year-olds for the murder of toddler Jamie Bulger, juvenile serious offenders, no matter what their age, are tried automatically in an adult court (for a brief synopsis of the case and its effects, see Torney 2011, or for a more detailed discussion, Scraton 1997). In the USA, the push for more punitive policies in many states has led to the rising use of the 'judicial waiver', whereby serious or mandatory charges are referred by a judge to the adult criminal court no matter what the individual circumstances of the young person might be (Feld 2006). Even in Denmark, which has a traditionally welfare-based system, serious offenders are now being transferred into adult criminal courts (Jepsen 2006).

The CROC places obligations on States Parties to ensure that children have a right to be heard, and a right to participate fully in all proceedings relating to them (see CRC GC No. 12, 2009). This is seen to be achievable by making proceedings informal, child-friendly and understandable, as well as ensuring that children have access to good-quality legal representation (CRC GC No. 12, 2009, paras 58–61). The failure of governments to provide children with the opportunity to participate fully in proceedings is seen as amounting to a breach of their right to a fair trial (Hamilton 2011).

The CRC prioritizes diversion from the formal court system as a key principle that should underpin the administration of juvenile justice (Article 40[3]). Diversion is known to reduce social harms and recidivism rates (Goldson 2009). The Committee calls for states to introduce a 'stepped' system of responding to children's criminality (CRC GC No. 10, 2007, para. 27). These steps are seen to include taking no further action, or using warnings, cautions, probation, therapeutic intervention, counselling, education, vocational work or other forms of pre-trial diversions, such as restorative justice (Hamilton 2011: 54). To avoid 'net widening', the CRC also considers that diversionary measures should only be imposed where 'there is compelling evidence' that the child has committed the offence, and where he or she has freely confessed his/her culpability, and should not be used for 'status' offences – that is, behaviour that may not be desirable, such as anti-social behaviour, truancy or sexual activity, but which is not actually criminal (see Hamilton 2011: 54). Goldson makes the point that one obvious way to divert children from the juvenile justice system in the UK would be to raise the age of criminal responsibility to 14 years (Goldson 2009).

11.7 Children in detention

Article 37 of the CROC stipulates that the detention of children should only be used as 'a measure of last resort' for the 'shortest period of time' when the possibility of diversionary options has been exhausted or the seriousness of the crime warrants a trial. The Beijing Rules call for the 'release' of the child into the community during the pre-trial period, and state that there should be a presumption in favour of release for children in all decisions (Hamilton 2011: 62). In many jurisdictions, it is common practice that first-time and minor offenders are dealt with in this way. However, in recent years concerns about 'risk', including the risk of re-offending; the desire of governments to appear to be tough on crime; and the impact of new managerialism on policing targets have been seen to lead to a situation where children are too readily placed in custody. For example, in NSW, from the 1990s, a series of reforms to bail and the policing of bail breaches was implemented that led to a significant rise in the numbers of young people (especially Indigenous young people) who were denied bail, or found to be in breach of bail conditions, and placed in custody on remand. On any one day there were over 200 unconvicted pre-trial children in custody. The majority of these detainees would not have faced a custodial sentence even if they had been convicted, and were released after their trial (Stubbs 2010; Wong *et al.* 2010; Child Rights Task Force 2011; Hamilton 2011).

All children in detention should be entitled to the same protections and rights afforded to those children living in the community. The CROC, the Beijing Rules and the Havana Rules stress the importance of children in detention having the same level of access to education in the community, vocational education, recreation and leisure, and medical, counselling and other rehabilitation services as is available to children in the community. The CROC Article 37(c), Havana Rules (61) and the CRC (GC No. 10) argue that sustained contact with family, including free communication and frequent visitation rights, is essential to the child's well-being and reintegration (Hamilton 2011). Article 19 of the CROC, which aims to protect children from neglect, abuse and exploitation, has been interpreted to mean that children should not be subject to non-violent disciplinary measures such as a reduction in diet, closed or solitary confinement, overcrowding, denial of contact with family, or hard labour (Hamilton 2011: 102).

As we have seen, international human rights instruments call for children in detention to be kept separately from adults, and treated in ways that are appropriate to their age and development. Yet children aged under 18 continue to be held in custody alongside adults, imprisoned in adult jails, or held in immigration detention with adults. According to Telford, the use of custody for those aged under 18 in the UK remains high in comparison to other European countries (Telford 2012). However, a recent High Court case in the UK successfully challenged the police practice of treating 17-year-olds as adults while in police custody ([2013] EWHC 982 [Admin]). The police had until that time been routinely holding 17-year-olds for up to 24 hours without contacting their families or having an independent adult present during questioning (Just For Kids 2013). In Australia, children are held in police custody alongside adults in remote and rural areas, because of the lack of alternative facilities. This results in the over-representation of many young Indigenous people in adult detention (see CRC GC No. 11).

In some poorer nations, such as Bolivia, non-offending children of all ages live in prisons alongside their parents, if through poverty or a lack of alternative care options there is nowhere else for them to live. La Paz jail has 1,500 inmates and children are subject to overcrowded, unsanitary conditions, experience the discipline of prison regimes, and become susceptible to physical and sexual abuse from other inmates, with a lack of access to education, health and other welfare services (see http://www.cyc-net.org/features/ft-bolivia.html).

Children are held in immigration detention as minors travelling on their own, or with another member of their family. This constitutes a clear breach of the country's human rights obligations. In Australia, children and their families, and unaccompanied minors, are held alongside adults in immigration detention, often in harsh, prison-like conditions in offshore and remote processing centres. Day-to-day, such children live alongside severely traumatized detainees who are awaiting refugee determination or deportation, and they witness adult self-harm and attempted suicide. This situation continues despite the fact that Australia has been subject to repeated critical commentary by the CRC (Child Rights Task Force 2011). As a 2011 Child Rights Task Force report notes, not only is the placement of children in such facilities in contravention of the CROC, but it is also injurious to their physical and mental health. Prolonged detention can lead to children and young people self-harming and in some cases attempting suicide (Child Rights Task Force 2011: 30). And children and young people in these circumstances have difficulty accessing health, education, recreation, leisure and child protection services on the same basis as other children in the community (ibid.).

The USA, which initially led the world in establishing juvenile courts and progressive attitudes towards delinquency (Jensen 2006), now provides us with a stark reminder of what happens when children's human rights are not fully incorporated into juvenile justice systems. For example, an average of 7,500 under-18-year-olds per day were incarcerated in adult jails in 2007 (Campaign for Youth Justice 2007: 4). Research shows that these young people are more likely to be victims of physical and sexual assault, and other forms of violence, and in consequence are particularly susceptible to trauma and self-harm (Campaign for Youth Justice 2007; ACLU/ Human Rights Watch 2012, Human Rights Watch 2013). Young offenders in adult prisons

Box 11.4   Age testing and children in Australian detention

To avoid children being placed inadvertently in the adult system, the CRC places an obligation on courts to give the benefit of the doubt if the age of a child is not easy to ascertain (CRC 2007, para. 35). However, the Australian Human Rights Commission found that, between 2008 and 2011, the Australian Government had not done so, and in consequence had breached the International Covenant on Civil and Political Rights, and CROC, on numerous occasions.

   As part of a series of 'get tough' measures designed to deter refugees arriving by boat, the government introduced heavy penalties for individuals accused of people smuggling (AHRC 2012). Some of the Indonesian crew members arrested for people smuggling told the authorities that they were under 18 years old; however, they were detained in adult prisons. The Australian Government thus imprisoned under-18-year-old Indonesian crew members accused of people smuggling in adult prisons (AHRC 2012). The government relied on the outdated and discredited technology of X-raying wrists to determine the skeletal maturity of the teenagers. They were held without charge in adult detention for periods of up to 10 months, and others whose cases were discontinued because of the lack of conclusive proof that they were 18 were still held in adult detention, with one individual spending 21 months there. Fifteen young crew members were sentenced to manda-tory terms of imprisonment that were only applicable to adults, and one of these detainees was held for almost three years in an adult facility. The government was found by the AHRC to have failed to take adequate meas-ures to secure age identification documentation from the Indonesian authorities, and to seek out the authentication of age from the young person's family and friends (AHRC 2012).

are often placed in segregation and solitary confinement for protection or punishment that can last for up to 22 hours per day, and can continue for years (ACLU/ Human Rights Watch 2012, Human Rights Watch 2013). Isolation can lead to mental disorders, paranoia and an increased risk of suicide (Campaign for Youth Justice 2007; ACLU/ Human Rights Watch 2012, Human Rights Watch 2013). If segregated, young people often have little access to education, work or leisure facilities, and some face lifelong separa-tion from their families (Campaign for Youth Justice 2007; ACLU/Human Rights Watch 2012, Human Rights Watch 2013). According to the Campaign for Youth Justice, in the USA in 2005, 21 per cent of inmate-on-inmate violence in jails was committed against youths aged under 18 – a high percentage considering that only 1 per cent of inmates in adult jails are juve-niles. A high percentage of those young people placed in adult custody while awaiting sentencing or trial ultimately do not receive adult convictions (Campaign for Youth Justice 2007).

Until 2005, the USA retained the use of capital punishment for under-18-year-olds. However, in the case of *Roper v Simmons* (543 US 551 [2005]), the Supreme Court concluded that it was unconstitutional to impose the death penalty on those convicted who were under 18 at the time of an offence. Young people in the USA continue to be sentenced to life without parole (LWP), which would amount to a contravention of Article 37(a) of the CROC. And children as young as 14 have been sentenced to stay in prison for the rest of their lives, even if they were only found to be accessories to crimes committed by others. In 2012, the US Supreme Court banned mandatory LWP sentences for juvenile offenders convicted of homicide. The Court considered that the sentence breached the 8th Amendment of the Constitution, since it did not take the age and circumstances of the young person into consideration. At the time of the judgment, 28 states and the federal jurisdiction sentenced teenagers to mandatory LWP. Now courts have to take the individual circumstances of young people into consideration as well as the nature of the crime committed; however, it is still within the discretion of judges to give an LWP sentence (National Center for Youth Law; see http://www.youthlaw.org/juvenile_justice/6/).

The treatment of children as adults not only contravenes international human rights instruments but also flies in the face of established criminological evidence on children's offending, and contemporary neuro-scientific and psychological evidence which shows that, on average, full adult reasoning competency is not realized until the age of 25 (Feld 2006; Goldson 2009; Kilkelly 2011; Telford 2012).

11.8 Reintegration and restorative justice

In 2007, the CRC reasserted the importance of rehabilitation and reintegration as strategies of juvenile justice, and called on States Parties to prioritize these, and restorative justice, over repression and retribution (CRC 2007, para. 10).

Restorative justice, youth justice conferencing and therapeutic justice are seen by many as the most effective means of providing young offenders with a greater opportunity to participate directly in decisions made about them, and to facilitate community reintegration. The Council of Europe, alongside the UN, has also recommended that restorative approaches, including diversion, mediation and alternative dispute resolution, should be prioritized (Goldson and Muncie 2012). Advocates of restorative practices consider that the flexible, discretionary, non-bureaucratic and de-professionalized qualities of the process can enhance children's participation and counter the failings of the formal judicial system (Goldson and Muncie 2012: 57). However, it is these very qualities that Goldson and Muncie argue can equally undermine other human rights principles such as proportionality, due process, best interests and protections against the excessive intrusion into children's lives (Goldson and Muncie 2012). According to Goldson and Muncie the discourse of responsibilization is still very strong within restorative justice, questions of power are airbrushed out, and simplistic narratives of victims and offenders mask the reality of the lives of many children who come into conflict with the law (2012: 59). Goldson and Muncie also make the point that, despite its perceived benefits, restorative conferencing has never really offered an alternative to the formal legal system, and tends to deal with a very small percentage of young offenders.

11.9 Conclusion

Over the years, children's human rights advocates and international human rights organizations have developed models, guidelines and reports that promote principles of best practice in relation to children's rights, and provide examples of innovative laws, policies and procedures (see Hamilton 2011 for guidelines on juvenile justice law and policy).

There has been a concerted push for governments and NGOs to 'mainstream' a children's human rights approach into all aspects of international and domestic policy formulation, law reform, programme development, resource allocation and service delivery, as well as systems of accountability and governance (Tobin 2011). This drive also includes expanding the idea of a child's 'right to be heard', so that children are involved in all decision-making that affects them (see CRC GC No. 12, 2009, paras 13, 14). There are already situations where children are involved in decision-making at a policy level, and there are children's advisory councils, children's parliaments, and direct consultations with children on legal and policy reforms. Children are involved in policy agenda setting, and in some European countries there are proposals to lower the voting age to strengthen children's citizenship rights (see Alston *et al.* 2005; Hamilton 2011; Tobin 2011). For the CRC, the expansion of children's participation marks the development of a new social contract that requires long-term changes in political, social, institutional and cultural structures (CRC 2009, para. 4). As Tobin argues, there is still work to be done on determining exactly what a 'children's human rights approach' might mean, but the mainstreaming of children's rights would lead to a situation where 'the place of children and their voice within the political economy can no longer be ignored, devalued or marginalised' (Tobin 2011: 89). It can only be hoped that this would have a positive impact on 'children in conflict with the law'.

Additional readings and materials

Defence for Children International.
 Available at: http://www.defenceforchildren.org/.
Invernizzi, A. and Williams, J. (eds) (2011) *The Human Rights of Children: From Visions to Implementation*, Farnham: Ashgate.
National Center for Youth Law.
 Available at: http://www.youthlaw.org/juvenile_justice/6/.
Pais, M.S. and Bissel, S. (2006) 'Overview and Implementation of the UN Convention on the Rights of the Child', *The Lancet*, 367: 389—90.
Sony Productions (2012) *The West Memphis Three*, documentary directed by Amy Berg.

Court cases cited

(IACtHR) *Guatemala Villagran Morales et al. v Guatemala Judgment of Nov. 19 1999 Inter-American Court of Human Rights (Ser.C) no. 63* (Central and South America).
(ECtHR) *A v United Kingdom Application No. 25599/94 23 Sept 1998* (Europe).
R [on the application of C] v Secretary of State for Justice [2008] (England).
 [2013] EWHC 982 [Admin] (England).
Roper v Simmons (543 US 551 [2005]) (US).

References

Abramson, B. (2006) 'Juvenile Justice: The Unwanted Child — Why the Potential of the Convention on the Rights of the Child is Not Being Realized, and What We Can Do About It', in E. L. Jensen and J. Jepsen (eds), *Juvenile Law Violators, Human Rights, and the Development of New Juvenile Justice Systems*, Oxford/Portland, OR: Hart Publishing, pp.15—38.
ACLU (American Civil Liberties Union) Human Rights Watch (2012) *Growing Up Locked Down: Youth in Solitary Confinement in Jails and Prisons Across the United States*, 10 October. Available at: http://www.hrw.org/reports/2012/10/03/growing-locked-down; accessed 22 February 2013.
AHRC (Australian Human Rights Commission) (2012) *An Age of Uncertainty: Inquiry into the Treatment of Individuals Suspected of People Smuggling Who Say That They Are Children*, Sydney: AHRC.
Alston, P., Tobin, J. and Darrow, M. (2005) *Laying the Foundations of Children's Rights: An Independent Study of Some Key Legal and Institutional Aspects of the Impact of the Convention on the Rights of the Child*, Florence: UNICEF Office of Research.

Campaign for Youth Justice (2007) *Jailing Juveniles: The Dangers of Incarcerating Youth in Adult Jails in America*. Available at: http://www.campaignforyouthjustice.org/documents/CFYJNR_JailingJuveniles.pdf; accessed 21 November 2012.

Child Rights Task Force (2011) *Listen to Children*, Child Rights NGO Report Australia, May.

Crawford, A. and Lister, J. (2007) 'The Use and Impact of Dispersal Orders', Joseph Rowntree Foundation. Available at: http://www.jrf.org.uk/sites/files/jrf/2135.pdf; accessed 3 April 2013.

CRC (United Nations Committee on the Rights of the Child) (2007) *General Comment No. 10: Children's Rights in Juvenile Justice, 44th Session, 15 January to 2 February*, Geneva: Office of the High Commissioner for Human Rights.

CRC (United Nations Committee on the Rights of the Child) (2009) *General Comment No. 11: Indigenous Children and their Rights Under the Convention*, Geneva: Office of the High Commissioner for Human Rights.

CRC (United Nations Committee on the Rights of the Child) (2009) *General Comment No. 12: On the Right of the Child to be Heard, 51st Session, 25 May to 12 June*, Geneva: Office of the High Commissioner for Human Rights.

Feld, B.C. (2006) 'The Inherent Tension of Social Welfare and Criminal Social Control: Policy Lessons from the American Juvenile Court Experience', in E.L. Jensen and J. Jepsen (eds), *Juvenile Law Violators, Human Rights, and the Development of New Juvenile Justice Systems*, Oxford/Portland, OR: Hart Publishing, pp. 407–42.

Freeman, M. (2011) 'The Value and Values of Children's Rights', in A. Invernizzi and J. Williams (eds), *The Human Rights of Children: From Visions to Implementation*, Farnham: Ashgate, pp. 21–36.

Gan (2011) 'The Role of Independent Children's Rights Institutions in Implementing the CRC', in A. Invernizzi and J. Williams (eds), *The Human Rights of Children: From Visions to Implementation*, Farnham: Ashgate, pp. 219–38.

Global Initiative to End All Corporal Punishment of Children (2012) *Ending Legalised Violence Against Children*. Available at: http://www.endcorporalpunishment.org/pages/pdfs/reports/GlobalReport2012.pdf; accessed 3 March 2013.

Goldson, B. (2009) 'COUNTERBLAST: "Difficult to understand or defend" — A Reasoned Case for Raising the Age of Criminal Responsibility', *The Howard Journal*, 48(5): 514–21.

Goldson, B. and Muncie, J.T. (2012) 'Towards a Global "Child Friendly" Juvenile Justice?', *International Journal of Law, Crime and Justice*, 40: 47–64.

Hamilton, C. (2011) *Guidance for Legislative Reform of Juvenile Justice,* New York: The Children's Legal Centre, UNICEF.

Human Rights Watch (2013) *Submission to the Inter-American Commission on Human Rights Re: Thematic Hearing on the Incarceration of Youth in US Adult Prisons*, 26 February.

Jensen, E.L. (2006) 'An Historical Overview of the American Juvenile Justice System', in E.L. Jensen and J. Jepsen (eds), *Juvenile Law Violators, Human*

Rights, and the Development of New Juvenile Justice Systems, Oxford/ Portland, OR: Hart Publishing, pp. 84—97.

Jensen, E.L. and Jepsen, J. (eds) (2006a), *Juvenile Law Violators, Human Rights, and the Development of New Juvenile Justice Systems*, Oxford/Portland, OR: Hart Publishing.

Jensen, E.L. and Jepsen, J. (2006b) 'Introduction', in E.L. Jensen and J. Jepsen (eds), *Juvenile Law Violators, Human Rights, and the Development of New Juvenile Justice Systems*, Oxford/Portland, OR: Hart Publishing, pp. 1—12.

Jepsen, J. (2006) 'Juvenile Justice in Denmark: From Social Work to Repression', in E.L. Jensen and J. Jepsen (eds), *Juvenile Law Violators, Human Rights, and the Development of New Juvenile Justice Systems*, Oxford/Portland, OR: Hart Publishing, pp. 213—62.

Just for Kids (2013) *The Divisional Court Rules Home Secretary's Treatment of 17-year-olds Unlawful*, Press Statement, 25 April. Available at: http://www.hja. net/legal-news/hja-news/appropriate-adult-ruling.aspx accessed 28 April 2013.

Kilkelly, U. (2008) 'Youth Justice and Children's Rights: Measuring Compliance with Human Rights Standards', *Youth Justice*, 8: 187—92.

Kilkelly, U. (2011) 'Using the Convention on the Rights of the Child in Law and Policy', in A. Invernizzi and J. Williams (eds), *The Human Rights of Children: From Visions to Implementation*, Farnham: Ashgate.

Liberty UK (no date) *Buzz Off Campaign*. Available at: http://www.liberty-human-rights.org.uk/campaigns/buzz-off/index.php; accessed 2 February 2013.

Liberty UK (no date) *Curfews*. Available at: http://www.liberty-human-rights.org.uk/human-rights/discrimination/young-people/curfews/index.php; accessed 2 February 2013.

Muncie, J. (2008) 'The "Punitive Turn" in Juvenile Justice: Cultures of Control and Rights Compliance in Western Europe and the USA', *Youth Justice*, 8: 107—21.

Muncie, J. (2009) *Youth & Crime*, 3rd edn, London: Sage.

Njungwe, E. (2009) 'International Protection of Children's Rights: An Analysis of African Attributes of the African Charter on the Rights and Welfare of the Child', *Cameroon Journal on Democracy and Human Rights*, 3(1): 4—25.

Pinheiro, P.S. (2006) *World Report on Violence against Children*, Geneva: United Nations.

Scraton, P. (1997) *Childhood in Crisis*, London: Routledge.

Stalford, H. (2012) *Children and the European Union: Rights, Welfare and Accountability*, Oxford/Portland, OR: Hart Publishing.

Stalford, H. and Drywood, E. (2011) 'Using the CRC to Inform EU Law and Policy Making', in A. Invernizzi and J. Williams (eds), *The Human Rights of Children: From Visions to Implementation*, Farnham: Ashgate, pp. 199—218.

Stubbs, J. (2010) 'Re-examining Bail and Remand for Young People in NSW', *Australian & New Zealand Journal of Criminology*, 43(3): 485—505.

Telford, M. (2012) The Criminal Responsibility of Children and Young People: An Analysis of Compliance with International Human Rights Obligations in England and Wales, *International Journal of Private Law*, 5(2): 107—20.

Tobin, J. (2011) 'Understanding a Human Rights Based Approach to Matters Involving Children: Conceptual Foundations and Strategic Considerations', in A. Invernizzi and J. Williams (eds), *The Human Rights of Children: From Visions to Implementation*, Farnham: Ashgate.

Tobin, J. (2013) 'Children's Rights in Australia: Confronting the Challenges', in P. Gerber and M. Castan (eds), *Contemporary Perspectives on Human Rights Law in Australia*, Pyrmont, NSW: Law Book Co. Thomson Reuters.

Torney, K. (2011) 'The Case Which Changed the Face of Youth Justice', *The Detail*, 8 May.

UNICEF (2013) *Children in Military Detention in Israel*. Available at: http://www.unicef.org/oPt/UNICEF_oPt_Children_in_Israeli_Military_Detention_Observations_and_Recommendations_-_6_March_2013.pdf.

Wong, K., Bailey, B. and Kenny, D. (2010) *Bail Me Out: NSW Young People and Bail*, Sydney: Youth Justice Coalition.

CHAPTER 12

Victims

> **Key concepts**
> Primary and secondary victimization — Prosecutorial tools — Restorative
> justice — Intersectionality

12.1 Introduction

The victims of crime compensation page of the Texas Department of Public Safety website informs the reader that 'an innocent victim of crime who suffers physical and/or emotional harm or death' may qualify for financial assistance (TDPS 2011). Similarly, compensation is offered in West Virginia ('compensation to innocent victims of crime', (CVCF 2013)) and New York State ('If you are an innocent victim of a crime within New York State you may be eligible to receive benefits from OVS [Office of Victim Services]' (OVS 2010)). Indeed, victim compensation schemes have been adopted by many US states as well as in other Western countries. There are, however, always conditions applicants must meet in order to qualify for compensation, thus reducing accessibility to these services and generating dissatisfaction among applicants (Elias 1984). Even if such compensation systems were improved significantly, to accept a broader range of applicants, it is clear from the examples above that one primary criterion is that applicants must be 'innocent' victims. The UK-based website, Victim Support (undated), states that 'when this [criminal injuries compensation] scheme was created it was not intended to literally compensate someone for their injuries but instead to be "an expression of public sympathy for *innocent* victims of violent crime"' (emphasis added).

This narrative of the innocent victim has heavily influenced the debate surrounding victimology. When is a victim 'innocent'? In general terms, it is believed that a victim is innocent when he or she did not precipitate the events that led to their victimization, yet the precipitation theory has been criticized for many years. Not only is the application of any benchmark of innocence open to interpretation, but the concept of the innocent victim has also produced distortions and expectations that have prevented any significant progress in an area still dominated by a conservative law and order policy. This is relevant because there is still a debate over whether the label of 'victim' should only cover victims of crime or be widened to include the victims of abuses of power, victims of accidents or events caused by people (as opposed to natural disasters), or victims of *all* forms of injustice (Garkawe 2004). Since the 1970s, victimology has been explored in the mainstream by policy-makers and academics in two main ways. First, it has been examined by drawing on conservative theoretical frameworks that posit a straightforward meaning of the term 'victim' based on notions of culpability, which is defined mainly from the ideas proposed by vocal victim movements. Second, victimology has been informed by liberal theoretical frameworks, which have begun to consider victims through the lens of human rights. This approach has favoured the examination of more hidden types of crime, such as white-collar crime and corporate crime, and has been informed by a broader interpretation of victims' human rights. Yet this approach to criminal victimization is largely confined to a rigid legalistic framework, limiting its potential and favouring the application of the label of deserving victim of crime, and occasionally the abuse of power. This narrow application has been tempered by a number of initiatives aimed at implementing a regime that recognizes victims' rights and focuses on restorative justice and improved communication between victims and criminal justice agencies. And while international human rights frameworks in this field have not encouraged a different approach over the decades, we can observe some changes along these lines in recent times, as highlighted in section 12.2. Here, the lack of binding international frameworks on crime victims is identified as a missed milestone, and one that is essential to building a more comprehensive top-down approach to broader victim rights. The second part of section 12.2 takes a closer look at some recent changes at the international, regional and domestic levels towards a recognition of the rights of victims of crime. Section 12.3 focuses on the UN-supported restorative justice principles as a mechanism that can provide victims with a better experience of the criminal justice process, thus reducing forms of secondary victimization. Finally, section 12.4 discusses the conservative and liberal approach to the role of victims, which has countered such progress, in emerging scenarios at the international level. Here, the 'black letter' human rights approach to victimhood – where only widely accepted principles are applied – is still embraced as the only possible way in which formal agreements can be achieved among multiple parties. The benchmark of 'innocence' is an ambitious threshold that has stimulated the development of a common definition of new categories of crime victims in the areas of transnational crime (such as victims of human trafficking) and international crime (such as crimes against humanity). However, its political use to advance certain policy agendas is also its biggest limitation, as the dominance of the concept of innocence weakens progressive discussion on victims' rights.

12.2 Crime victims, offenders and the role of the state

12.2.1 'After all, victims are human too'

Wemmers (2012: 74) questions why international human rights instruments do not explicitly embrace the rights of victims of crime, but include protections for the offender, observing, 'after all, victims are human too'. Indeed, international binding obligations in this area have yet to be achieved. It is nevertheless recognized that the voiceless victims of various forms of discrimination have been targets of intervention for the international community since the end of the Second World War. The 1948 Universal Declaration of Human Rights does not refer explicitly to victims, yet it is recognized as a response of the newly established United Nations (UN) to the atrocities carried out by the Nazi regime, which saw individuals left with no protection against a totalitarian state. In the years following the war, the international community proceeded to agree on more conventions and treaties that targeted groups of people deemed to be in need of special attention because of the weak position they had within their communities (see further discussion on collective rights and discrimination in Chapter 4). These years saw the emergence of the following strategic conventions aimed at imposing top-down standards on nation-states:

- the 1951 Convention Relating to the Status of Refugees, aimed at protecting asylum seekers;
- the 1965 Convention on the Elimination of All Forms of Racial Discrimination, targeting any form of exclusion based on race, colour, descent, or national or ethnic origin;
- the 1979 Convention on the Elimination of All forms of Discrimination against Women, focused on equal opportunities for women and men;
- the 1989 Convention on the Rights of the Child, aimed at guaranteeing the protection of people younger than 18 years old (also see Chapter 11 on juvenile justice);
- the 1984 Convention against Torture and Other Cruel, Inhuman or Degrading Treatment or Punishment, aimed at the removal of any form of inhuman treatment or punishment; and

- the 2006 Convention on the Rights of Persons with Disabilities, targeting people who are disadvantaged as a result of mental or physical impairment.

This process continued with the establishment of a permanent International Criminal Court (ICC) in 2000 (via the Rome Statute) for the punishment of genocide and crimes against humanity. The Rome Statute represents a public stand against states that turn against their own people, even if it has mainly, and controversially, focused on states in the African continent, which are considered to be less important geo-political players.

The violation of granted human rights, as stated in the conventions listed above, is the essential event that produces the status of victimhood, which ought to be recognized at the international, regional and national level. For example, Article 34 of the European Convention on Human Rights (ECHR) refers to the right of petition to anyone claiming to be 'the victim of a violation' of the Convention. A similar point can be found under Article 1 of the Optional Protocol to the International Covenant on Civil and Political Rights, and in national human rights charters, such as the UK's Human Rights Act 1998 (under Section 7). Further, Doak (2008) claims that the ECHR and national provisions such as the UK's Human Rights Act can progress the rights of crime victims even if only in an indirect manner, because such legislation has the power to send a signal to criminal justice agencies (police, prosecution and others) to act in accordance with human rights frameworks.

However, crime victims have not been recognized openly by the international community as a homogenous group that is at a disadvantage and in need of focused, mandatory protection. This lack of recognition is even more pronounced when juxtaposed with the range of rights guaranteed to offenders. As argued by Wemmers (2012), human rights frameworks that protect the offender against the state are found everywhere. For example, international human rights agreements contain explicit reference to the right of the person 'charged with a criminal offence'. And the same can be found at the national level, such as in the 1982 Canadian Charter of Rights and Freedoms, and the UK's Human Rights Act. At the regional level, we can trace a similar trend. For example, the 2000 Charter of Fundamental Rights of the European Union makes no mention of the rights of victims, but clearly states the rights of the offenders. And even if there is an underlying logic that offenders are relatively powerless subjects at the mercy of the powerful state, there should be space to warrant protection and access to justice for those millions of people who are victims of crime every year. They suffer physical and psychological harm at the hands of offenders (primary victimization), and of an uncaring criminal justice system driven by a focus on the offender (secondary victimization). Their hardship and lack of access to services and rights are no different, according to Garkawe (2005), from that experienced by other groups of people who are subjected routinely to discrimination. Yet it is conspicuous that references to victims' human rights in international agreements have been sporadic. Wemmers (2012: 74) suggests that this is a result of the historical development of criminal law whereby 'the state replaced the victim in the legal process' (see also McBarnett 1983; and for a different view, Kirchengast 2006). The role of victims has been instrumental to other purposes, and for many years now in Western legal systems reduced to that of a witness in a criminal case against the state, a prosecutorial tool used if and when needed to give evidence. Thus victims 'have been rendered powerless against an omnipotent state that has the power to force them to testify as well as the power to shut them out' (Wemmers 2012: 75). The role and visibility of victims in the criminal justice system has attracted a great deal of attention in the literature in recent decades (for an overview, see Cook *et al.* 1999). Garkawe (2005) suggests that the instrumentalized role of victims in the legal system partially explains why it remains challenging to recognize victims as a uniform group deserving protection. The fact that victims do not share any distinct characteristic (for example, related to gender, race, religion or otherwise) that would allow for their easy identification also does not facilitate a call for action against discrimination to raise awareness.

It is evident that the international community is more concerned with human rights law that focuses on state violations (through any of its agencies or agents, such as the police), while at the national level the focus of the criminal justice system is on violations perpetrated by individuals. Common to both scenarios is that the powerful party (the state in the first place and the offender second) is scrutinized more closely for the purpose of re-establishing peace within the community. The victim becomes a secondary element, a prosecutorial tool, to achieve this aim. Further, international obligations are often invoked for the protection of the offender, who is recognized as a victim of the state. In these cases, the international human rights framework steps in to protect the rights of the offender to a fair trial and the prohibition against torture. Exemplary here is the 1999 *Selmouni v France* case before the European Court of Human Rights (ECtHR), involving a victim of police violence. A Dutch-Moroccan man, Ahmed Selmouni, was arrested by the police for an alleged offence and later sentenced to 15 years' imprisonment for drug trafficking. France was forced to pay US$100,000 (500,000 French francs) to Selmouni because the state police extorted his confession via torture (including by inflicting permanent disability, and rape) while he was held in police custody for four days. Thus this case illustrates how the offender who transgresses under national law can become a victim of state violence, and thus actioning the humanitarian protection in his defence.

12.2.3 *The movement towards formal recognition of victims' rights*

A dramatic step forward for victims' rights came with the 1985 UN Declaration of Basic Principles of Justice for Victims of Crime and Abuse of Power. Even though a declaration is 'soft law', and therefore not binding, as is a convention, it promotes debate and action. The 1985 Declaration has certainly helped to establish a platform at the international level to encourage a focus on the right to dignity and respect for the needs of victims of trauma. It has acted as a top-down standard, inspiring improvements to national criminal justice systems, and furthering transparency and accountability. Though not much progress was initially made either in Europe or North America (Wemmers 2012), some progress has been seen more recently in many national criminal justice systems, with the recognition of victims' hardship and improved access to services for victims (Cook *et al.* 1999).

This process of sensitization towards victims' rights has also been evident in a number of cases before the ECtHR, in particular the 1996 *Doorson* v. *Netherlands* case. On that occasion, the Court decided on an extended interpretation of Article 6 (right to a fair trial) of the ECHR to include the protection of victims who are providing testimony for the case:

> It is true that Article 6 does not explicitly require the interests of witnesses in general, and those of victims called upon to testify in particular, to be taken into consideration. However their life, liberty or security of person may be at stake, as may interests coming generally within the ambit of Article 8 [right to a private life]. Such interests of witnesses and victims are in principle protected by other, substantive provisions of the Convention, which imply that Contracting States should organise their criminal proceedings in such a way that those interests are not unjustifiably imperilled. Against this background, principles of fair trial also require that in appropriate cases the interests of the defence are balanced against those of witnesses or victims called upon to testify. (para. 70)

The 1998 Rome Statute also embraces this new attitude of respect for victims, highlighting that the prosecutor should take every step to ensure that victims of mass atrocities are protected (Article 54.1), and that their views and concerns are considered at all stages of the proceedings (Article 68.3). In this vein, the ICC has produced a 'Guide for the participation of victims in the proceedings of the court' (ICC undated), which mirrors very closely several national guides that offer information to victims of crime (see Box 12.1). Alongside this greater participation of victims in court proceedings, there has been a tangible turn towards embracing a human-rights-grounded policy approach to addressing

---

Box 12.1   Extract from 'Guide for the participation of victims in the proceedings of the court' (application process)

1. Victims are informed about their rights and how to apply to participate in ICC proceedings

2. Victims obtain and complete application forms with the assistance of individuals or organisations trained by the ICC

3. Victims submit their applications to the VPRS at the Headquarters or a Field Office

4. VPRS receives an application and provides the applicant with a reference number to the contact address provided or to the legal representative, if the applicant has appointed one

5. VPRS files the application with the Chamber of Judges.

6. Judges review and decide if the application is successful or rejected and the applicant is notified

7. If successful, applicant receives information, including about legal representation. If rejected applicant is allowed to apply again later in the proceedings

(ICC undated, box 8, p. 20)

---

past wrongs, based on restorative justice and reparation policy. International recognition of victims' rights reflects the belief that forgiveness of unfair treatment allows victims to look towards the future rather than back to the past (Arendt 1958), which is encapsulated in the 2005 UN Basic Principles and Guidelines on the Right to a Remedy and Reparation for Victims of Gross Violations of International Human Rights Law and Serious Violations of International Humanitarian Law (hereafter, the UN Basic Principles). The UN Basic Principles include a definition of the victim, as follows:

> Victims are persons who individually or collectively suffered harm, including physical or mental injury, emotional suffering, economic loss or substantial impairment of their fundamental rights, through acts or omissions that constitute gross violations of international human rights law, or serious violations of international humanitarian law.
>
> Where appropriate, and in accordance with domestic law, the term 'victim' also includes the immediate family or dependants of the direct victim and persons who have suffered harm in intervening to assist victims in distress or to prevent victimization.
>
> A person shall be considered a victim regardless of whether the perpetrator of the violation is identified, apprehended, prosecuted, or convicted

and regardless of the familial relationship between the perpetrator and the victim. (Articles 8 and 9, section V)

The 2008 apology of the Australian Prime Minister Kevin Rudd to Aboriginals and Torres Strait Islanders is an example of reparation for past wrongdoing (see Box 12.2), caused by the forced separation of Indigenous children from their families. In this regard, the term 'Stolen Generations' refers to the Indigenous Australian children who were removed by force from their families by past Australian governments from the late 1800s to the 1970s for the purpose of racial assimilation. The prime minister's apology can be seen as a direct application of the UN Basic Principle, Chapter 9 (Reparation for harm suffered), Article 22.e, which states:

> Satisfaction should include, where applicable, any or all of the following:
> ...
> (e) Public apology, including acknowledgement of the facts and acceptance of Responsibility.

These restorative-justice-infused UN Basic Principles, combined with the 1985 UN Declaration, have influenced the regional and national narrative on victims of domestic crimes. In October 2012, the Parliament and the Council of the EU reached an agreement on 'Minimum standards on the rights, support and protection of victims of crime'. Improved treatment of victims within domestic criminal justice systems is suggested by the statement in these standards that 'crime is a wrong against society *as well as* a violation of the individual rights of victims' (point 9, emphasis added). These standards mark an impressive step forward in embracing concrete and well-defined principles, an example of which is the right to have a presence before, during and after trial, rather than merely being considered a tool of the court. This right to a presence is enunciated in many Articles, such as Article 3 of the minimum standards, which stipulates the 'right to understand and to be understood'; or under the several rights to participate in criminal proceedings, including the 'right to safeguards in the context of restorative justice services' (Article 12). These minimum standards have been adopted as a Directive, which means that such provisions are directly enforceable by EU Member States, and that each Member State has three years (until 16 November 2015) to implement the provisions within their national laws. This top-down approach will ensure their applicability at the national level, and will set a standard for other regional areas.

In the USA, a proposed amendment to the US Constitution to protect the rights of crime victims was first discussed, with poor results, at the 112th

Box 12.2   Federal Parliament's full apology to the Stolen Generations delivered by the then Prime Minister Kevin Rudd, 13 February 2008

'Today we honour the Indigenous peoples of this land, the oldest continuing cultures in human history.

We reflect on their past mistreatment.

We reflect in particular on the mistreatment of those who were Stolen Generations — this blemished chapter in our nation's history.

The time has now come for the nation to turn a new page in Australia's history by righting the wrongs of the past and so moving forward with confidence to the future.

We apologise for the laws and policies of successive Parliaments and governments that have inflicted profound grief, suffering and loss on these our fellow Australians.

We apologise especially for the removal of Aboriginal and Torres Strait Islander children from their families, their communities and their country.

For the pain, suffering and hurt of these Stolen Generations, their descendants and for their families left behind, we say sorry.

To the mothers and the fathers, the brothers and the sisters, for the breaking up of families and communities, we say sorry.

And for the indignity and degradation thus inflicted on a proud people and a proud culture, we say sorry.

We the Parliament of Australia respectfully request that this apology be received in the spirit in which it is offered as part of the healing of the nation.

For the future we take heart; resolving that this new page in the history of our great continent can now be written.

We today take this first step by acknowledging the past and laying claim to a future that embraces all Australians.

A future where this Parliament resolves that the injustices of the past must never, never happen again.

A future where we harness the determination of all Australians, Indigenous and non-Indigenous, to close the gap that lies between us in life expectancy, educational achievement and economic opportunity.

A future where we embrace the possibility of new solutions to enduring problems where old approaches have failed.

A future based on mutual respect, mutual resolve and mutual responsibility.

A future where all Australians, whatever their origins, are truly equal partners, with equal opportunities and with an equal stake in shaping the next chapter in the history of this great country, Australia.'

Source: http://australia.gov.au/about-australia/our-country/our-people/apology-to-australias-indigenous-peoples. Reproduced under terms of the Creative Commons Attribution 3.0 Australia.

Congress in 2012. However, during the 113th Congress, in April 2013, the bill was reassigned to a congressional committee for its consideration. The amendment suggests the introduction of an Article whose first section includes the following:

> Section 1. The rights of a crime victim to fairness, respect, and dignity, being capable of protection without denying the constitutional rights of the accused, shall not be denied or abridged by the United States or any State. The crime victim shall, moreover, have the rights to reasonable notice of, and shall not be excluded from, public proceedings relating to the offense, to be heard at any release, plea, sentencing, or other such proceeding involving any right established by this article, to proceedings free from unreasonable delay, to reasonable notice of the release or escape of the accused, to due consideration of the crime victim's safety and privacy, and to restitution. (US Government 2013)

This provision would therefore apply constitutional status to the right of a victim to be heard at any release, plea or sentencing, and to receive information regarding his or her case at all times. Those who oppose this amendment, such as the CATO Institute, argue that this provision could interfere with the presumption of innocence of the accused. The juxtaposing of victims' rights with the rights of the accused is rather problematic (this will be discussed further in the next section). However, the proposed amendment is positive as it encourages a debate on victims' rights at the constitutional level. This, combined with the 2012 EU Minimum Standards, the 2005 UN Basic Principles and the 1985 UN Declaration, will also facilitate the possible introduction of a UN convention on victims' rights, as a binding document for all UN signatory parties. Garkawe has been arguing for such a convention since 2005, and in recent years the World Society of Victimology and the University of Tilburg have organized several meetings to draft such document.

12.3 Victimization and restorative justice

The emphasis at the international level on principles of restorative justice was clear when the UN Economic and Social Council endorsed a declaration on the Basic Principles on the Use of Restorative Justice Programmes in Criminal Matters (hereafter, UN Basic Principles) in July 2002. This point in time crystallized the recognition of alternative ways of responding to crime, which actively involve the victim in the process. Recognition of the condition and characteristics of victims has contributed to the advancement since the early 1990s of redistributive justice initiatives, such as restorative and indigenous justice. The aim of these alternative platforms is to ensure that demographic, cultural and other differences are taken into account, and that more space is given to victims to communicate their feelings and responses to the crime or trauma directly to the offender. National surveys of crime and other methods of statistical analysis are often used to construct a better understanding of victims and their characteristics (Zedner 1997; Coleman and Moynihan 2003). And while these instruments are limited in that they tend to categorize victims according to traditional methods and national types of criminal offences, and do not add a new narrative (Green 2007), they do allow for the identification of the characteristics of victims of crime.

While this chapter lacks the scope to discuss this further, it is recognized that the analysis of available data at the national level suggests that people in disadvantaged positions (intersectional (in)visibility) are often the victims of crime, and that this trend is common across many Western countries (for example, see Personal Crimes 2002; Harrell 2007; ABS 2011; Truman 2011).

Restorative justice is intended to create an environment where these conditions of structural disadvantage, and others inherently connected to the criminal justice system, may be taken in consideration. Dignan (2005) argues that restorative justice can contribute to a better experience of the criminal justice process for the victim – an experience that allows him or her to be treated with dignity, and power imbalances to be considered and addressed. This experience would be more in line with the 2002 UN Basic Principles, which state that procedural safeguards should guarantee fairness for the victim as much as for the offender and other parties. A balance between victims' and offenders' rights is the ultimate target of the UN Basic Principles. In fact, referring to crime victims' rights in opposition to offenders' rights would suggest that, if a platform of rights were offered to victims, such as the right to be protected and the right to access a fair trial, this would take away from the other parties' rights (Groenhuijsen 1996). Ashworth (2002: 584) addresses this issue by focusing on three principles: the principle of compensation and reparation for the victim; the principle of proportionality in the sentencing process; and the principle of independence and impartiality. In relation to each, Ashworth states that victims' rights have to be recognized, and, yet, a balancing process between victims' and offenders' rights needs to be followed more carefully, in the light of human rights obligations.

According to Strang and Sherman (2003), victims may wish to access information, participate, have their emotional and psychological trauma treated with respect and dignity as much as their material loss, and receive an apology as a form of closure rather than, or alongside, a financial settlement: '[victims want] that emotional harm is healed, as opposed to compensated for, only by an act of emotional repair' (ibid.: 22). Emotional healing is critically important to address a victim's post-traumatic experience and help them renegotiate their existence with a reduced sense of vulnerability, especially when their home has been invaded or their routine disturbed. Yet, as Strang and Sherman (2003) point out, in many Western legal systems there is no space for direct interaction between victims and offenders, or for apologies; rather, the harm is reduced to a measurable outcome that can be counted in 'monetary metric'. Forms of alternative justice offer victims an opportunity to better understand the offender and to alleviate any anxiety caused by the harm done to them. And yet, Ashworth (2002: 585) questions whether in restorative justice mechanisms 'the victim's legitimate interest goes beyond reparation or compensation ... and extends to the question of punishment'. Linked to this is the direct and potentially influential involvement of the victims in the sentencing process. This level of involvement impacts two basic rights: the proportionality principle and the impartiality principle. The test of proportionality suggests that the extent of punishment ought to be linked directly to the severity of the offence. Ashworth argues that the application of this principle should not involve the victim, 'because the views of victims may vary' (2002: 586). Therefore, a proportionate sentence may not be in line with the outcomes of a restorative process. The question about how to align the victims' expectations created by any restorative mechanism and the proportionality test needs to be explored further. Moreover, as Ashworth (2002) points out, the right to a fair trial needs to be considered. With this in mind, it can be asked whether a restorative process is independent and impartial when the victim's response to a situation may not be impartial.

In conclusion, Doak (2008) claims that the issues raised above are inherent to the structure and values of the current criminal justice system. He advocates for judicial reform that can allow for reconsideration of the role of victims within a system driven by principles of restorative justice.

12.4 Victims' agency in transnational and international crimes

Despite calls for a UN convention on crime victims' rights, Letschert and van Dijk (2012) argue that the focus on crime has become increasingly internationalized, in particular since the events of 11 September 2001 (hereafter, 9/11), and discussion about such a convention has been sidelined by other priorities. Making reference to the 2004 UN-coined term 'human security' (UN 2004: 15), van Dijk and Letschert (2012) claim that the 'globalization [process] produces new categories of victims and complicates their access to justice' (p. 303). It is evident that the progress made in the past few years in recognizing the agency of victims of crime has been minimized when it comes to victims of transnational and international crimes. The conservative approach to victimhood embraced at the international level alienates a more inclusive understanding of suffering in a globalized society. At the international level, victims of crime are often either ignored or used as political tools to serve an agenda: there is not much space left between these two positions. Denying people the label of victim is amplified by the geo-political nature and dynamics of the compromises involved in negotiation around the definition of crime. And when they are not ignored, victims are depicted in a conservative manner to fit with a transnational neo-liberal agenda of law and order. Exemplary here is the linking of a victim's credibility to their naivety, such as in the case of victims of human trafficking, who have to appear to have been in no way compliant with their traffickers to be classified as eligible for a humanitarian visa. These complex issues thus become simplified by such constructions of victimhood as being linked to culpability. The contradiction in the discretionary application of the victim label to those with little or no agency, but who hold enough social credibility to claim status as a genuine victim, has been identified by many commentators (see, in particular, Christie 1986). The ideal victim who is powerless to resist the violence perpetrated against him or her is a construct used to justify the creation of an ideal offender: someone who is evil, culpable and not known to the victim. In reality, the victim–offender relationship is more complex (Crawford and Goodey 2000), but has traditionally been explored to highlight the level of involvement – or blame – the victim has in the criminal act (Cook *et al.* 1999). The transnational criminal justice system uses an approach that has been criticized at the national level since the early 1970s: the victim is used as a tool to resolve the dispute in favour of, or against, the defendant (the human trafficker, in this case). Discrediting victims and their characters in court, particularly women, is not uncommon, and has a long history in rape and sexual assault trials (Amir 1967; Lees 1997). At the national level, feminist, radical and critical theories of victimology have been challenging the conservative view on the characteristics of victims and their role in the criminal event by highlighting the oppressive structural processes facing victimized minority groups and underprivileged people (Spalek 2006). Commentators have argued that the social construction of the victim through the lens of law and order is problematic, and partial to the interests of the powerful (Mawby and Walklate 1994). However, we are far from applying this discourse to issues at the international level. Some advancement is evident in the recognition of the negative experiences of stigmatized women who want to access justice in international courts (Dolgopol 2012), and the focus within reparation programmes on victims of sexual and reproductive violence (Rubio Marin 2009). Yet there is a degree of resistance to understanding human rights violations as being similar to traditional forms of crime, and progress made at the national level seems not to be translating to the international context.

One cannot deny that this is partially linked to how these violations and their victims are explained, via text and images, and who holds the power to respond to such representations of violence (Wilson and Brown 2009). The narrative around some crimes is selective and generates descriptions of victims that produce targeted responses. The treatment of human rights and victims at the international level usually positions victims, especially of transnational and international crimes, as being stuck in a triangulation of 'savages', 'victims' and 'saviours' (Mutua 2001), with the aim of fulfilling certain geo-political agendas of power and justice. Within this triangulation, the perpetrator is the savage, or evil other: in transnational crimes the perpetrator is the terrorist, human or drug trafficker, or people smuggler; in international crimes, such as genocide or crimes against humanity, the perpetrator is the enemy state or rebel non-state actors. Little matter their story, or the circumstances under which their status of friend-turned-foe occurred, as in the case of Libya and Colonel Gaddafi in 2011. The saviour is usually depicted as the Western world, represented by the state (or its agents) at the national or international level. The passive or heroic victim needs to be perceived as innocent to close the triangle. This was evident after the Second World War in relation to the victims of the Holocaust. And this is still the case at the time of writing, with the first ICC ruling against the Congolese warlord Thomas Lubanga Dyilo, where all the other forms of violence, abuse, rape and killing of adult (often male) victims were set aside, together with the Western-dominated history of the Congo, to make space for a rhetoric of salvation about child soldiers. The ICC (2012) verdict read as follows:

> Enlisting and conscripting of children under the age of 15 years into the Force Patriotique pour la Libération du Congo [Patriotic Force for the Liberation of Congo] (FPLC) and using them to participate actively in hostilities in the context of an armed conflict not of an international character from 1 September 2002 to 13 August 2003 (punishable under article 8(2)(e)(vii) of the Rome Statute).

The same discourse of victimization applies in other transnational matters. The victims of 9/11 and other terrorist events that followed have been labelled as passive victims. Victims of sex or labour trafficking have to be seen as passive to be accepted as credible. Heroic victims such as Aung San Suu Kyi, the Burmese opposition politician who was under house arrest for more than 15 years, are perceived as peaceful fighters and therefore still innocent. The law-and-order fabrication of victimhood and the exaggeration of victims' experiences serves political interests, which are amplified by a co-opted media. As observed by Strang and Sherman in relation to traditional forms of crime (2003: 17):

> Claims are frequently made about victims' views of the criminal justice system by the media, elected officials, lobbyists, and civil libertarians. Victims' views are usually assumed to be more punitive than those of the general public. Such claims have been used to support more retributive criminal justice policies.

This discourse finds application at the international level, where the black letter human rights approach to victims of transnational and international crime has been dominated by a combination of conservative and liberal frameworks. A critical approach to human rights and 'global' victims can help to broaden understanding of victimhood at the international level. It can also encourage the recognition that supranational policies (such as immigration, environmental and crime control policies) may at times be responsible for human suffering.

12.5 Conclusion

Currently, there is no UN binding document to protect victims' rights. Despite this, recent developments at the international, regional and domestic level are aimed at rebalancing victims' rights with those of the offender. Such developments are encouraging, since they promote restorative justice principles and access to fair treatment. However, progress has been slow, as the debate surrounding victims' rights has been dominated by a law-and-order approach. A black letter legal approach to the term and concept of the victim has influenced – and limited – the trajectory and potentialities of such rights. The influential discourses that have dominated the narrative of victimhood can be divided into two main groups: the legalistic human rights framework approach; and the criminal justice approach.

The legalistic human rights framework is still heavily influenced by the legacy of the lessons learnt from the post-1945 Nuremburg trials, which identified the so-called powerless victims of an evil state. This vision of the passive and heroic victim is perpetuated in many international agreements that promote a law-and-order approach, and was epitomized by the first verdict of the permanent ICC. In this approach, the agency of the victim is constrained by artificial limitations defined by the characteristics of being either deserving or blameworthy. However, the interventions of supranational courts such as the ECtHR and the Inter-American Court of Human Rights to punish fundamental human rights violations by the state have made some progress in the field of victims' rights. This has in turn influenced further international developments inspired by principles of restorative justice.

Under the criminal justice approach, the concept that the state is acting in the interests of society is applied to court proceedings. It is the criminal justice system's approach to victimhood as oppositional (offenders against victims) that limits the full potential of a debate on victims' agency. Proponents of a restorative-justice-driven system, such as Doak (2008), suggest that victims whose agency is recognized are less likely to experience secondary victimization at the hands of criminal justice agencies.

Additional reading and materials

Dignan, J. (2005) *Understanding Victims and Restorative Justice*, Maidenhead: Open University Press.

EU (European Union) (2012) 'Minimum Standards on the Rights, Support and Protection of Victims of Crime', *Official Journal of the European Union*, 14 November, L 315/58. Available at: http://eur-lex.europa.eu/LexUriServ/ LexUriServ.do?uri=OJ:L:2012:315:0057:0073:EN:PDF.

Letschert, R. and van Dijk, J. (eds) (2012) *The New Faces of Victimhood*, Dordrecht: Springer.

Maryland Crime Victims' Resource Center.
Available at: http://www.mdcrimevictims.org/.

United Nations (1985) *Declaration of Basic Principles of Justice for Victims of Crime and Abuse of Power*. Available at: http://www.un.org/documents/ga/res/ 40/a40r034.htm.

United Nations Office for Drug Control and Crime Prevention (1999) *Handbook on Justice for Victims*, United Nations Office for Drug Control and Crime Prevention, Centre for International Crime Prevention. Available at http://www. uncjin.org/Standards/9857854.pdf.

World Society of Victimology.
Available at: http://www.worldsocietyofvictimology.org/.

Court cases cited

Selmouni v France, Application number 00025803/94, 28/07/1999, *European Court of Human Rights* (Europe).

Doorson v Netherlands, Application number 20524/92, 26/03/1996, *European Court of Human Rights* (Europe).

References

ABS (Australian Bureau of Statistics) (2011) 'Recorded Crime — Victims, 4510.0 Australian Bureau of Statistics. Available at: http://www.abs.gov.au/ausstats/abs@.nsf/Lookup/0FA9FF7C8E9F17B3CA257A150018FAE0?opendocument.

Amir, M. (1967) 'Victim Precipitated Forcible Rape', *Journal of Criminal Law, Criminology and Police Science*, 58(4): 493—502.

Arendt, H. (1958) *The Human Condition*, Chicago: Chicago University Press.

Ashworth, A. (2002) 'Responsibilities, Rights and Restorative Justice', *British Journal of Criminology*, 42(3): 578—95.

Christie, N. (1986) 'The Ideal Victim', in E. Fattah (ed.), *From Crime Policy to Victim Policy*, London: Macmillan, pp. 17—30.

Coleman, C. and Moynihan, J. (2003) *Understanding Crime Data*, Maidenhead: Open University Press

Cook, B., David, F. and Grant, A. (1999) *Victims' Needs, Victims' Rights: Policies and Programs for Victims of Crime in Australia*, Canberra: Australian Institute of Criminology Research and Public Policy Series, No. 19.

Crawford, A. and Goodey, J. (eds) (2000) *Integrating a Victim Perspective within Criminal Justice: International Debates*, Aldershot: Ashgate.

CVCF, Crime Victims Compensation Fund (2013), West Virginia Legislature's Crime Victims Compensation Fund. Available at: http://www.legis.state.wv.us/Joint/victims.cfm.

Dignan, J. (2005) *Understanding Victims and Restorative Justice*, Maidenhead: Open University Press.

Doak, J. (2008) *Victims' Rights, Human Rights and Criminal Justice: Reconceiving the Role of Third Parties*, Oxford: Hart Publishing.

Dolgopol, U. (2012) 'A Role for the Rome Statute System in Gender-Focused Reform of Criminal Laws and Procedures in the Pacific Islands', *Australian Journal of Human Rights*, 18(2): 109—37.

Elias R. (1984) 'Alienating the Victim: Compensation and Victim Attitudes', *Journal of Social Issues*, 40: 103—16.

Garkawe, S. (2004) 'Revisiting the Scope of Victimology: How Broad a Discipline Should It Be?', *International Review of Victimology*, 11: 275—94.

Garkawe, S. (2005) 'The Need for a Victims Convention', *The Victimologist*, 9: 4—6.

Green, S. (2007) 'Crime, Victimisation and Vulnerability', in S. Walklate (ed.), *Handbook of Victims and Victimology*, Uffculme, Devon: Willan Publishing, ch. 4.

Groenhuijsen, M. (1996) 'Conflicts of Victims' Interests and Offenders' Rights in the Criminal Justice System: A European Perspective', in *International Victimology: Selected Papers from the 8th International Symposium*, Canberra: Australian Institute of Criminology, pp. 163—76. Available at: http://www.aic.gov.au/media_library/publications/proceedings/27/groenhuijsen.pdf.

Harrell, E. (2007) *Black Victims of Violent Crime*, Bureau of Justice Statistics Special Report, Office of Justice Programs, US Department of Justice, NCJ 214258.

Kirchengast, T. (2006) *The Victim in Criminal Law and Justice*, Basingstoke: Palgrave Macmillan.

ICC (International Criminal Court) (2012) *The Prosecutor v. Thomas Lubanga Dyilo*, ICC-01/04-01/06. Available at: http://www.icc-cpi.int/en_menus/icc/situations%20and%20cases/situations/situation%20icc%200104/related%20cases/icc%200104%200106/Pages/democratic%20republic%20of%20the%20congo.aspx.

ICC (International Criminal Court) (undated), Guide for the participation of victims in the proceedings of the court. Available at: http://www.icc-cpi.int/NR/rdonlyres/C029F900-C529-46DB-9080-60D92B25F9D2/282477/160910VPRS BookletEnglish3.pdf.

Lees, S. (1997) *Ruling Passions: Sexual Violence, Reputation and the Law*, Buckingham: Open University Press.

Letschert, R. and van Dijk, J. (Eds) (2012) *The New Faces of Victimhood: Globalization, Transnational Crimes and Victim Rights* (Studies in Global Justice, Vol. 8), Dordrecht: Springer.

Mawby, R. and Walklate, S. (1994), *Critical Victimology: International Perspectives*, London: Sage.

McBarnett, D. (1983), 'Victim in the Witness Box: Confronting Victimology's Stereotype', *Contemporary Crises*, 7: 279—93.

Mutua, M. (2001), 'Savages, Victims, and Saviors: The Metaphor of Human Rights', *Harvard International Law Journal*, 42(1): 201—45.

OVS, Office of Victim Services (2010) Compensation, New York State. Available at: http://www.ovs.ny.gov/services/VictimCompensation.aspx.

Personal Crimes (2002), 'Number of Victimizations and Victimization Rates for Persons Age 12 and Over, by Type of Crime and Gender and Race of Victims', in *Criminal Victimization in the United States*, 2002 Statistical Tables, US Department of Justice, Office of Justice Programs, Bureau of Justice Statistics, Washington, DC.

Rubio Marin, R. (2009) *The Gender of Reparation*, Cambridge: Cambridge University Press.

Spalek, B. (2006) *Crime Victims: Theory, Policy and Practice*, New York: Palgrave Macmillan.

Strang, H. and Sherman, L. (2003) 'Repairing the Harm: Victims and Restorative Justice', *Utah Law Review*, 15(1): 15—42.

TDPS, Texas Department of Public Safety (2011), Crime Victims' Compensation. Available at: http://www.dps.texas.gov/administration/staff_support/victim services/pages/crimevictimscompensation.htm.

Truman, J. (2011) *Criminal Victimization*, 2010 National Crime Victimization Survey, Bureau of Justice Statistics Special Report, Office of Justice Programs, US Department of Justice, NCJ 235508.

United Nations (2004) *A More Secure World: Our Shared Responsibility*, Report of the High level Panel on Threats, Challenges, and Change, http://iis-db.stanford.edu/pubs/20806/A_More_Secure_World_.pdf.

US Government (2013) 'H.J.Res. 40: Proposing an amendment to the Constitution of the United States to protect the rights of crime victims', 113th Congress, 2013–2015. Text as of 23 Apr, 2013 (Introduced). Available at: http://www.govtrack.us/congress/bills/113/hjres40/text.

van Dijk, J. and Letschert, R. (2012) 'Reconstructing Victim-centered Justice on a Global Scale', in R. Letschert and J. van Dijk (eds), *The New Faces of Victimhood: Globalization, Transnational Crimes and Victim Rights* (Studies in Global Justice, Vol. 8), Dordrecht: Springer, pp. 3–14.

Victim Support (undated) Compensation, UK. Available at: http://www.victim support.org.uk/help-for-victims/how-crime-can-affect-you/compensation.

Wemmers, J. (2012) 'Victims' Rights Are Human Rights: The Importance of Recognizing Victims as Persons', *Temida*, 15(2): 71–83.

Wilson, R. and Brown, R. (2009) *Humanitarianism and Suffering: The Mobilization of Empathy through Narrative*, New York: Cambridge University Press.

Zedner, L. (1997) 'Victims', in M. Maguire, R. Morgan and R. Reiner (eds), *The Oxford Handbook of Criminology*, Oxford: Oxford University Press, pp. 577–611.

A Criminology for Human Rights

In the final chapter we identify some key themes within criminology that illustrate the increasing relevance of human rights as a discursive tool and analytical framework for the discipline.

Many of these themes arise from the rapid social and technological changes associated with globalization, and highlight the need for both criminology and human rights to adapt to new challenges under transformed conditions of governance.

We argue that human rights have particular resonance where governments are confronted by problems of order and inclusion concerning those who are not their citizens; where asocial means of control diminish opportunities to recognize the humanity of the subjects of governance; and where calls for collective security eclipse considerations of individual and minority group rights.

Ultimately, a criminology for human rights may take many forms, but it is recognizable by the primacy it accords to the well-being of all individuals and the social groups to which they belong.

CHAPTER 13

Future Directions

Key concepts

Globalization — risk — securitization — criminology of the other — decentring of the state

---

13.1 Introduction

In earlier chapters we reviewed some existing criminological scholarship that has applied human rights perspectives. In this final chapter we identify some of the key criminological themes of our time which raise significant human rights issues that are likely to demand criminological attention well into the future. While these 'big picture' themes and debates are not always expressed in the language of human rights, and may not refer to specific international legal norms and standards, a brief review of some selected themes brings the human rights dimension into view.

13.2 A criminology for human rights: key themes

13.2.1 Risk, punitivism and securitization

The social and economic insecurities generated by rapid global change pose a range of challenges for criminology and human rights. As Hogg explains: 'Human rights as universal ethic has trouble competing with nationalism and other sources of identity and security' that fuel a 'hardening of familiar solidarities in the face of fear and insecurity' (Hogg 2002: 210). The obsession with risk and the pursuit of security manifests across many domains of contemporary governance and has been analysed within criminology in terms of popular punitivism (Pratt *et al.* 2005), containment (Feeley and Simon 1992), a culture of control (Garland 2001), pre-criminology (Zedner 2007) and micro-level risk management (Hannah-Moffat 2010), all of which raise significant human rights concerns around equity, proportionality and due process. On the other hand, it has been suggested that new ways of thinking about both risk and rights could identify opportunities for a rapprochement between these competing paradigms. For example, Whitty (2011) has proposed that realization of the consequences of the failure to protect human rights and dignity within prison settings could create circumstances in which increased human rights protection is seen by prison managers as reducing their 'organizational risk' (Whitty 2011). This instrumental language may not appeal to those who are committed to human rights norms as moral imperatives, but nevertheless opens up a middle ground from which to challenge damaging risk-based practices.

13.2.2 Criminology of the other

Closely associated with the politics of fear and risk is the appearance of contradictory strands within criminology and criminal justice administration, which Garland (2001) refers to as the 'criminology of the self' and the 'criminology of the other'. The first is invoked to portray crime as routine and criminals as solitary, rational actors who are not so different from the rest of us; and the second to demonize particular offenders and support calls for harsh punishment and exclusion. Neither discourse supports the rehabilitative objective expressed in many human rights instruments, nor the contextualized analysis of offending that characterizes what Garland calls 'social democratic criminology'. The criminology of the other depicts offenders as 'dangerous others who threaten our safety and have no calls on our fellow feeling. The appropriate reaction for society is one of social defence: we should defend ourselves against these dangerous enemies rather than concern ourselves with their welfare and prospects for rehabilitation' (Garland 2001: 184). Risk management techniques feed into this process by identifying certain groups as 'presumptively dangerous populations' destined for social and physical exclusion (Simon 2007). Jamieson and McEvoy (2005: 517) have observed that discursive processes of 'juridical othering', which identify groups 'to whom normal rules do not apply', facilitate human rights violations by states and their agents, marking the criminology of the other as an important theme for human rights criminology.

13.2.3 Border control and citizenship

Border control is another emerging theme within criminology. Critical border control studies respond to the new set of global conditions arising from globalization (see, for example, Pickering and Weber 2006; Aas 2007; Bosworth and Guild 2008). The study of transnational crimes such as trafficking of human beings, cross-border trade in illicit goods, and environmental destruction opens up important new frontiers in criminological inquiry, and invites researchers, practitioners and students to engage with international legal instruments and UN-sanctioned crime prevention techniques. However, the criminological critique of contemporary border control practices themselves (rather than cross-border transgressions more readily identified as transnational crimes) goes still further and exposes the limits of both the sovereign state and the international human rights system that has developed in tandem with it (Gready 2004). As Dauvergne has noted, '[f]or extralegal migrants seeking legal protection or redress for harms, the status of "illegal" has been almost insurmountable. This will eventually prove to be one of the most important tests of the global spread of human rights' (Dauvergne 2008: 19). And citizenship theorist, Linda Bosniak, has noted that 'the rights undocumented immigrants formally enjoy in the sphere of territorial personhood are often rendered irrelevant, as a practical matter, by operation of the nation's border-regulatory authority' (Bosniak 2006: 70). These fundamental structural changes, and the future shifts in global governance that they presage, are transforming the territorially bounded subject matter of criminology. A key challenge for a human rights criminology is to consider how security may be achieved for all, and not only for those who are formally recognized as citizens or legal residents.

13.2.4 Justice reinvestment

Since the 1980s there has been a retreat from welfare and developmental expenditure and an increasing reliance on an inappropriately equipped criminal justice system to respond to the failures of economic, social and public policy (Garland 2001; Currie 2013). It is possible that justice reinvestment might provide the catalyst for a criminal justice future that not only reduces recidivism and crime rates but also enhances human rights and well-being (Brown *et al.* 2012). The support for justice reinvestment comes from disparate sources. There are those who prioritize the fiscal benefits resulting from reducing expenditure on prisons, but who may not be willing to reinvest adequately in social and public policy programmes, and for whom cost cutting is the goal. Whereas other advocates see that justice reinvestment provides opportunities for community development and capacity building, which leads subsequently to a reduction in crime and harm, such that the push for greater cost efficiency and effectiveness provides a means to a social justice end. There is potential for justice reinvestment to be the moment when a window of policy opportunity opens, enabling a human rights perspective to add a normative base to an evidence-based, politically appealing and forward-looking policy agenda.

13.2.5 Restorative justice

Restorative justice and other alternative justice mechanisms aim at redistributing and balancing power among voiceless parties. Court environments that can offer holistic alternatives to formal court settings, and diversification of outcomes to fit individual cases, are now no longer described as 'experimental'. The 1990 UN Tokyo Rules (non-custodial measures), revisited recently under the 2006 Compendium of United Nations Standards and Norms in Crime Prevention and Criminal Justice (alternatives to imprisonment and restorative justice), are further evidence of an alternative legal system with well-established principles, which recognizes the rights of dignity and fairness of trial as basic human rights values. This modernist approach to law as a therapeutic tool also allows for normative acceptance that the law can generate or exacerbate traumas (that is, have an anti-therapeutic effect): a shared understanding among criminologists and legal practitioners. Restorative justice and therapeutic jurisprudence may offer a human rights platform to address individual cases in a manner that respects diversity and constraints, and at the same time acts as an instrument to reconsider the whole criminal justice system.

13.2.6 Technology and surveillance

The space of governance is also being reconfigured radically by rapid advances in technology (see Zureik and Salter 2005; Mattelart 2010; Aas 2011; Coleman and McCahill 2011) in ways that raise new concerns for a human rights criminology. Human rights standards – both existing and evolving – provide a basis for judgements about specific applications of new technologies of governance. Lyon (2001) sees the advent of the 'surveillance society' as neither a generalized threat to individual liberty nor a promise of utopia. However, Krasmann (2012: 382) notes that rights have proved to be ineffective in thwarting trends which she claims are 'making private space accessible to surveillance in a way that would have been unimaginable decades ago'. At the same time, she argues that rights are needed to regulate (rather than thwart) these new surveillance practices, which may require the application of the very same technologies. Where surveillance does present an identifiable threat to human rights it will often be the case that non-state actors are responsible for creating or applying the technologies. This takes us to another key theme for a human-rights-aware criminology – the rise of transnational corporations.

13.2.7 Transnational corporations and the decentring of the state

Criminologists have charted significant trends in the devolution of state power through complex chains of public and private actors at both the domestic and transnational levels (see, for example, Garland 1996; Wood and Shearing 2007). This opens up possibilities for the commission of 'state crime by proxy' (Jamieson and McEvoy 2005), which presents new challenges for a human-rights-based criminology. Jamieson and McEvoy (2007) note that the partial decentring of state power is occurring at multiple levels 'above' the state, such as transnational policing; 'alongside' the state, as with privatized policing; and 'below' the state, with the involvement of community volunteers. They conclude that this 'shared sovereignty over justice ... requires a broader, deeper and less "state-centric" human rights perspective if the potential for more moral action is to be realized' (Jamieson and McEvoy 2007: 434). The evolution of global capitalism is also of central importance in this context because of the potential for under-regulated corporations to commit human rights abuses both at home or, more likely, abroad, through worker exploitation, illegal trading or environmental destruction, sometimes with the complicity of governments.

13.3 Conclusion

In this book we have sought to demonstrate the benefits, pitfalls and limitations of applying human rights concepts and legal frameworks within criminology. While vague appeals to human rights can sometimes amount to little more than sloganeering, the brief survey of major themes in this final chapter illustrates some important contexts in which more focused human rights thinking could make a significant contribution to our understanding. In fact, considering the current pace of social and technological change, it may become increasingly difficult to tackle critical topics in criminology without a clear grasp of the relevance of human rights within a global context.

While criminologists of different persuasions may hold vastly different views about the value and validity of human rights law and thinking, there is space within the discipline for engagement with human rights at a range of levels. We attempted to illustrate this diversity of human rights scholarship within criminology in Chapter 5. In turn, a critical and globally aware criminology can help to expand the horizons of human rights by highlighting the increasing prevalence of transnational corporations and other non-state actors as perpetrators of major human rights abuses, and the manifold limitations of the current state-based approach to protecting individual and group rights within the present international system. The starting point for criminologists with an eye to the future is to become more knowledgeable about the origin and meaning of human rights as law, philosophy, politics and practice. The goal of this book has been to provide a foundation and catalyst for that process.

References

Aas, K. (2007) *Globalization and Crime*, London: Sage.

Aas, K. (2011) '"Crimmigrant" Bodies and Bona Fide Travelers: Surveillance, Citizenship and Global Governance', *Theoretical Criminology*, 15(3): 331–46.

Bosniak, L. (2006) *The Citizen and the Alien: Dilemmas of Contemporary Membership*, Princeton, NJ: Princeton University Press.

Bosworth, M. and Guild, M. (2008) 'Governing through Migration Control: Security and Citizenship in Britain', *British Journal of Criminology*, 48(6): 703–19.

Brown, D., Schwartz, M. and Boseley, L. (2012) *The Promise of Justice Re-Investment*. Available at: http://papers.ssrn.com/sol3/papers.cfm?abstract_id= 2078715; accessed 24 April 2013.

Coleman, R. and McCahill, M. (2011) *Surveillance and Crime*, London: Sage.

Currie, E. (2013) 'The Sustaining Society', in K. Carrington, M. Ball, E. O'Brien and J. Tauri (eds), *Crime, Justice and Social Democracy: International Perspectives*, Basingstoke: Palgrave Macmillan, pp. 3–15.

Dauvergne, C. (2008) *Making People Illegal: What Globalization Means for Migration and Law*, New York: Cambridge University Press.

Feeley, S. and Simon, J. (1992) 'The New Penology: Notes on the Emerging Strategy of Corrections and Its Implications', *Criminology*, 30(4): 449–74.

Garland, D. (1996) 'The Limits of the Sovereign State: Strategies of Crime Control in Contemporary Society', *British Journal of Criminology*, 36(4): 445–71.

Garland, D. (2001) *The Culture of Control: Crime and Social Order in Contemporary Society*, Oxford: Oxford University Press.

Gready, P. (2004) 'Conceptualising Globalisation and Human Rights: Boomerangs and Borders', *International Journal of Human Rights*, 8(3): 345–54.

Hannah-Moffat, K. (2010) 'Sacrosanct or Flawed: Risk, Accountability and Gender-Responsive Penal Politics', *Current Issues in Criminal Justice*, 22(2): 193–215.

Hogg, R. (2002) 'Criminology beyond the Nation State: Global Conflicts, Human Rights and the "New World Disorder"', in K. Carrington and R. Hogg (eds), *Critical Criminology: Issues, Debates, Challenges*, Uffculme, Devon: Willan Publishing.

Jamieson, R. and McEvoy, K. (2005) 'State Crime by Proxy and Juridical Othering', *British Journal of Criminology – Special Issue on State Crime*, 45(4): 504–27.

Jamieson, R. and McEvoy, K. (2007) 'Conflict, Suffering and the Promise of Human Rights', in D. Downes, P. Rick, C. Chinkin and C. Gearty (eds), *Crime, Social Control and Human Rights: From Moral Panics to States of Denial – Essays in Honour of Stanley Cohen*, Uffculme, Devon: Willan Publishing.

Krasmann, S. (2012) 'Law's Knowledge: On the Susceptibility and Resistance of Legal Practices to Security Matters', *Theoretical Criminology*, 16(4): 379–94.

Lyon, D. (2001) *Surveillance Society: Monitoring Everyday Life*, Buckingham: Open University Press.

Mattelart, A. (2010) *The Globalization of Surveillance*, Cambridge: Polity Press.

Pickering, S. and Weber, L. (2006) *Borders, Mobility and Technologies of Control*, Amsterdam: Springer.

Pratt, J., Brown, D., Brown, M., Hallsworth, S. and Morrison, J. (2005) *The New Punitiveness: Trends, Theories, Perspectives*, Uffculme, Devon: Willan Publishing.

Simon, J. (2007) *Governing through Crime: How the War on Crime Transformed American Democracy and Created a Culture of Fear*, New York: Oxford University Press.

Whitty, N. (2011) 'Human Rights as Risk: UK Prisons and the Management of Risks and Rights', *Punishment and Society*, 13(2): 123—48.

Wood, J. and Shearing, C. (2007) *Imagining Security*, Uffculme, Devon: Willan Publishing.

Zedner, L. (2007) 'Pre-Crime and Post-Criminology?', *Theoretical Criminology*, 11(2): 261—81.

Zureik, E. and Salter, M. (2005) *Global Surveillance and Policing: Borders, Security, Identity*, Uffculme, Devon: Willan Publishing.

Index

CPSIA information can be obtained
at www.ICGtesting.com
Printed in the USA
LVHW080610120821
694861LV00004B/33